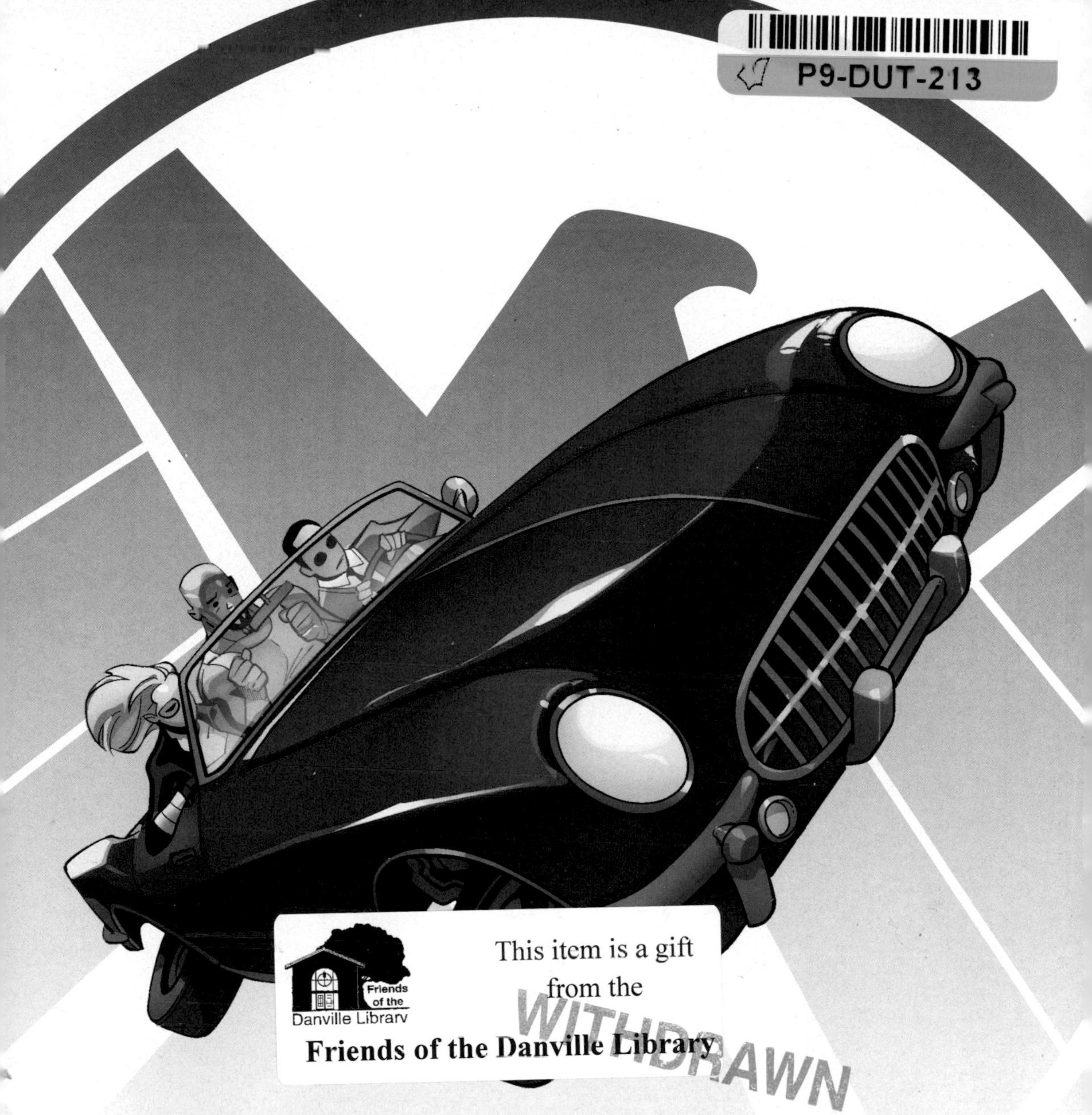

STRATEGIC HOMELAND INTERVENTION ENFORCEMENT LOGISTICS DIVISION

S.H.I.E.L.D.

THE MAN CALLED D.E.A.T.H.

S.H.I.E.L.D. VOL. 2: THE MAN CALLED D.E.A.T.H. Contains material originally published in magazine form as S.H.I.E.L.D. #7-12. First printing 2016. ISBN# 978-0-7851-9363-0. Published by MARVEL WORLDWIDE, INC., a subsidiary of MARVEL ENTERTAINMENT, LLC. OFFICE OF PUBLICATION: 135 West 50th Street, New York, NY 10020. Copyright © 2016 MARVEL No similarity between any of the names, characters, persons, and/or institutions in this magazine with those of any living or dead person or institution is intended, and any such similarity which may exist is purely coincidental. **Printed in Canada.** ALAN FINE, President, Marvel Entertainment; DAN BUCKLEY, President, TV, Publishing and Brand Management; JOE QUESADA, Chief Creative Officer; TOM BREVOORT, SVP of Publishing; DAVID BOGART, SVP of Operations & Procurement, Publishing; C.B. CEBULSKI, VP of International Development & Brand Management; DAVID GABRIEL, SVP Print, Sales & Marketing; JIM O'KEEFE, VP of Operations & Logistics; DAN CARR, Executive Director of Publishing Technology; SUSAN CRESPI, Editorial Operations Manager; ALEX MORALES, Publishing Operations Manager; STAN LEE, Chairman Emeritus. For information regarding advertising in Marvel Comics or on Marvel.com, please contact Jonathan Rheingold, VP of Custom Solutions & Ad Sales, at jrheingold@marvel.com. For Marvel subscription inquiries, please call 800-217-9158. **Manufactured between 12/4/2015 and 1/11/2016 by SOLISCO PRINTERS, SCOTT, QC, CANADA.**

10 9 8 7 6 5 4 3 2 1

STRATEGIC HOMELAND INTERVENTION ENFORCEMENT LOGISTICS DIVISION

S.H.I.E.L.D.

THE MAN CALLED D·E·A·T·H

WRITER
MARK WAID

ISSUE #7

ARTIST
GREG SMALLWOOD

COLOR ARTIST
GURU-eFX

ISSUE #8

PENCILER
PACO MEDINA

INKER
JUAN VLASCO

COLOR ARTIST
DAVID CURIEL

ISSUE #9

ARTIST
LEE FERGUSON

COLOR ARTIST
PAUL MOUNTS

ADDITIONAL MATERIAL
**JACK KIRBY,
JIM STERANKO,
JOHN SEVERIN &
STAN LEE**

ISSUE #10

ARTIST
EVAN "DOC" SHANER

COLOR ARTIST
MATTHEW WILSON

ISSUE #11

ARTIST
HOWARD CHAYKIN

COLOR ARTIST
EDGAR DELGADO

ISSUE #12

PENCILER
JOE BENNETT

INKER
ALEJANDRO SICAT WITH
ED TADEO & WALDEN WONG

COLOR ARTIST
RACHELLE ROSENBERG

LETTERER
VC'S JOE CARAMAGNA

COVER ART
JULIAN TOTINO TEDESCO

ASSISTANT EDITOR
**JON MOISAN
& ALANNA SMITH**

EDITOR
TOM BREVOORT

SPECIAL THANKS TO JEPH LOEB
AND MEGAN THOMAS BRADNER

S·H·I·E·L·D· CREATED BY
STAN LEE & JACK KIRBY

COLLECTION EDITOR
JENNIFER GRÜNWALD

ASSISTANT EDITOR
SARAH BRUNSTAD

ASSOCIATE MANAGING EDITOR
ALEX STARBUCK

EDITOR, SPECIAL PROJECTS
MARK D. BEAZLEY

SENIOR EDITOR, SPECIAL PROJECT
JEFF YOUNGQUIST

SVP PRINT, SALES & MARKETING
DAVID GABRIEL

BOOK DESIGNER
ADAM DEL RE

EDITOR IN CHIEF
AXEL ALONSO

CHIEF CREATIVE OFFICER
JOE QUESADA

PUBLISHER
DAN BUCKLEY

EXECUTIVE PRODUCER
ALAN FINE

7.

ACTIVE MISSION:

THE STRANGE CASE OF DAISY JOHNSON AND MR. HYDE

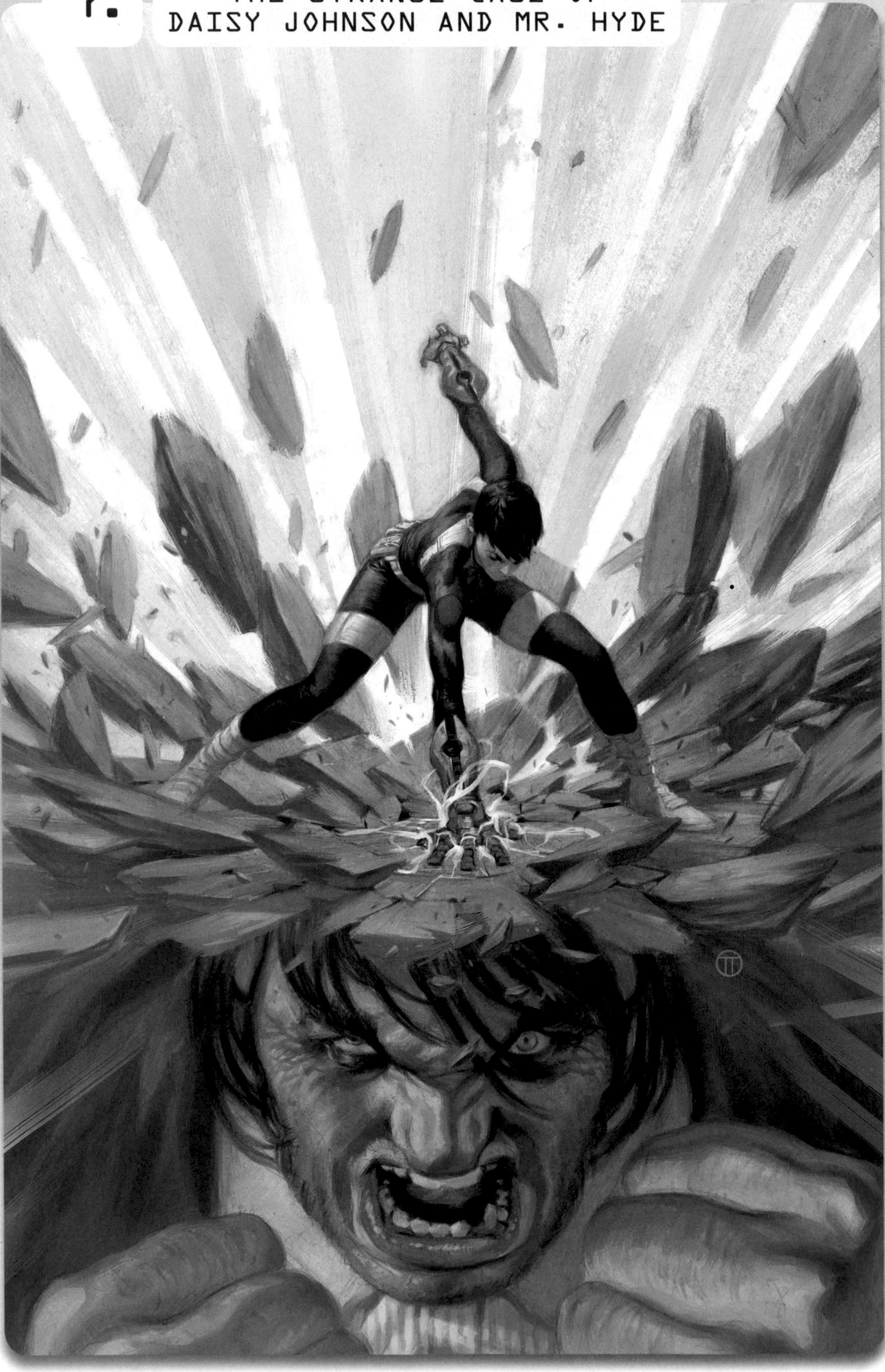

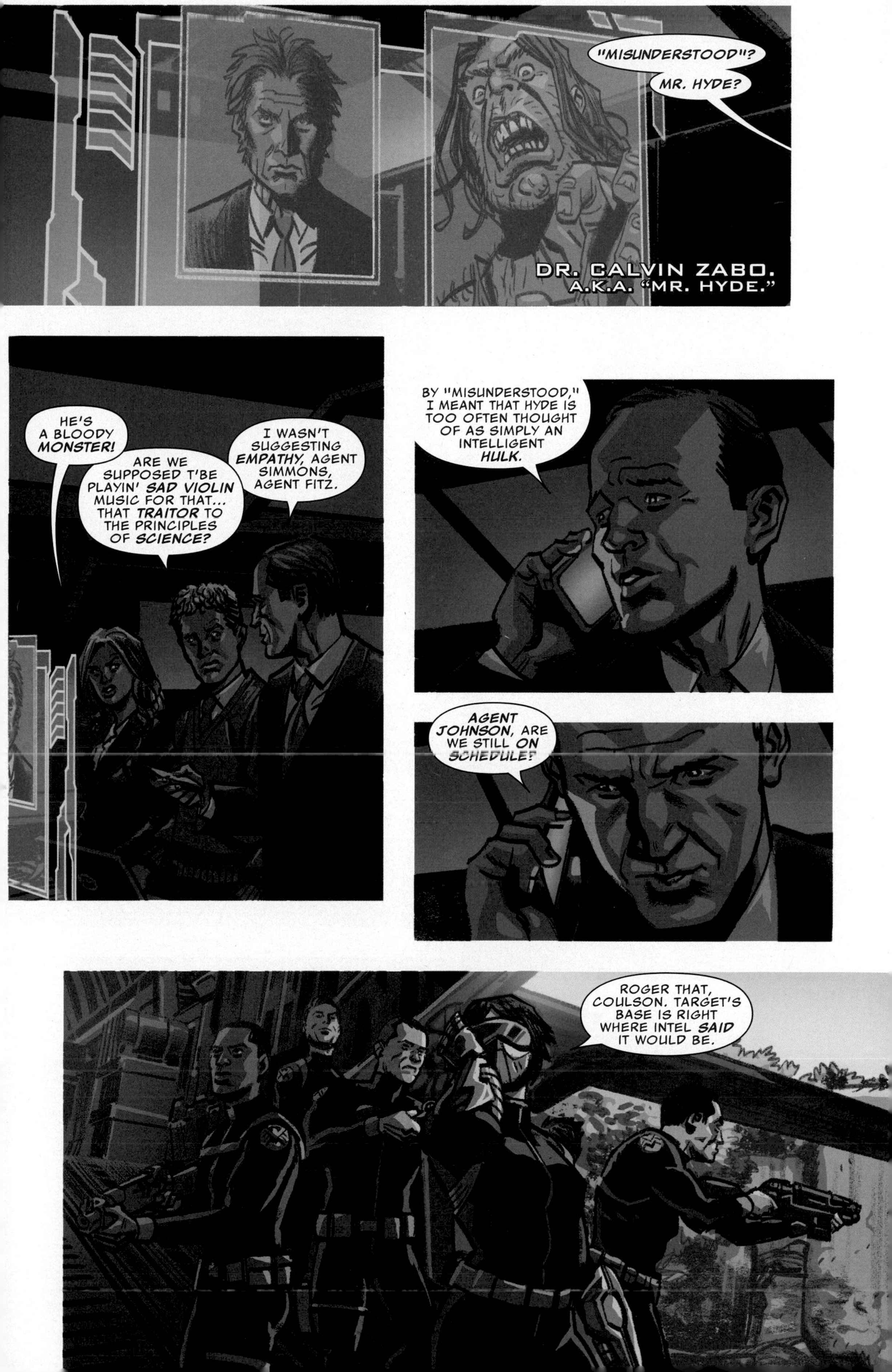
"MISUNDERSTOOD"?
MR. HYDE?
DR. CALVIN ZABO.
A.K.A. "MR. HYDE."
HE'S A BLOODY MONSTER!
ARE WE SUPPOSED T'BE PLAYIN' SAD VIOLIN MUSIC FOR THAT... THAT TRAITOR TO THE PRINCIPLES OF SCIENCE?
I WASN'T SUGGESTING EMPATHY, AGENT SIMMONS, AGENT FITZ.
BY "MISUNDERSTOOD," I MEANT THAT HYDE IS TOO OFTEN THOUGHT OF AS SIMPLY AN INTELLIGENT HULK.
AGENT JOHNSON, ARE WE STILL ON SCHEDULE?
ROGER THAT, COULSON. TARGET'S BASE IS RIGHT WHERE INTEL SAID IT WOULD BE.

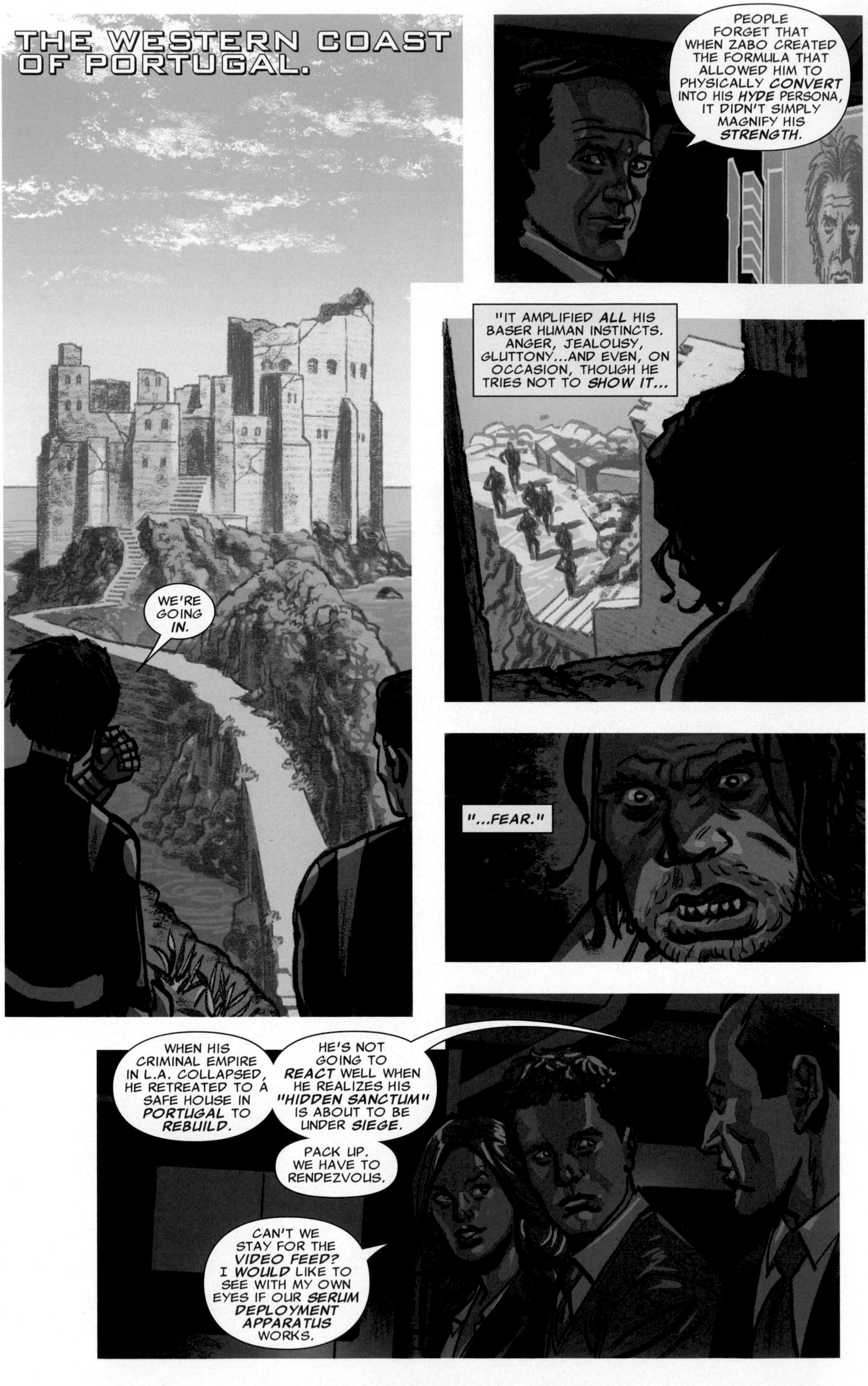
THE WESTERN COAST OF PORTUGAL.
WE'RE GOING IN.
PEOPLE FORGET THAT WHEN ZABO CREATED THE FORMULA THAT ALLOWED HIM TO PHYSICALLY CONVERT INTO HIS HYDE PERSONA, IT DIDN'T SIMPLY MAGNIFY HIS STRENGTH.
"IT AMPLIFIED ALL HIS BASER HUMAN INSTINCTS. ANGER, JEALOUSY, GLUTTONY...AND EVEN, ON OCCASION, THOUGH HE TRIES NOT TO SHOW IT...
"...FEAR."
WHEN HIS CRIMINAL EMPIRE IN L.A. COLLAPSED, HE RETREATED TO A SAFE HOUSE IN PORTUGAL TO REBUILD.
HE'S NOT GOING TO REACT WELL WHEN HE REALIZES HIS "HIDDEN SANCTUM" IS ABOUT TO BE UNDER SIEGE.
PACK UP. WE HAVE TO RENDEZVOUS.
CAN'T WE STAY FOR THE VIDEO FEED? I WOULD LIKE TO SEE WITH MY OWN EYES IF OUR SERUM DEPLOYMENT APPARATUS WORKS.

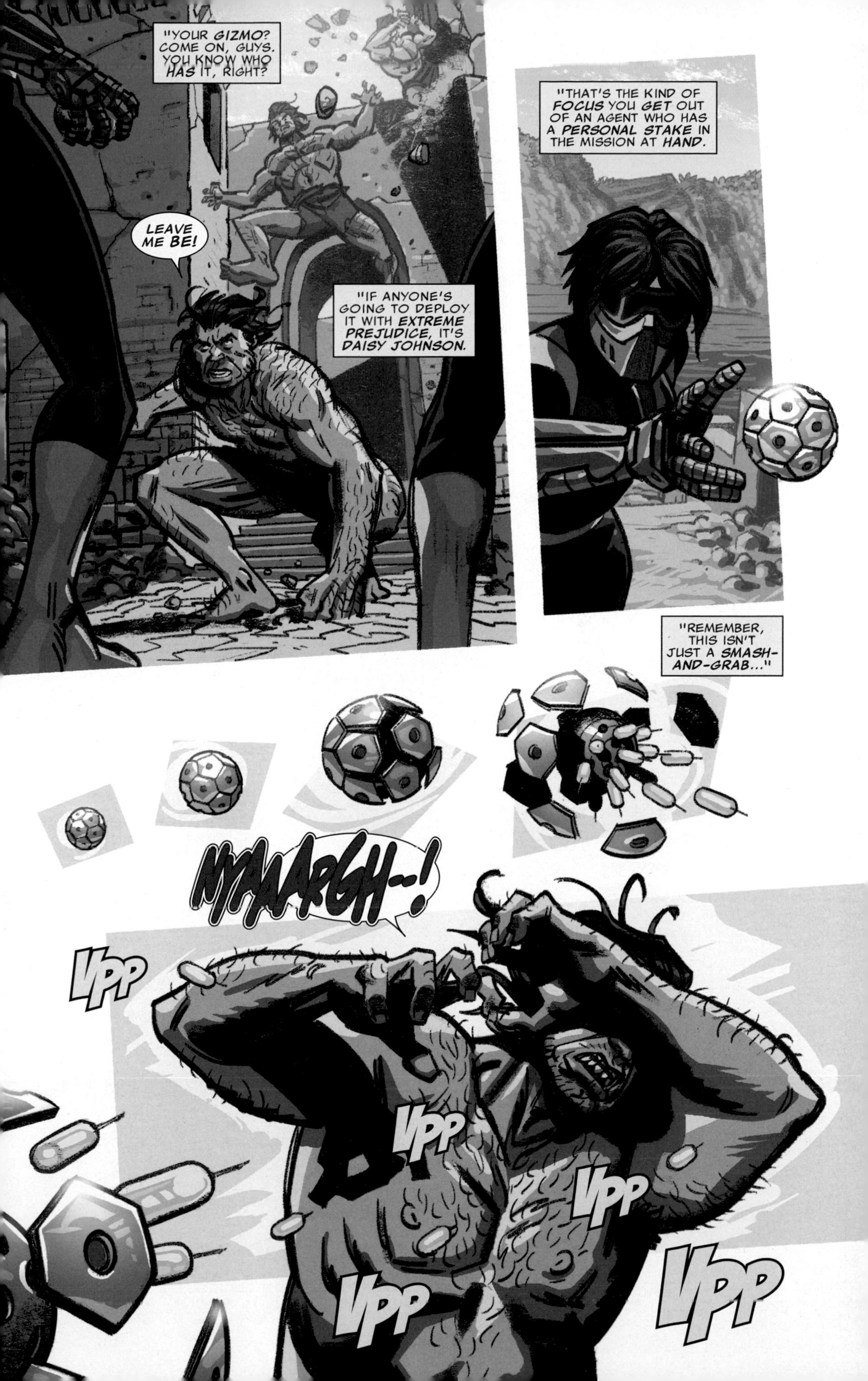
"YOUR GIZMO? COME ON, GUYS. YOU KNOW WHO HAS IT, RIGHT?
LEAVE ME BE!
"IF ANYONE'S GOING TO DEPLOY IT WITH EXTREME PREJUDICE, IT'S DAISY JOHNSON.
"THAT'S THE KIND OF FOCUS YOU GET OUT OF AN AGENT WHO HAS A PERSONAL STAKE IN THE MISSION AT HAND.
"REMEMBER, THIS ISN'T JUST A SMASH-AND-GRAB..."
NYAAARGH--!
VPP
VPP
VPP
VPP
VPP

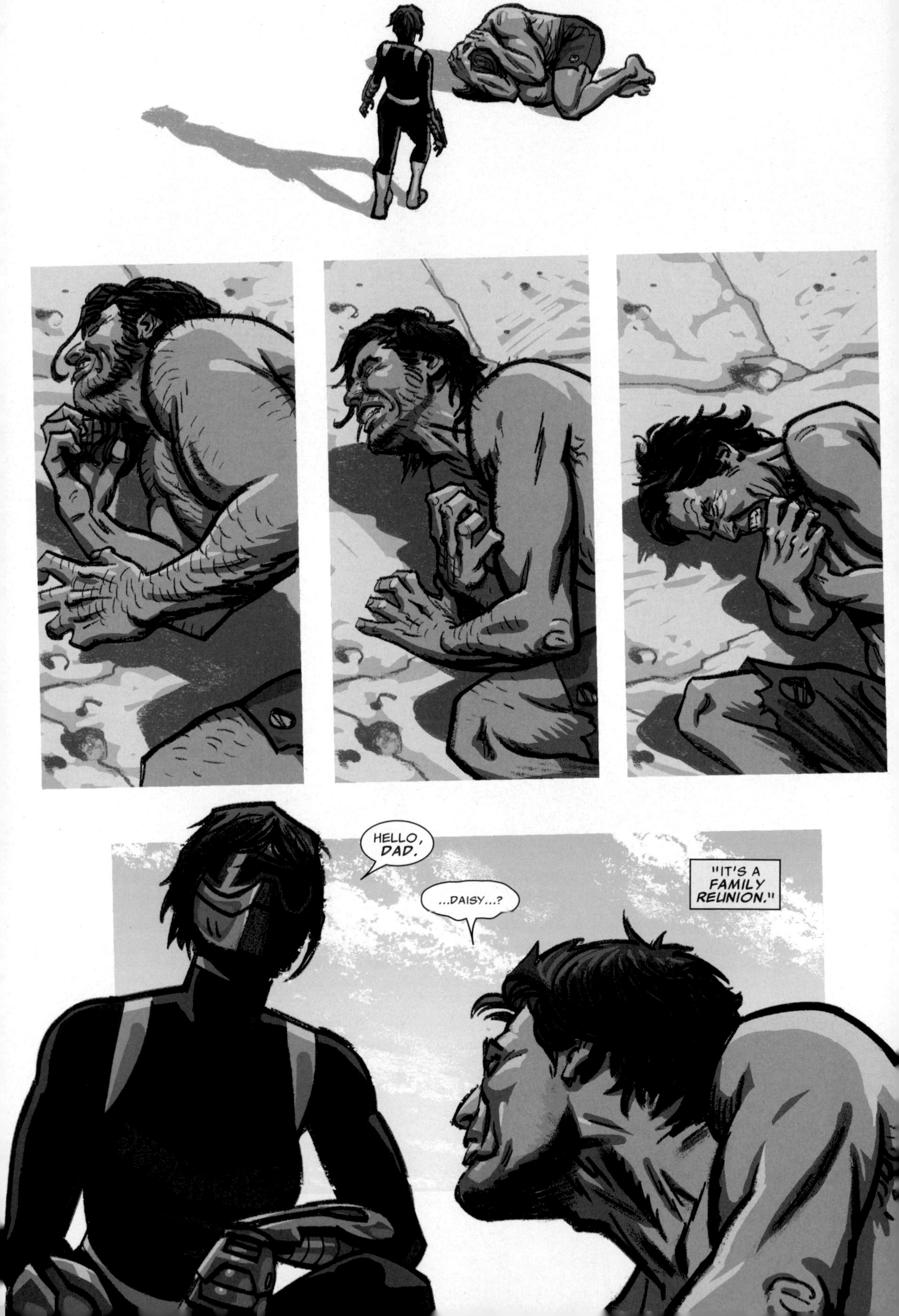
HELLO, DAD.
...DAISY...?
"IT'S A FAMILY REUNION."

ACCESS GRANTED...

STRATEGIC HOMELAND INTERVENTION ENFORCEMENT LOGISTICS DIVISION

S.H.I.E.L.D.

ACTIVE MISSION:

THE STRANGE CASE OF DAISY JOHNSON AND MR. HYDE

PAST MISSION:

S.H.I.E.L.D., the Strategic Homeland Intervention, Enforcement and Logistics Division. Mitigates and confronts threats to the security of the Earth and its people. Led by Director Phil Coulson, its highly-trained agents include Jenna Simmons, Leo Fitz and Daisy "Quake" Johnson, who has the ability to create earthquakes. Together, they detect and defend against any menace that might rear its head against our world. Coulson and his S.H.I.E.L.D. agents encounter mutants, monsters, villains, gods, and the best and worst of humanity on a daily basis as they endeavor to carry out S.H.I.E.L.D.'s mission and save our world.

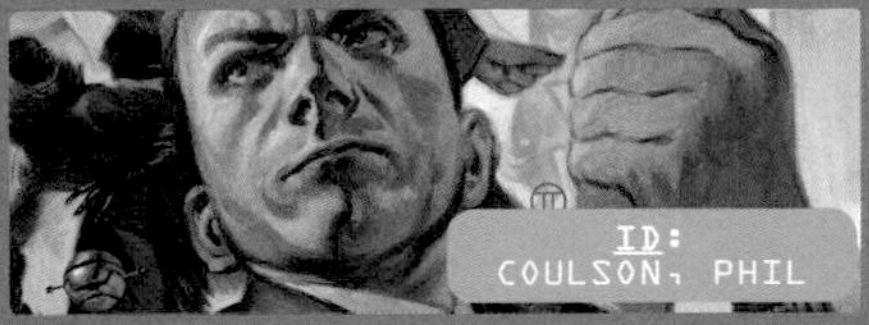
ID:
COULSON, PHIL

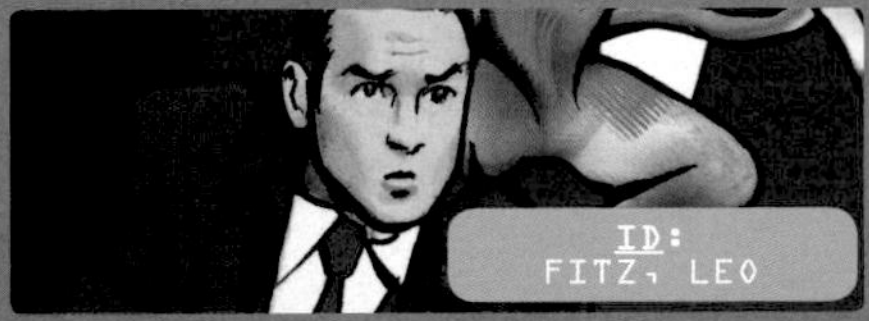
ID:
FITZ, LEO

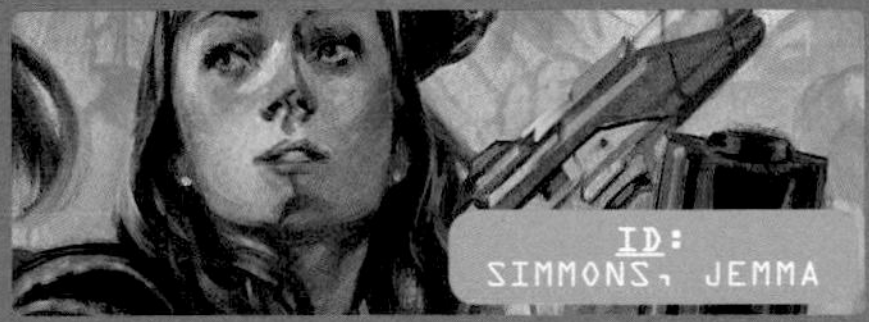
ID:
SIMMONS, JEMMA

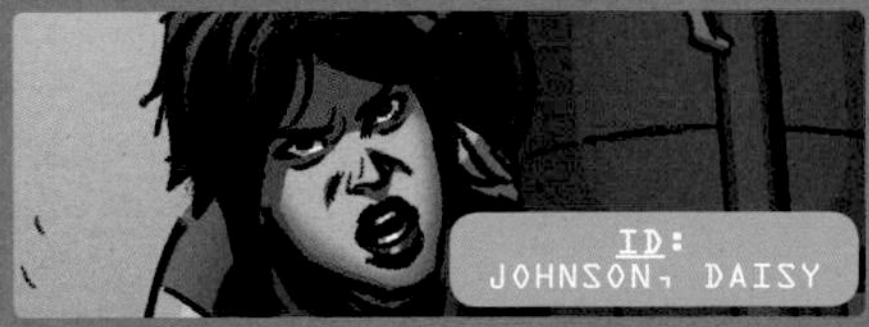
ID:
JOHNSON, DAISY

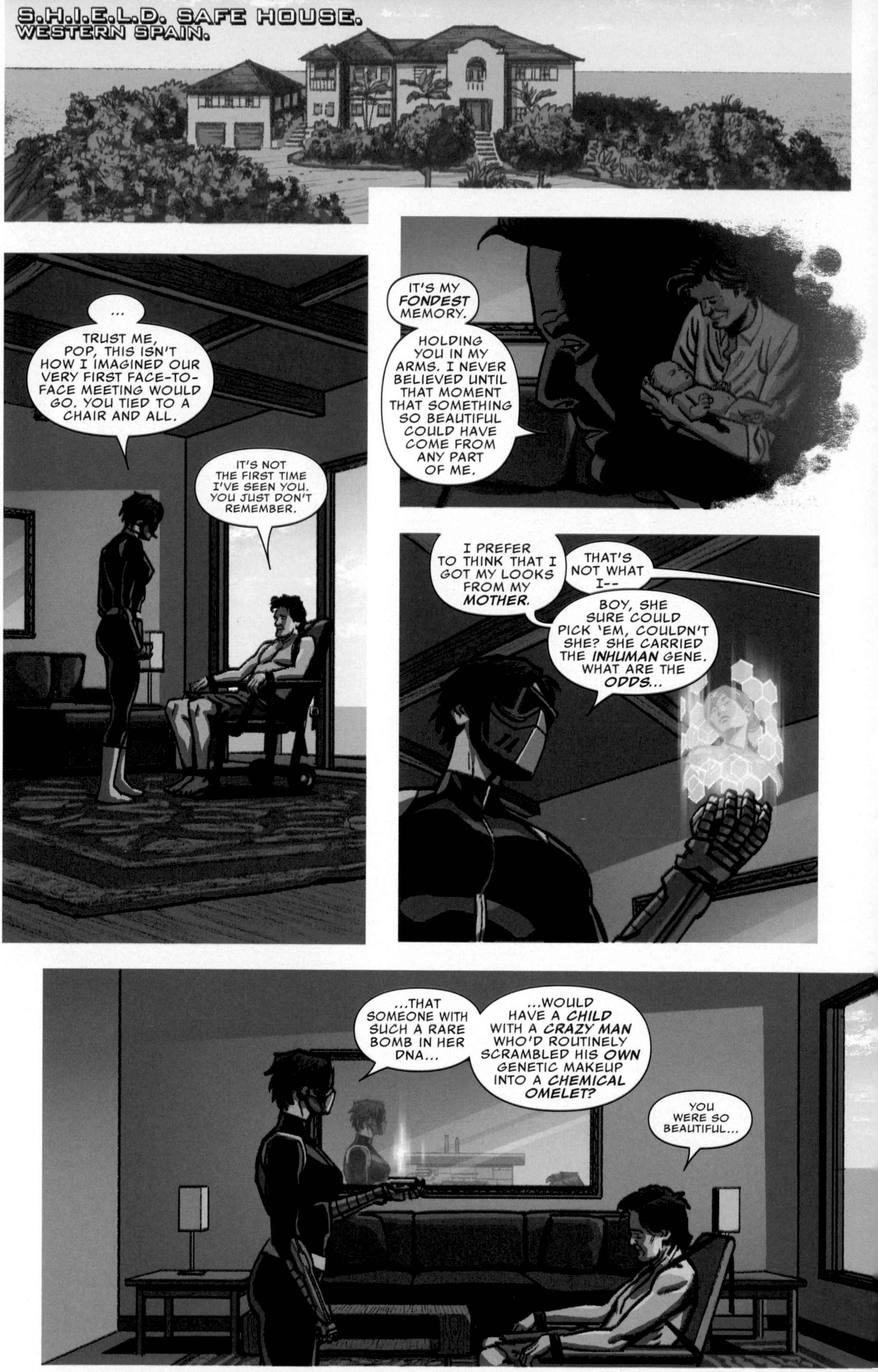
S.H.I.E.L.D. SAFE HOUSE. WESTERN SPAIN.
...
TRUST ME, POP, THIS ISN'T HOW I IMAGINED OUR VERY FIRST FACE-TO-FACE MEETING WOULD GO. YOU TIED TO A CHAIR AND ALL.
IT'S NOT THE FIRST TIME I'VE SEEN YOU. YOU JUST DON'T REMEMBER.
IT'S MY FONDEST MEMORY.
HOLDING YOU IN MY ARMS. I NEVER BELIEVED UNTIL THAT MOMENT THAT SOMETHING SO BEAUTIFUL COULD HAVE COME FROM ANY PART OF ME.
I PREFER TO THINK THAT I GOT MY LOOKS FROM MY MOTHER.
THAT'S NOT WHAT I--
BOY, SHE SURE COULD PICK 'EM, COULDN'T SHE? SHE CARRIED THE INHUMAN GENE. WHAT ARE THE ODDS...
...THAT SOMEONE WITH SUCH A RARE BOMB IN HER DNA...
...WOULD HAVE A CHILD WITH A CRAZY MAN WHO'D ROUTINELY SCRAMBLED HIS OWN GENETIC MAKEUP INTO A CHEMICAL OMELET?
YOU WERE SO BEAUTIFUL...

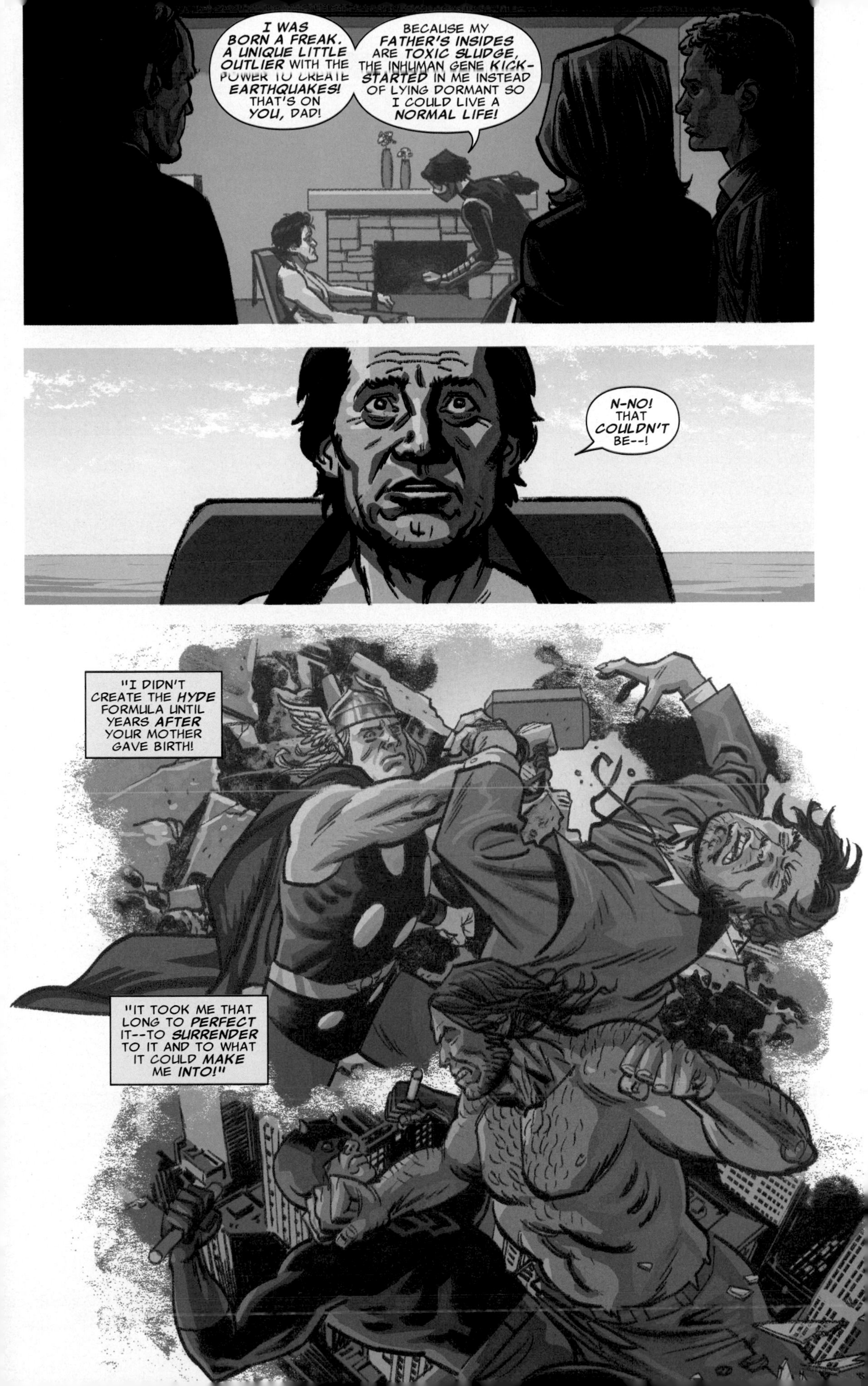
I WAS BORN A FREAK. A UNIQUE LITTLE OUTLIER WITH THE POWER TO CREATE EARTHQUAKES! THAT'S ON YOU, DAD!
BECAUSE MY FATHER'S INSIDES ARE TOXIC SLUDGE, THE INHUMAN GENE KICK-STARTED IN ME INSTEAD OF LYING DORMANT SO I COULD LIVE A NORMAL LIFE!
N-NO! THAT COULDN'T BE--!
"I DIDN'T CREATE THE HYDE FORMULA UNTIL YEARS AFTER YOUR MOTHER GAVE BIRTH!
"IT TOOK ME THAT LONG TO PERFECT IT--TO SURRENDER TO IT AND TO WHAT IT COULD MAKE ME INTO!"

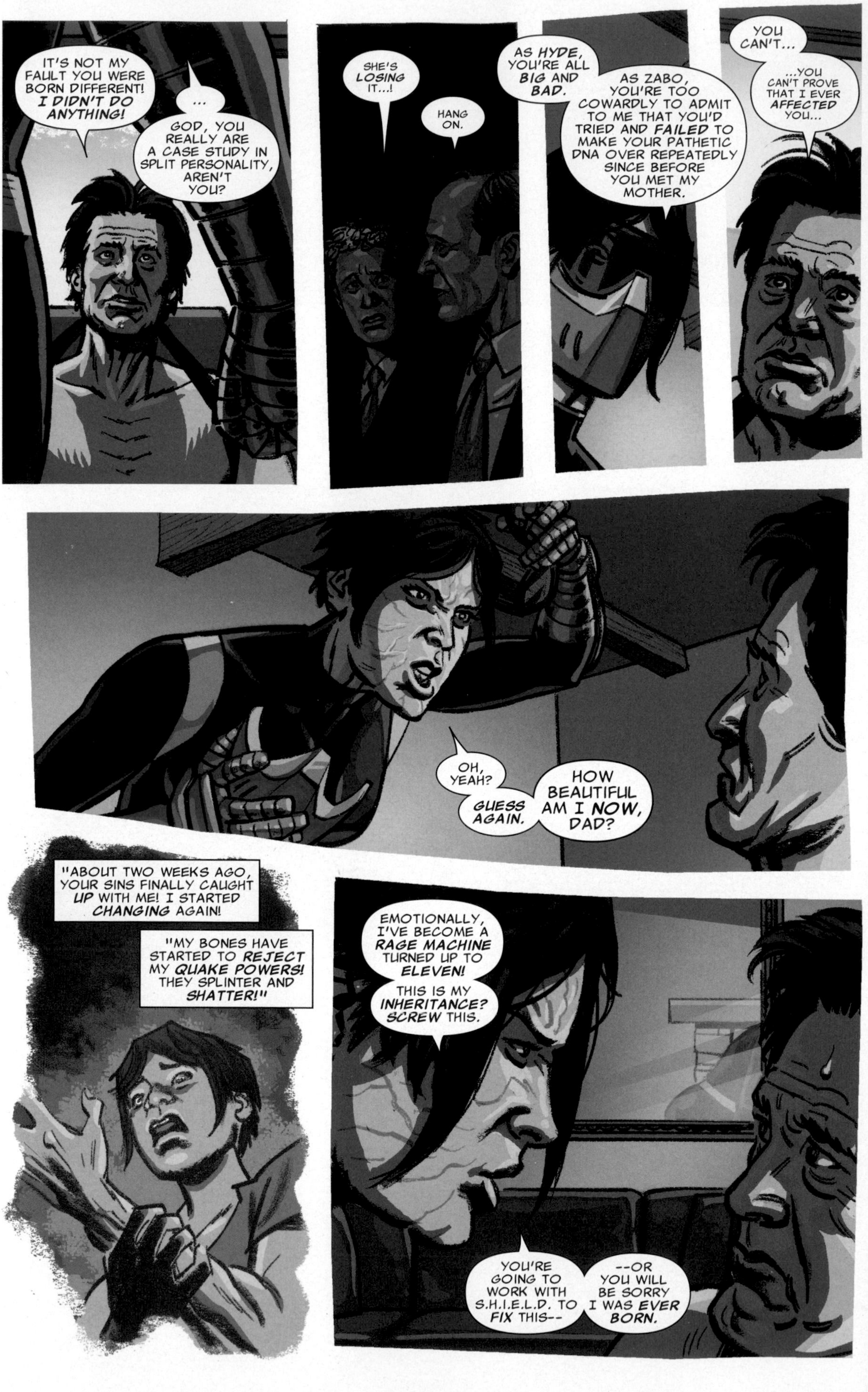

IT'S NOT MY FAULT YOU WERE BORN DIFFERENT! I DIDN'T DO ANYTHING!
...
GOD, YOU REALLY ARE A CASE STUDY IN SPLIT PERSONALITY, AREN'T YOU?
SHE'S LOSING IT...!
HANG ON.
AS HYDE, YOU'RE ALL BIG AND BAD.
AS ZABO, YOU'RE TOO COWARDLY TO ADMIT TO ME THAT YOU'D TRIED AND FAILED TO MAKE YOUR PATHETIC DNA OVER REPEATEDLY SINCE BEFORE YOU MET MY MOTHER.
YOU CAN'T...
...YOU CAN'T PROVE THAT I EVER AFFECTED YOU...
OH, YEAH?
GUESS AGAIN.
HOW BEAUTIFUL AM I NOW, DAD?
"ABOUT TWO WEEKS AGO, YOUR SINS FINALLY CAUGHT UP WITH ME! I STARTED CHANGING AGAIN!
"MY BONES HAVE STARTED TO REJECT MY QUAKE POWERS! THEY SPLINTER AND SHATTER!"
EMOTIONALLY, I'VE BECOME A RAGE MACHINE TURNED UP TO ELEVEN!
THIS IS MY INHERITANCE? SCREW THIS.
YOU'RE GOING TO WORK WITH S.H.I.E.L.D. TO FIX THIS--
--OR YOU WILL BE SORRY I WAS EVER BORN.

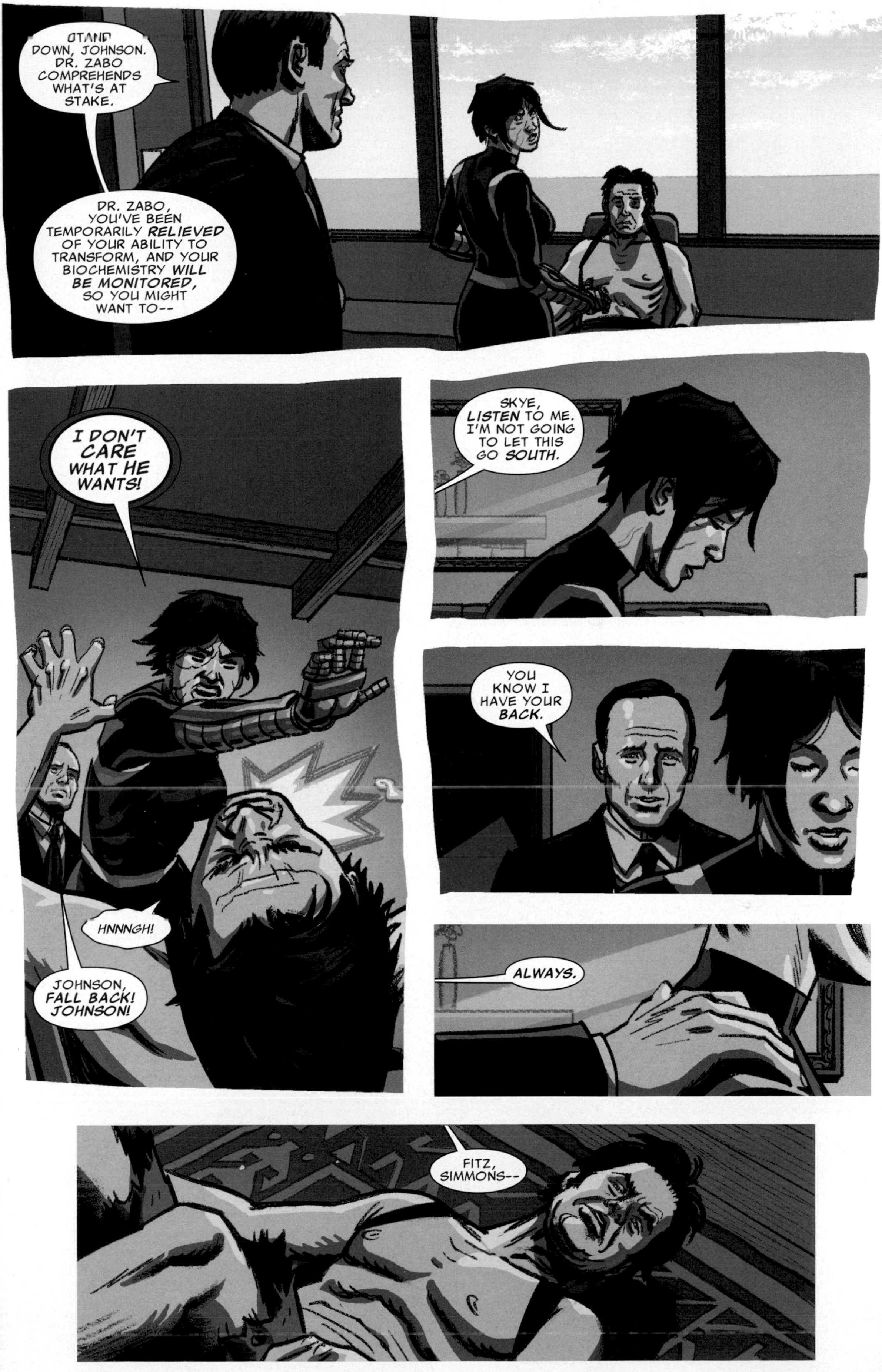
STAND DOWN, JOHNSON. DR. ZABO COMPREHENDS WHAT'S AT STAKE.
DR. ZABO, YOU'VE BEEN TEMPORARILY RELIEVED OF YOUR ABILITY TO TRANSFORM, AND YOUR BIOCHEMISTRY WILL BE MONITORED, SO YOU MIGHT WANT TO--
I DON'T CARE WHAT HE WANTS!
HNNNGH!
JOHNSON, FALL BACK! JOHNSON!
SKYE, LISTEN TO ME. I'M NOT GOING TO LET THIS GO SOUTH.
YOU KNOW I HAVE YOUR BACK.
ALWAYS.
FITZ, SIMMONS--

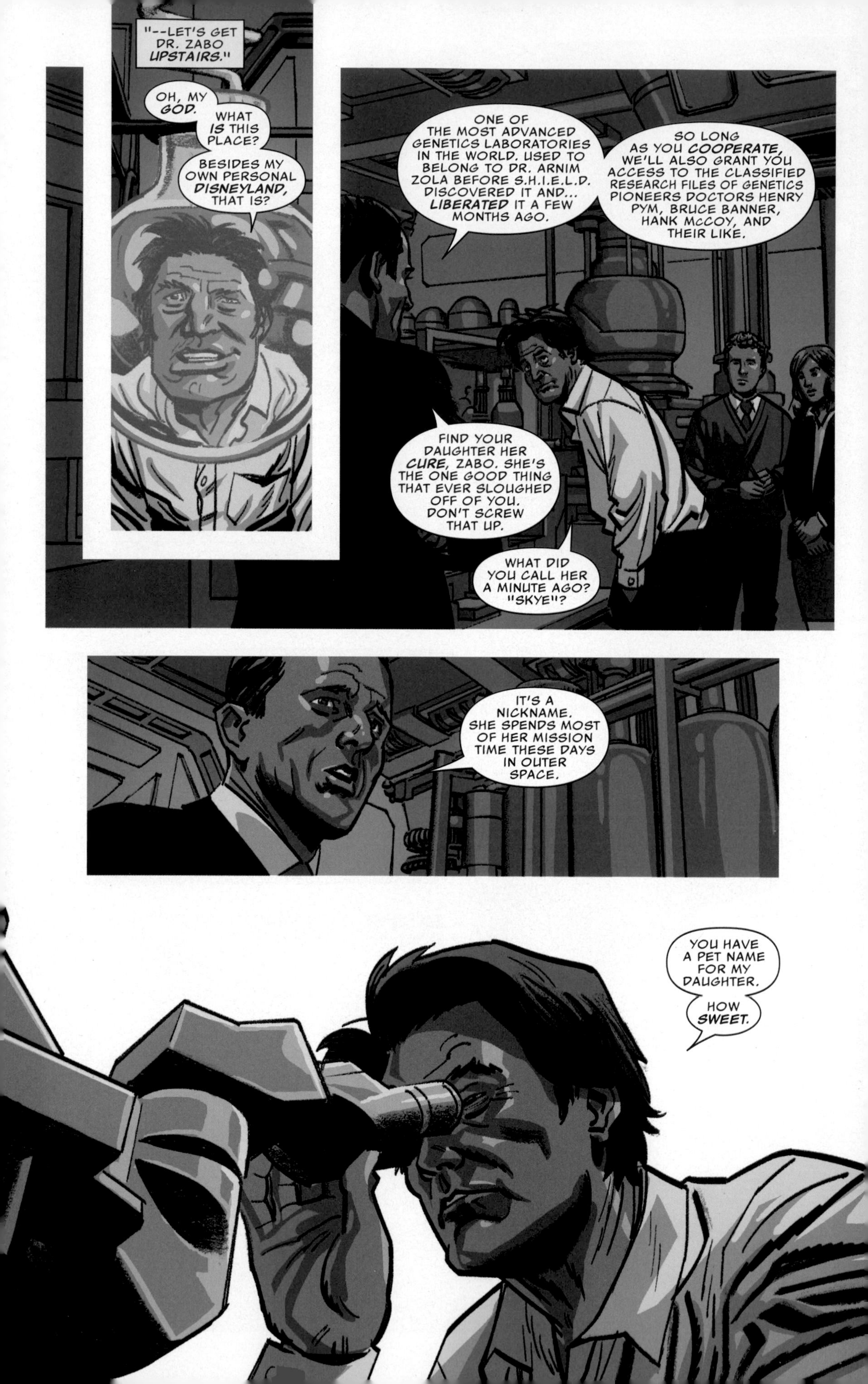
"--LET'S GET DR. ZABO UPSTAIRS."
OH, MY GOD.
WHAT IS THIS PLACE?
BESIDES MY OWN PERSONAL DISNEYLAND, THAT IS?
ONE OF THE MOST ADVANCED GENETICS LABORATORIES IN THE WORLD. USED TO BELONG TO DR. ARNIM ZOLA BEFORE S.H.I.E.L.D. DISCOVERED IT AND... LIBERATED IT A FEW MONTHS AGO.
SO LONG AS YOU COOPERATE, WE'LL ALSO GRANT YOU ACCESS TO THE CLASSIFIED RESEARCH FILES OF GENETICS PIONEERS DOCTORS HENRY PYM, BRUCE BANNER, HANK McCOY, AND THEIR LIKE.
FIND YOUR DAUGHTER HER CURE, ZABO. SHE'S THE ONE GOOD THING THAT EVER SLOUGHED OFF OF YOU. DON'T SCREW THAT UP.
WHAT DID YOU CALL HER A MINUTE AGO? "SKYE"?
IT'S A NICKNAME. SHE SPENDS MOST OF HER MISSION TIME THESE DAYS IN OUTER SPACE.
YOU HAVE A PET NAME FOR MY DAUGHTER.
HOW SWEET.

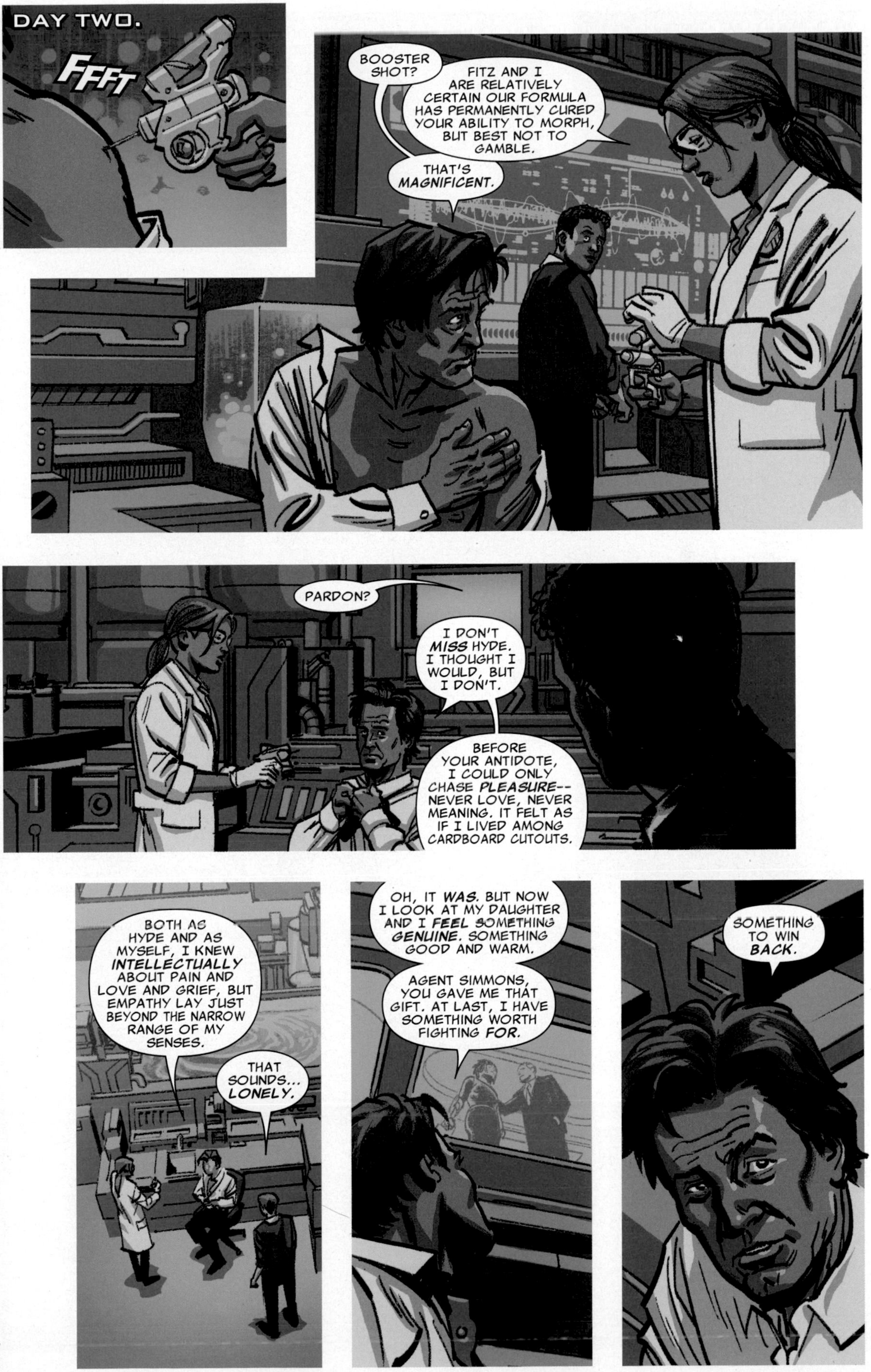
DAY TWO.
FFFT
BOOSTER SHOT?
FITZ AND I ARE RELATIVELY CERTAIN OUR FORMULA HAS PERMANENTLY CURED YOUR ABILITY TO MORPH, BUT BEST NOT TO GAMBLE.
THAT'S MAGNIFICENT.
PARDON?
I DON'T MISS HYDE. I THOUGHT I WOULD, BUT I DON'T.
BEFORE YOUR ANTIDOTE, I COULD ONLY CHASE PLEASURE-- NEVER LOVE, NEVER MEANING. IT FELT AS IF I LIVED AMONG CARDBOARD CUTOUTS.
BOTH AS HYDE AND AS MYSELF, I KNEW INTELLECTUALLY ABOUT PAIN AND LOVE AND GRIEF, BUT EMPATHY LAY JUST BEYOND THE NARROW RANGE OF MY SENSES.
THAT SOUNDS... LONELY.
OH, IT WAS. BUT NOW I LOOK AT MY DAUGHTER AND I FEEL SOMETHING GENUINE. SOMETHING GOOD AND WARM.
AGENT SIMMONS, YOU GAVE ME THAT GIFT. AT LAST, I HAVE SOMETHING WORTH FIGHTING FOR.
SOMETHING TO WIN BACK.

DAY THREE.

FFFT

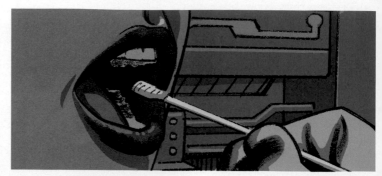

NNGGHH--

HANG *ON*, SKYE. IT'LL PASS.

DAY FOUR.

FFFT

AAAA!

I KNOW. I *KNOW*. DEEP BREATHS, SKYE. JUST LIKE WE'VE BEEN DOING. IT'LL *PASS*.

...

BRING MY DAUGHTER DOWN. HURRY.

I'VE GOT THE CURE.

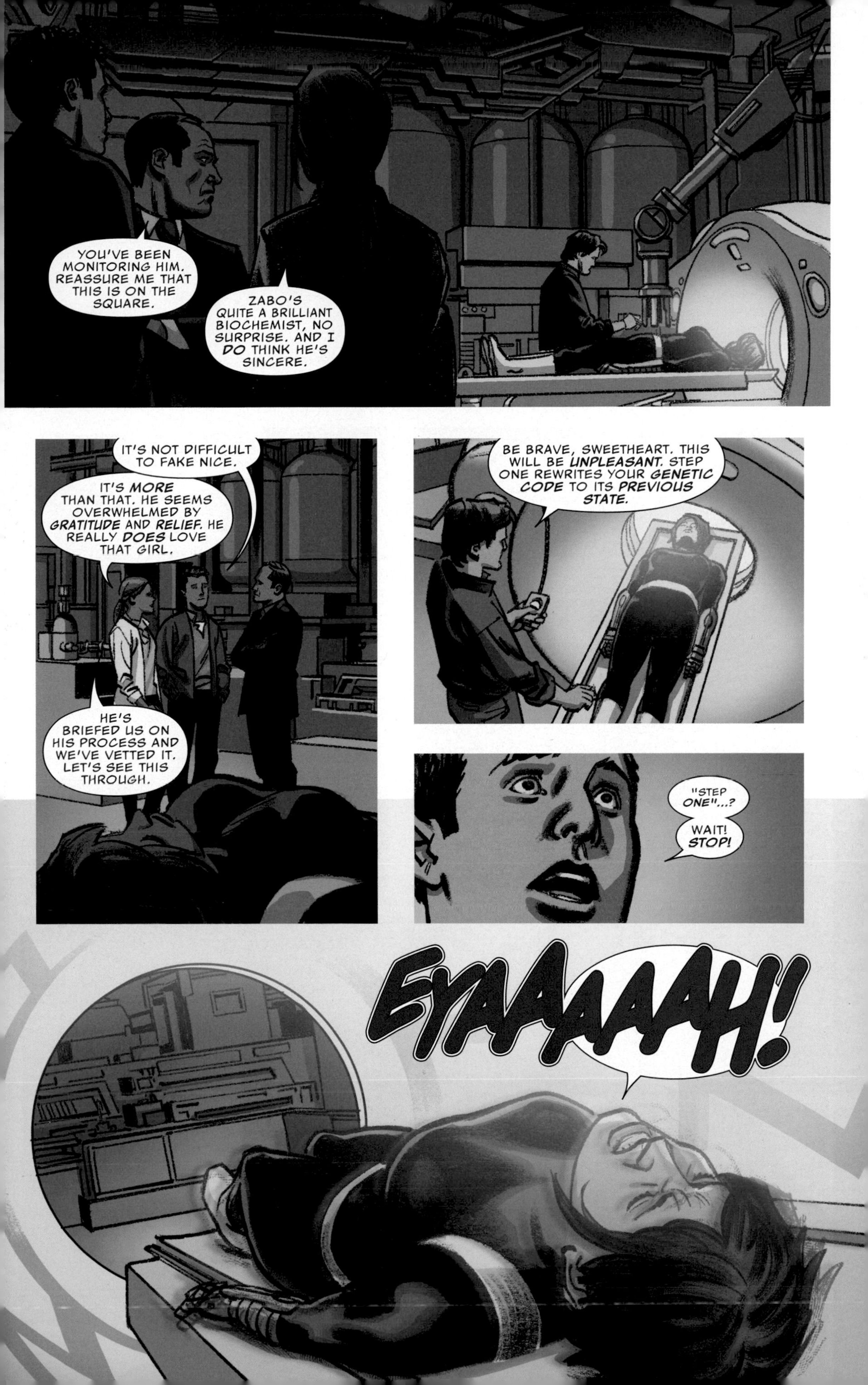

YOU'VE BEEN MONITORING HIM. REASSURE ME THAT THIS IS ON THE SQUARE.
ZABO'S QUITE A BRILLIANT BIOCHEMIST, NO SURPRISE. AND I *DO* THINK HE'S SINCERE.
IT'S NOT DIFFICULT TO FAKE NICE.
IT'S *MORE* THAN THAT. HE SEEMS OVERWHELMED BY *GRATITUDE* AND *RELIEF*. HE REALLY *DOES* LOVE THAT GIRL.
HE'S BRIEFED US ON HIS PROCESS AND WE'VE VETTED IT. LET'S SEE THIS THROUGH.
BE BRAVE, SWEETHEART. THIS WILL BE *UNPLEASANT*. STEP ONE REWRITES YOUR *GENETIC CODE* TO ITS *PREVIOUS STATE*.
"STEP *ONE*"...?
WAIT! *STOP!*
EYAAAAAH!

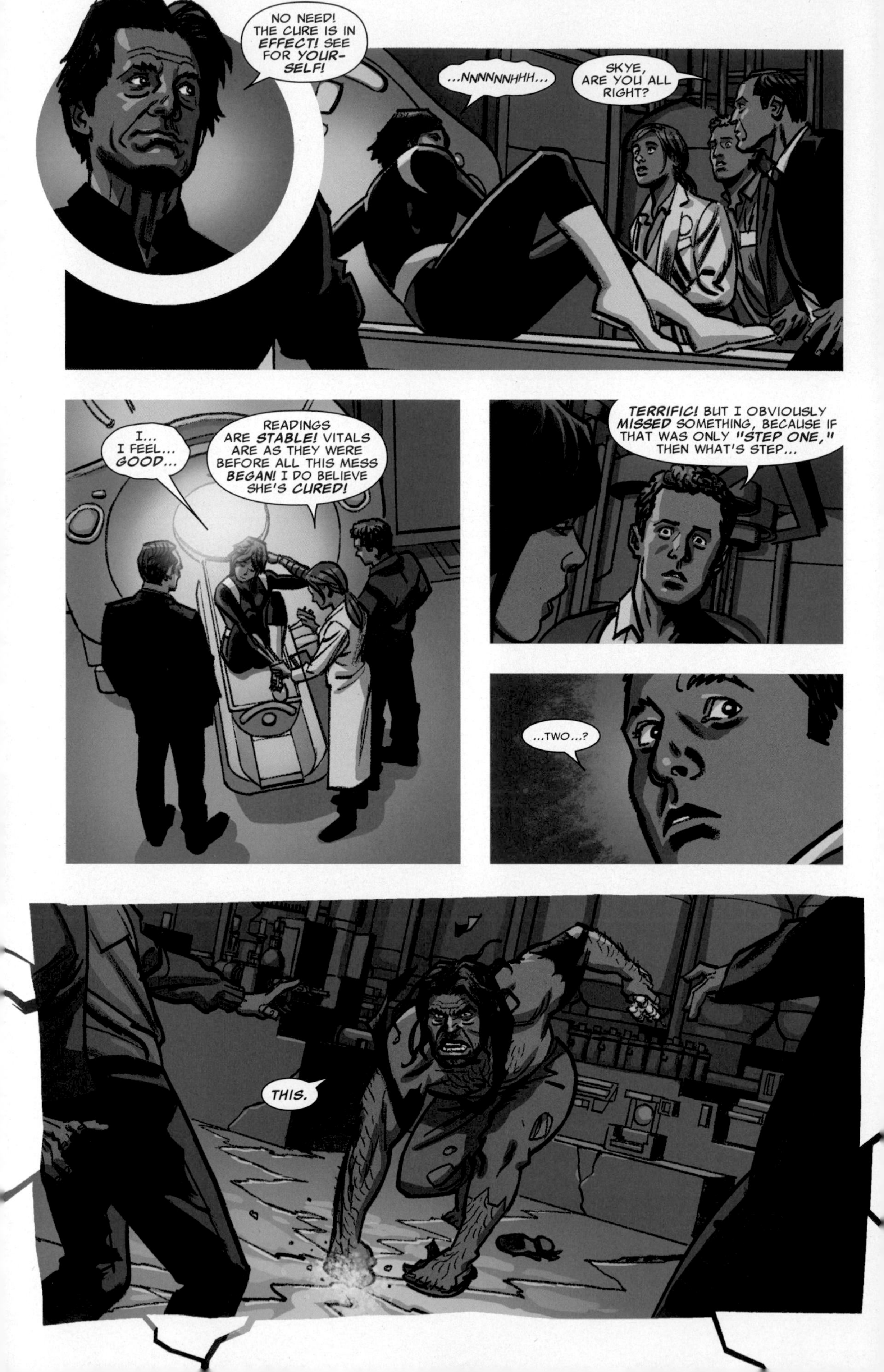
NO NEED! THE CURE IS IN EFFECT! SEE FOR YOURSELF!
...NNNNNNHHH...
SKYE, ARE YOU ALL RIGHT?
I... I FEEL... GOOD...
READINGS ARE STABLE! VITALS ARE AS THEY WERE BEFORE ALL THIS MESS BEGAN! I DO BELIEVE SHE'S CURED!
TERRIFIC! BUT I OBVIOUSLY MISSED SOMETHING, BECAUSE IF THAT WAS ONLY "STEP ONE," THEN WHAT'S STEP...
...TWO...?
THIS.

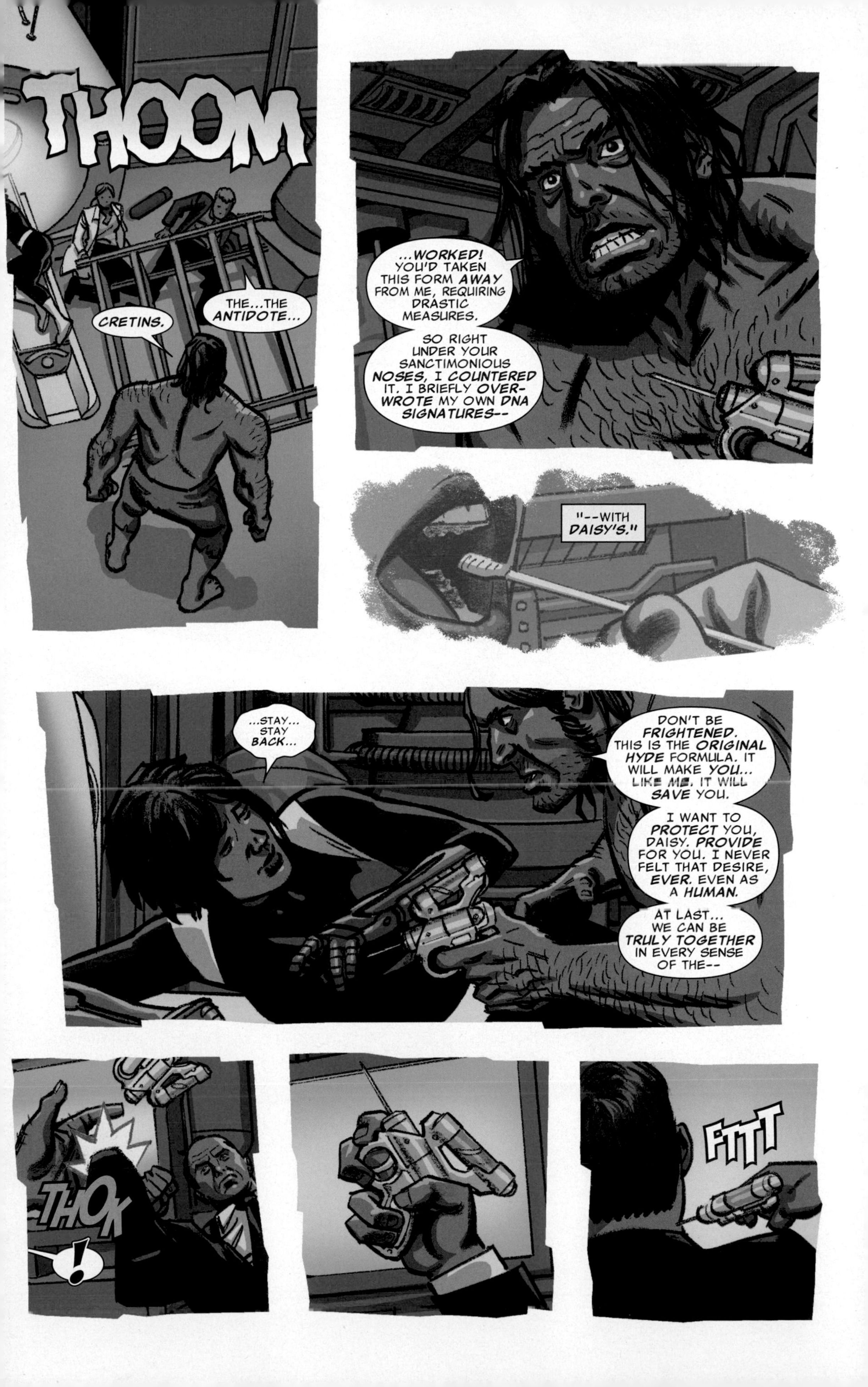
THOOM
CRETINS.
THE...THE ANTIDOTE...
...WORKED! YOU'D TAKEN THIS FORM AWAY FROM ME, REQUIRING DRASTIC MEASURES.
SO RIGHT UNDER YOUR SANCTIMONIOUS NOSES, I COUNTERED IT. I BRIEFLY OVER-WROTE MY OWN DNA SIGNATURES--
"--WITH DAISY'S."
...STAY... STAY BACK...
DON'T BE FRIGHTENED. THIS IS THE ORIGINAL HYDE FORMULA. IT WILL MAKE YOU... LIKE ME. IT WILL SAVE YOU.
I WANT TO PROTECT YOU, DAISY. PROVIDE FOR YOU. I NEVER FELT THAT DESIRE, EVER. EVEN AS A HUMAN.
AT LAST... WE CAN BE TRULY TOGETHER IN EVERY SENSE OF THE--
THOK
!
FTTT

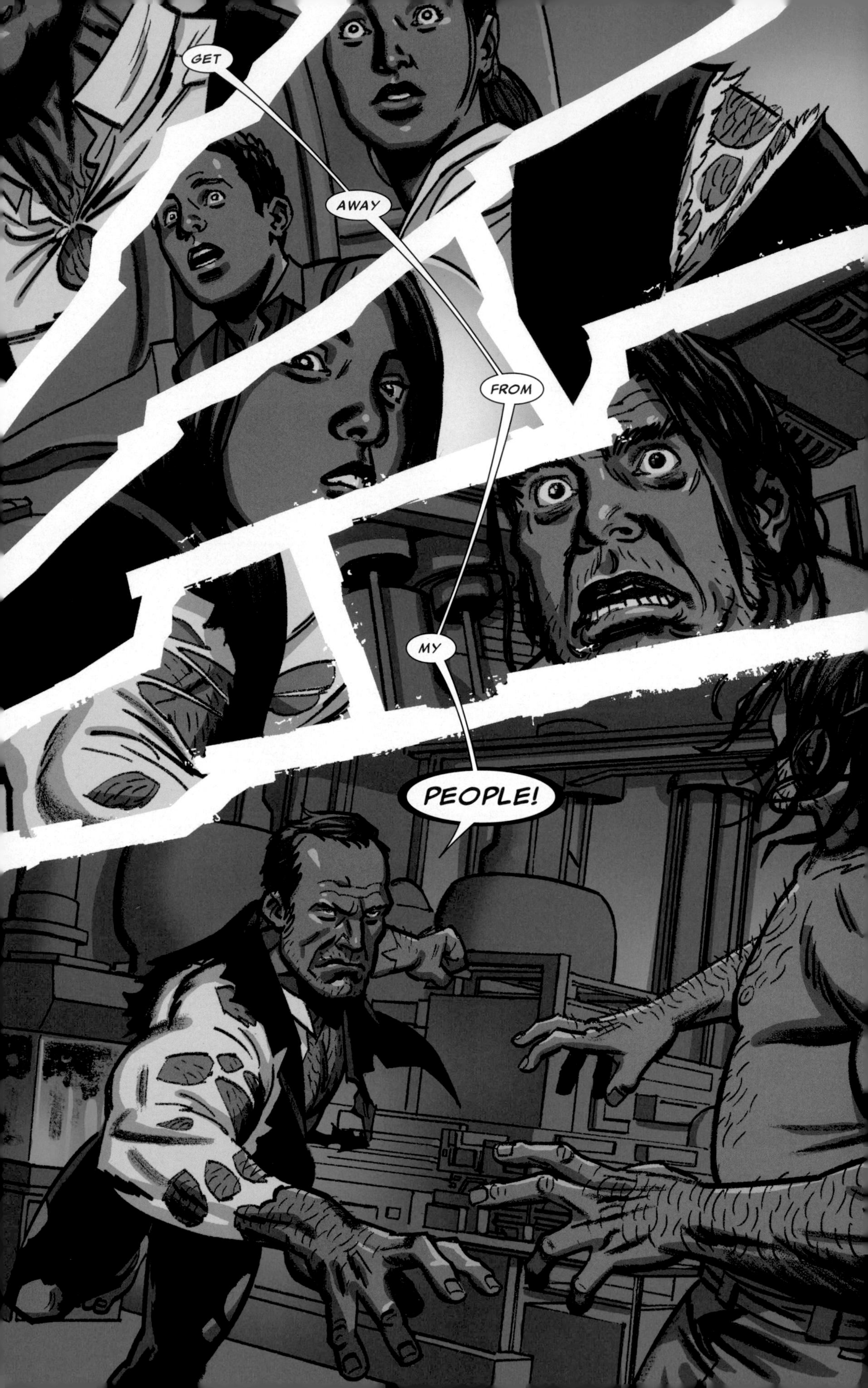
GET
AWAY
FROM
MY
PEOPLE!

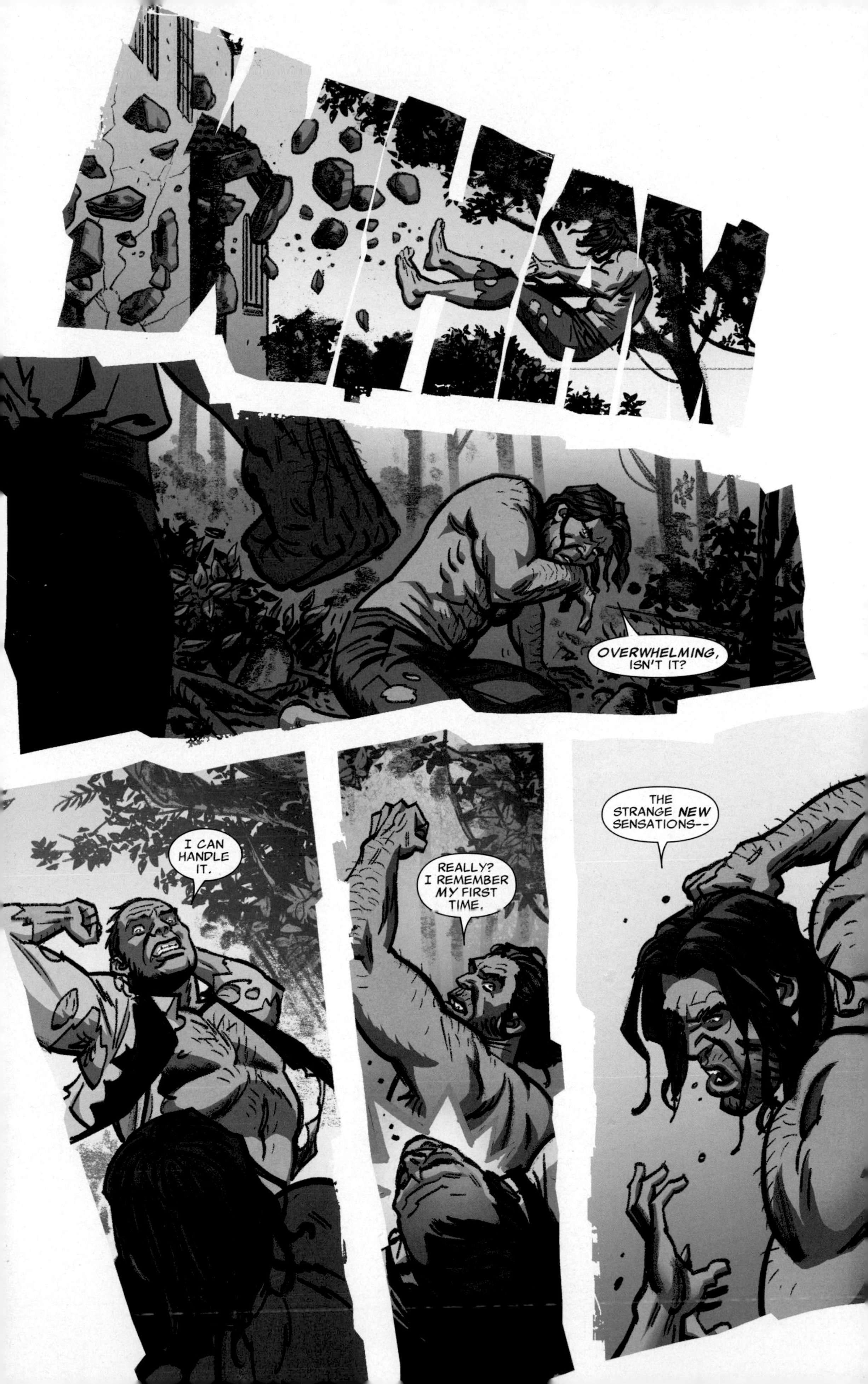
OVERWHELMING, ISN'T IT?
I CAN HANDLE IT.
REALLY? I REMEMBER MY FIRST TIME.
THE STRANGE NEW SENSATIONS--

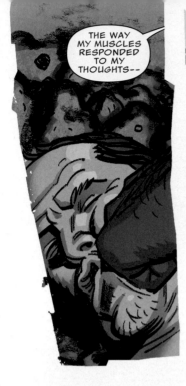

THE WAY MY MUSCLES RESPONDED TO MY THOUGHTS--

--THE AWKWARDNESS--

--IT TOOK QUITE SOME TIME TO ADJUST.

OH, MY GOD...HE'S LOSING! HYDE'S KILLING HIM!

DO SOMETHING! QUAKE HIM--!

I'M...TRYING...! I JUST...NEED A MOMENT...!

TIME I WON'T GIVE YOU.

PHIL! I'VE GOT HIM!

FITZ, NO!

WHAT ARE YOU DOING?

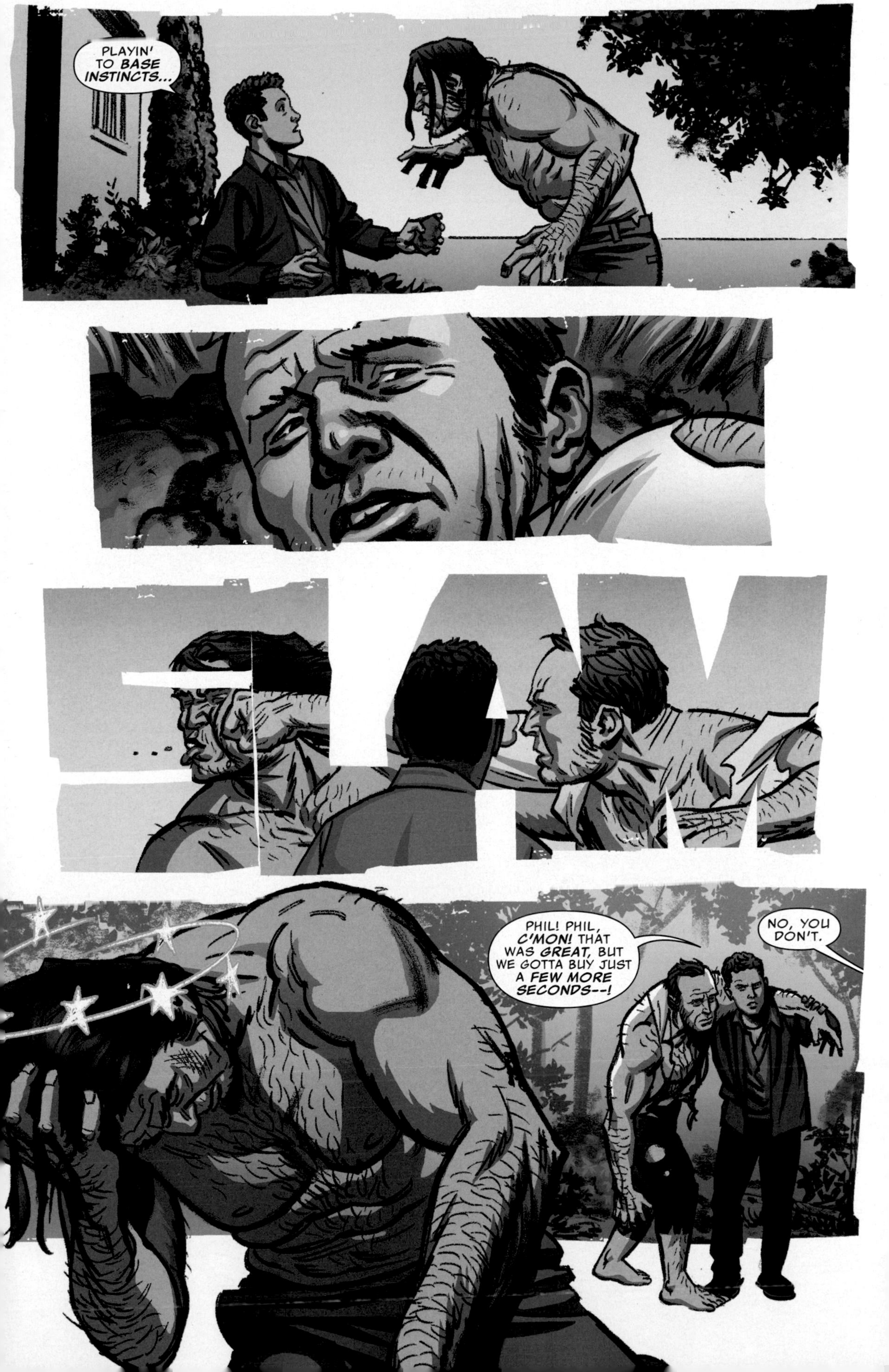
PLAYIN' TO BASE INSTINCTS...
...
PHIL! PHIL, C'MON! THAT WAS GREAT, BUT WE GOTTA BUY JUST A FEW MORE SECONDS--!
NO, YOU DON'T.

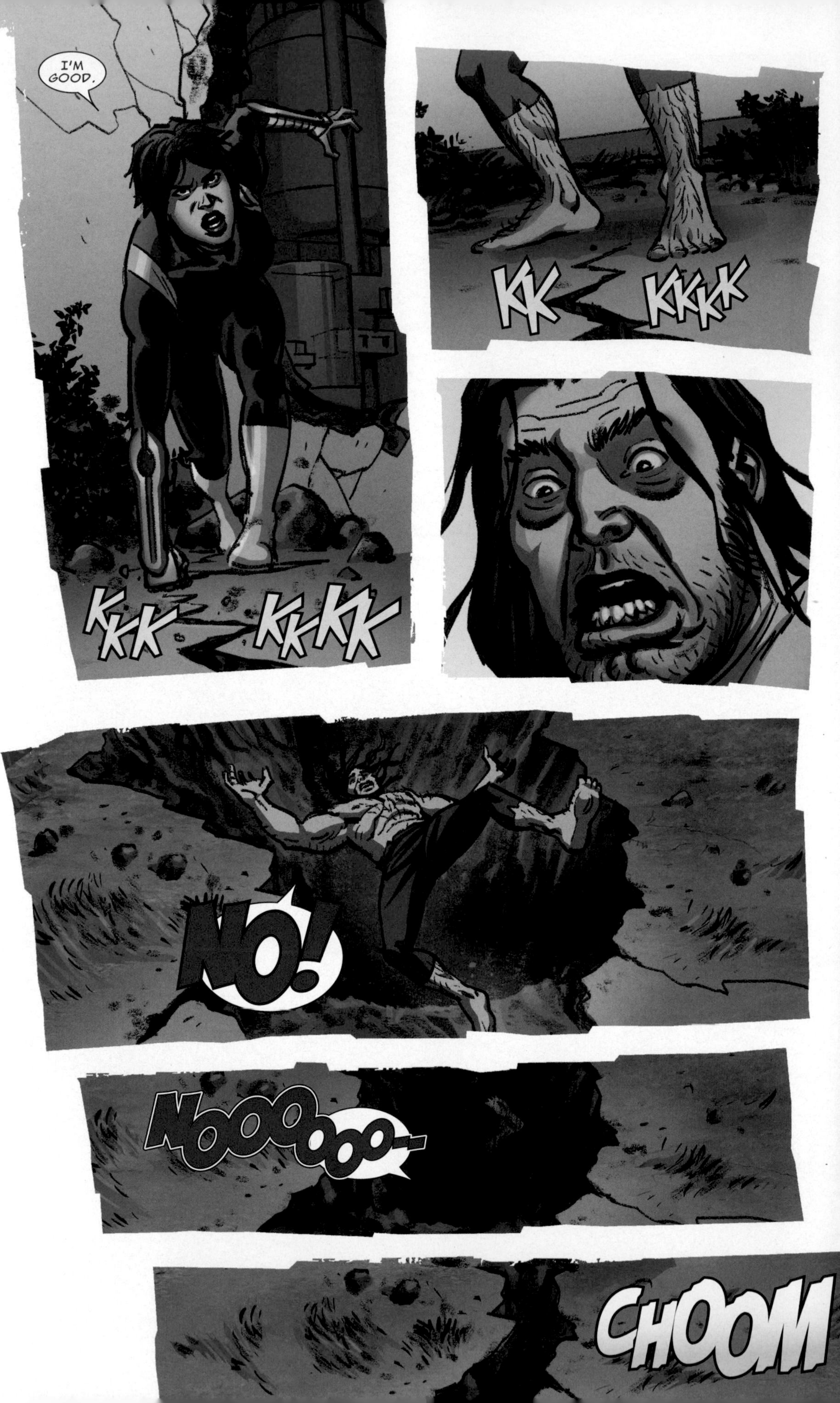
I'M GOOD.
KKK KKKKK
KK KKKK
NO!
NOOOOOOO--
CHOOM

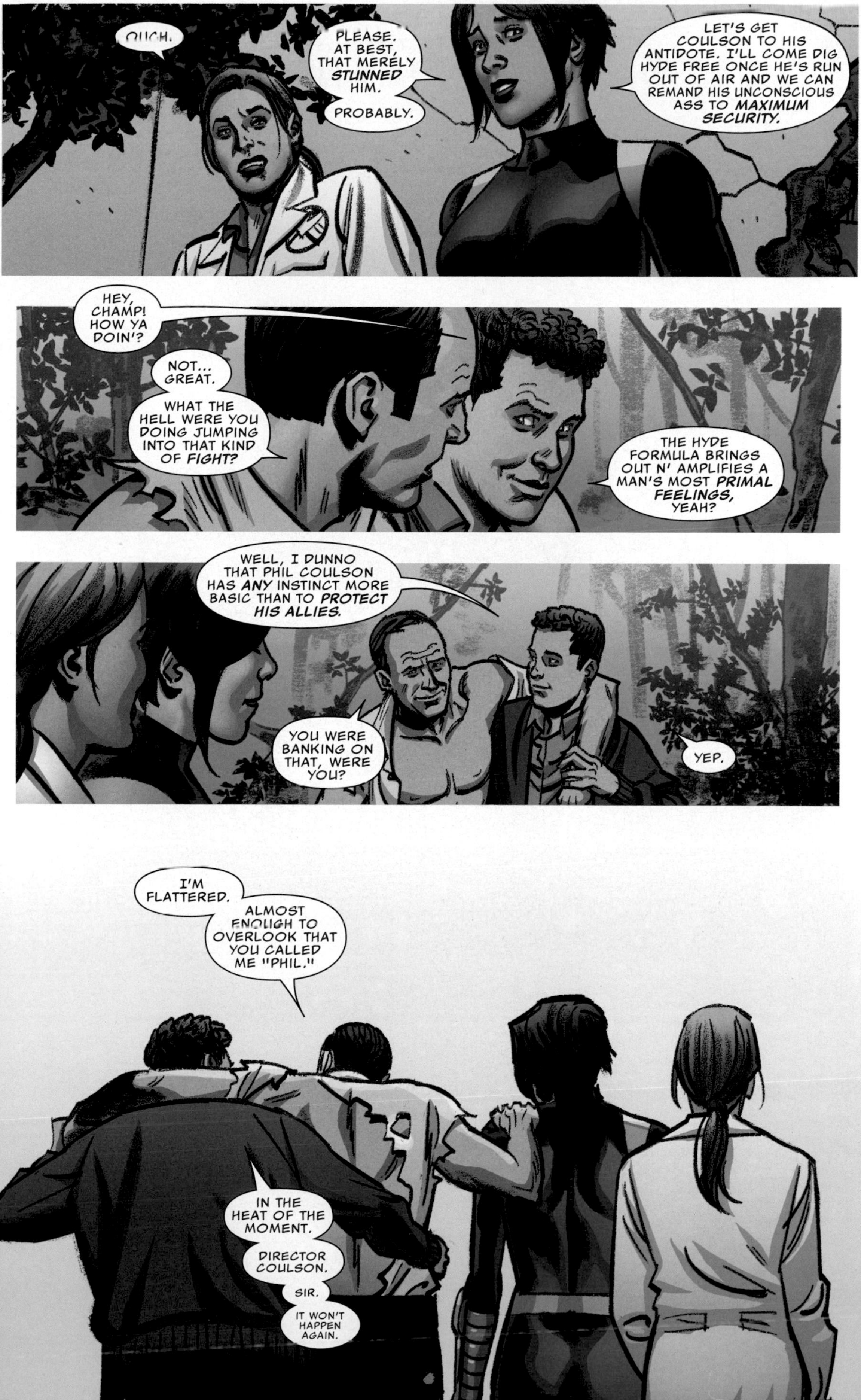
OUCH.
PLEASE. AT BEST, THAT MERELY STUNNED HIM.
PROBABLY.
LET'S GET COULSON TO HIS ANTIDOTE. I'LL COME DIG HYDE FREE ONCE HE'S RUN OUT OF AIR AND WE CAN REMAND HIS UNCONSCIOUS ASS TO MAXIMUM SECURITY.
HEY, CHAMP! HOW YA DOIN'?
NOT... GREAT.
WHAT THE HELL WERE YOU DOING JUMPING INTO THAT KIND OF FIGHT?
THE HYDE FORMULA BRINGS OUT N' AMPLIFIES A MAN'S MOST PRIMAL FEELINGS, YEAH?
WELL, I DUNNO THAT PHIL COULSON HAS ANY INSTINCT MORE BASIC THAN TO PROTECT HIS ALLIES.
YOU WERE BANKING ON THAT, WERE YOU?
YEP.
I'M FLATTERED.
ALMOST ENOUGH TO OVERLOOK THAT YOU CALLED ME "PHIL."
IN THE HEAT OF THE MOMENT.
DIRECTOR COULSON.
SIR.
IT WON'T HAPPEN AGAIN.

8.

ACTIVE MISSION:

NO ANGEL

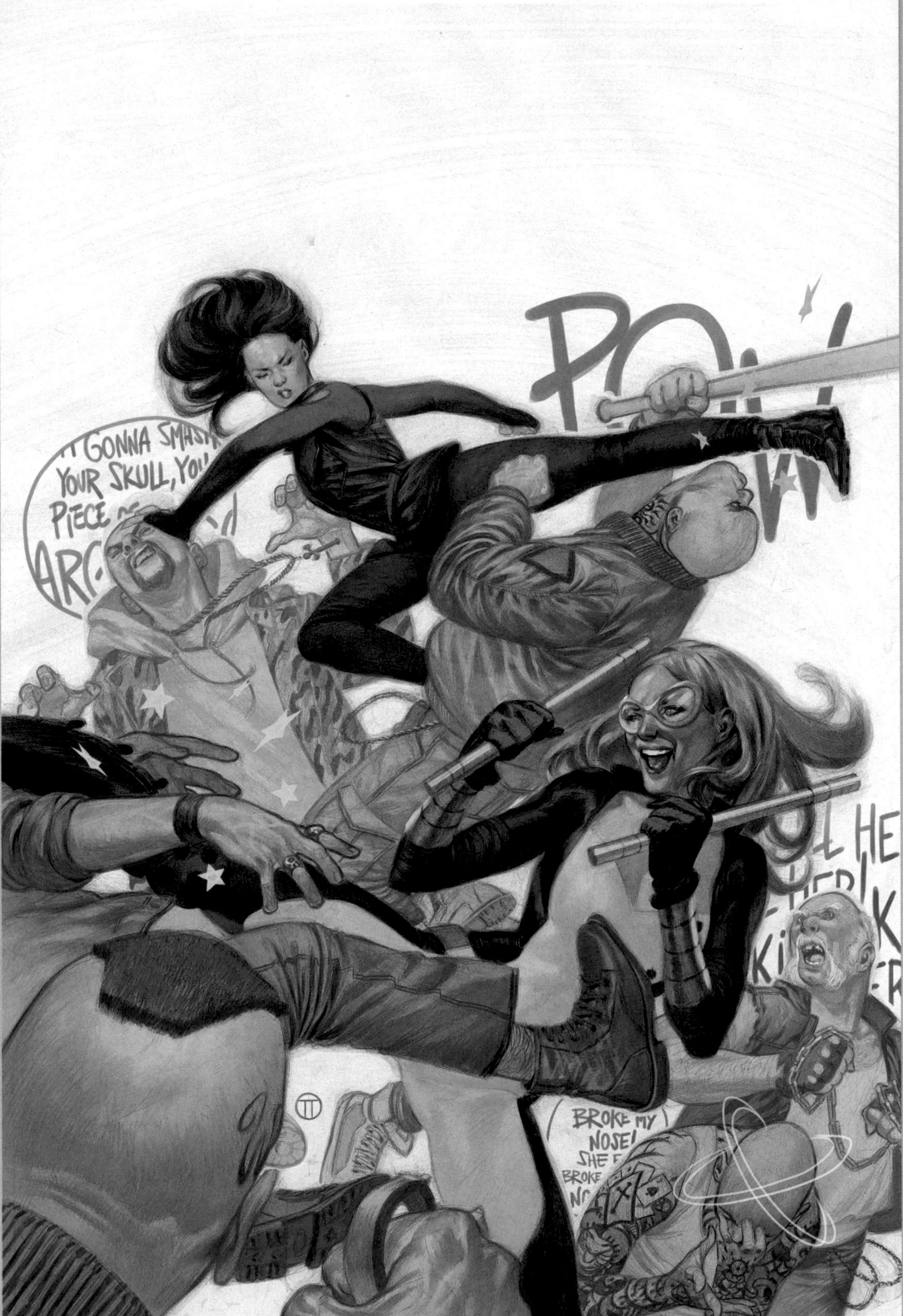
GONNA SMASH
YOUR SKULL, YOU
PIECE
POW
BROKE MY NOSE!
SHE
BROKE

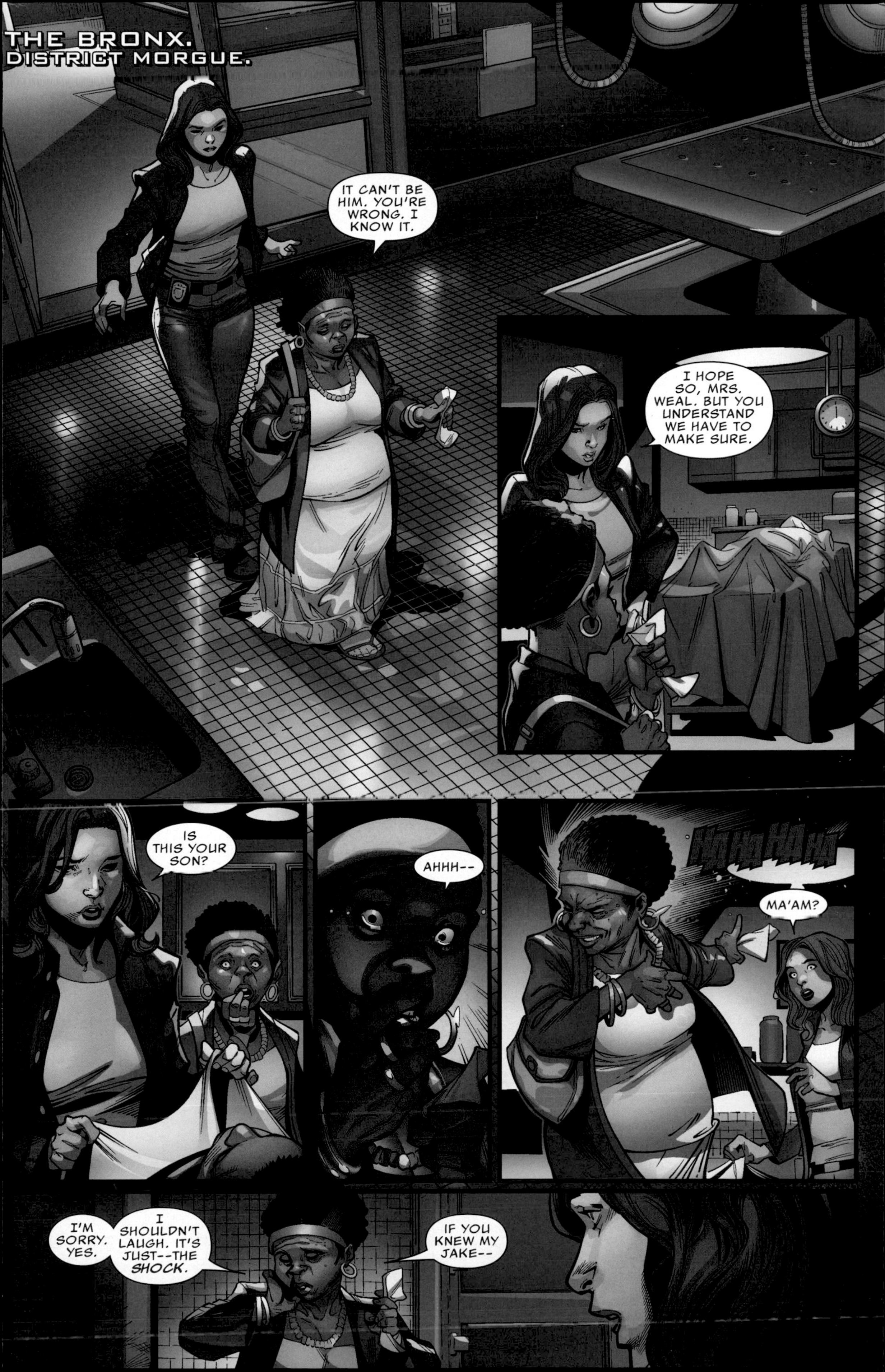
THE BRONX.
DISTRICT MORGUE.
IT CAN'T BE HIM. YOU'RE WRONG. I KNOW IT.
I HOPE SO, MRS. WEAL. BUT YOU UNDERSTAND WE HAVE TO MAKE SURE.
IS THIS YOUR SON?
AHHH--
HA HA HA HA
MA'AM?
I'M SORRY. YES.
I SHOULDN'T LAUGH. IT'S JUST--THE SHOCK.
IF YOU KNEW MY JAKE--

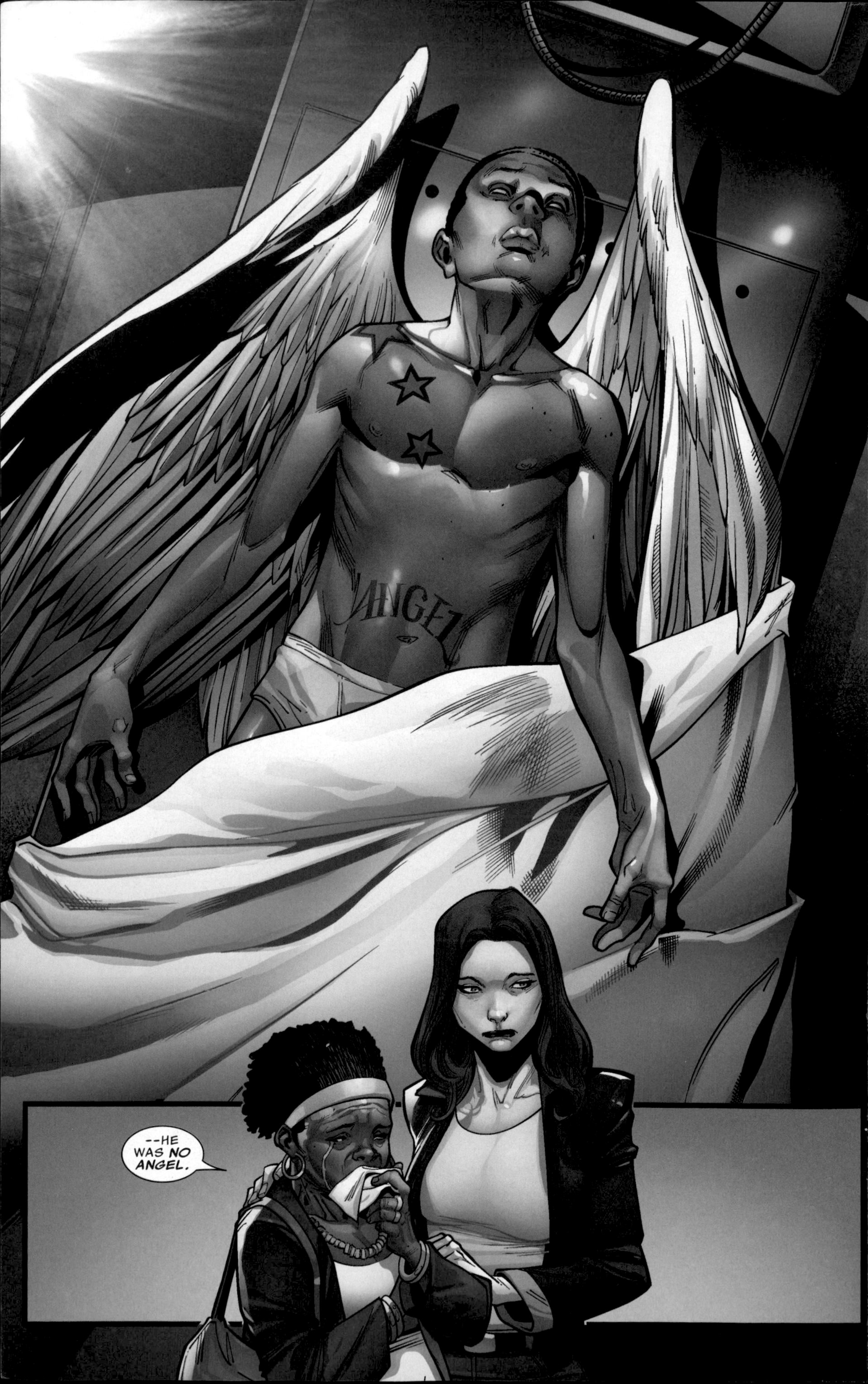
--HE WAS NO ANGEL.

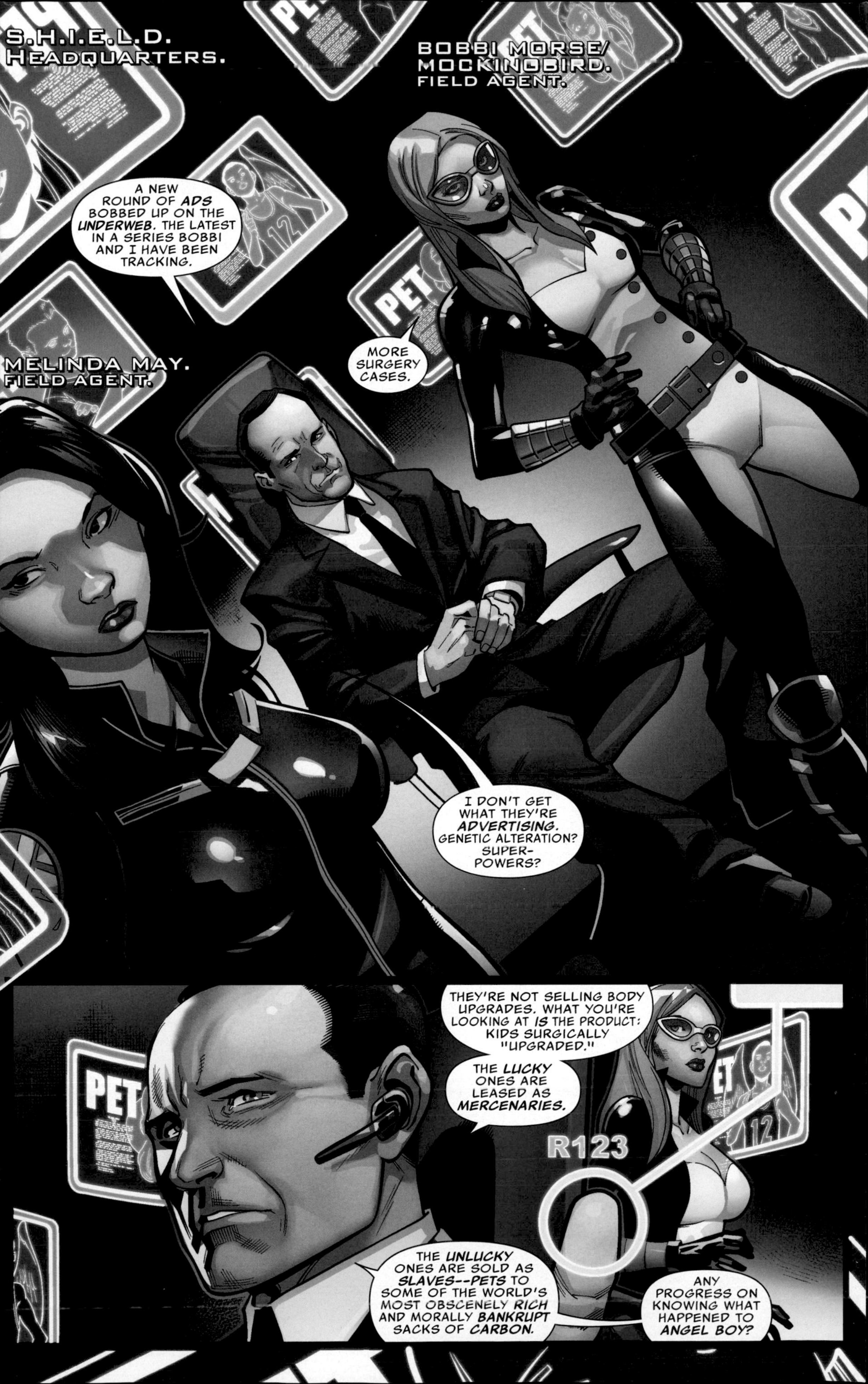
S.H.I.E.L.D. HEADQUARTERS.
BOBBI MORSE/ MOCKINGBIRD. FIELD AGENT.
A NEW ROUND OF ADS BOBBED UP ON THE UNDERWEB. THE LATEST IN A SERIES BOBBI AND I HAVE BEEN TRACKING.
MORE SURGERY CASES.
MELINDA MAY. FIELD AGENT.
I DON'T GET WHAT THEY'RE ADVERTISING. GENETIC ALTERATION? SUPER-POWERS?
THEY'RE NOT SELLING BODY UPGRADES. WHAT YOU'RE LOOKING AT IS THE PRODUCT: KIDS SURGICALLY "UPGRADED."
THE LUCKY ONES ARE LEASED AS MERCENARIES.
R123
THE UNLUCKY ONES ARE SOLD AS SLAVES--PETS TO SOME OF THE WORLD'S MOST OBSCENELY RICH AND MORALLY BANKRUPT SACKS OF CARBON.
ANY PROGRESS ON KNOWING WHAT HAPPENED TO ANGEL BOY?

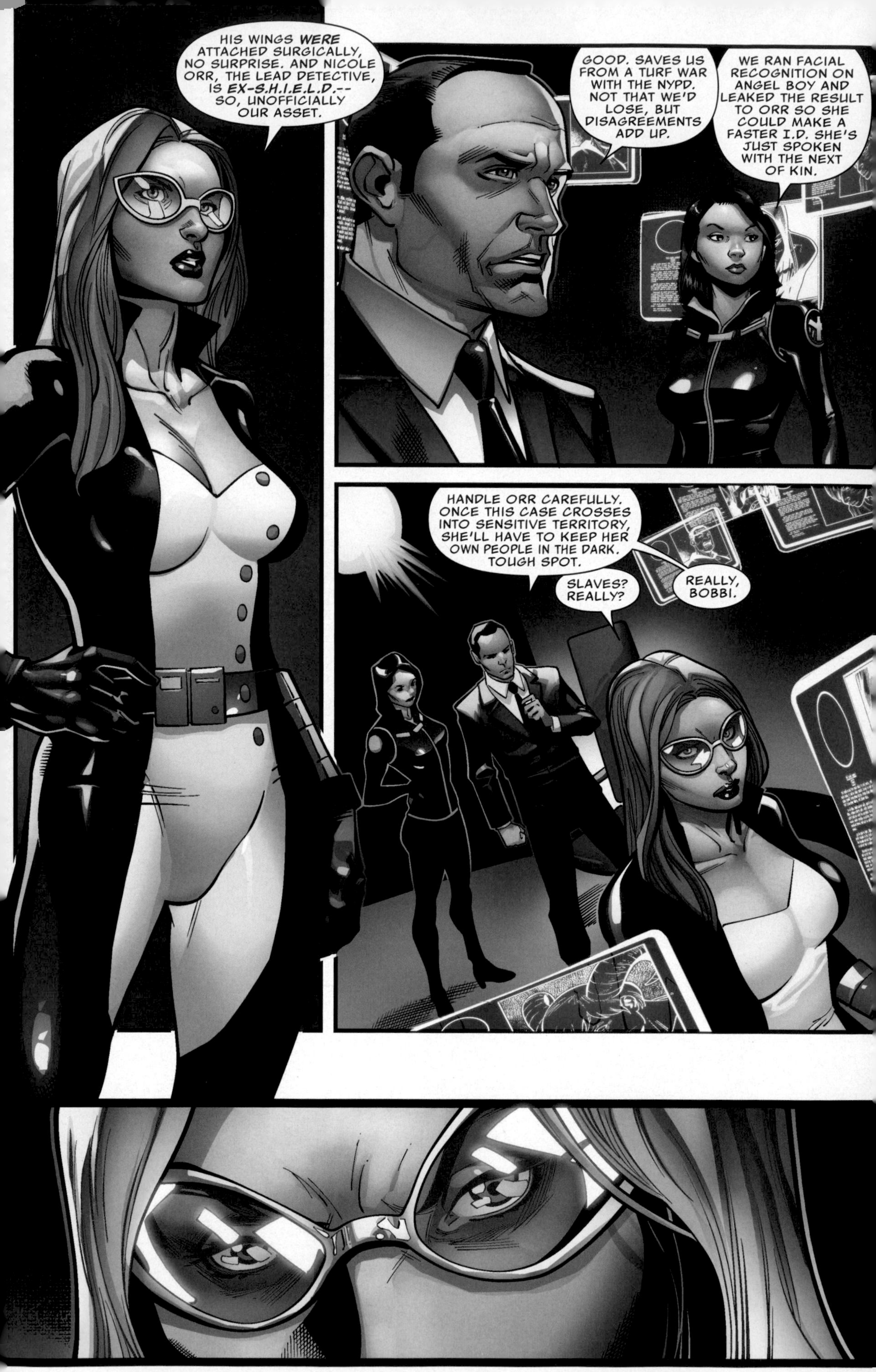
HIS WINGS **WERE** ATTACHED SURGICALLY, NO SURPRISE. AND NICOLE ORR, THE LEAD DETECTIVE, IS ***EX-S.H.I.E.L.D.***-- SO, UNOFFICIALLY OUR ASSET.
GOOD. SAVES US FROM A TURF WAR WITH THE NYPD. NOT THAT WE'D LOSE, BUT DISAGREEMENTS ADD UP.
WE RAN FACIAL RECOGNITION ON ANGEL BOY AND LEAKED THE RESULT TO ORR SO SHE COULD MAKE A FASTER I.D. SHE'S JUST SPOKEN WITH THE NEXT OF KIN.
HANDLE ORR CAREFULLY. ONCE THIS CASE CROSSES INTO SENSITIVE TERRITORY, SHE'LL HAVE TO KEEP HER OWN PEOPLE IN THE DARK. TOUGH SPOT.
SLAVES? REALLY?
REALLY, BOBBI.

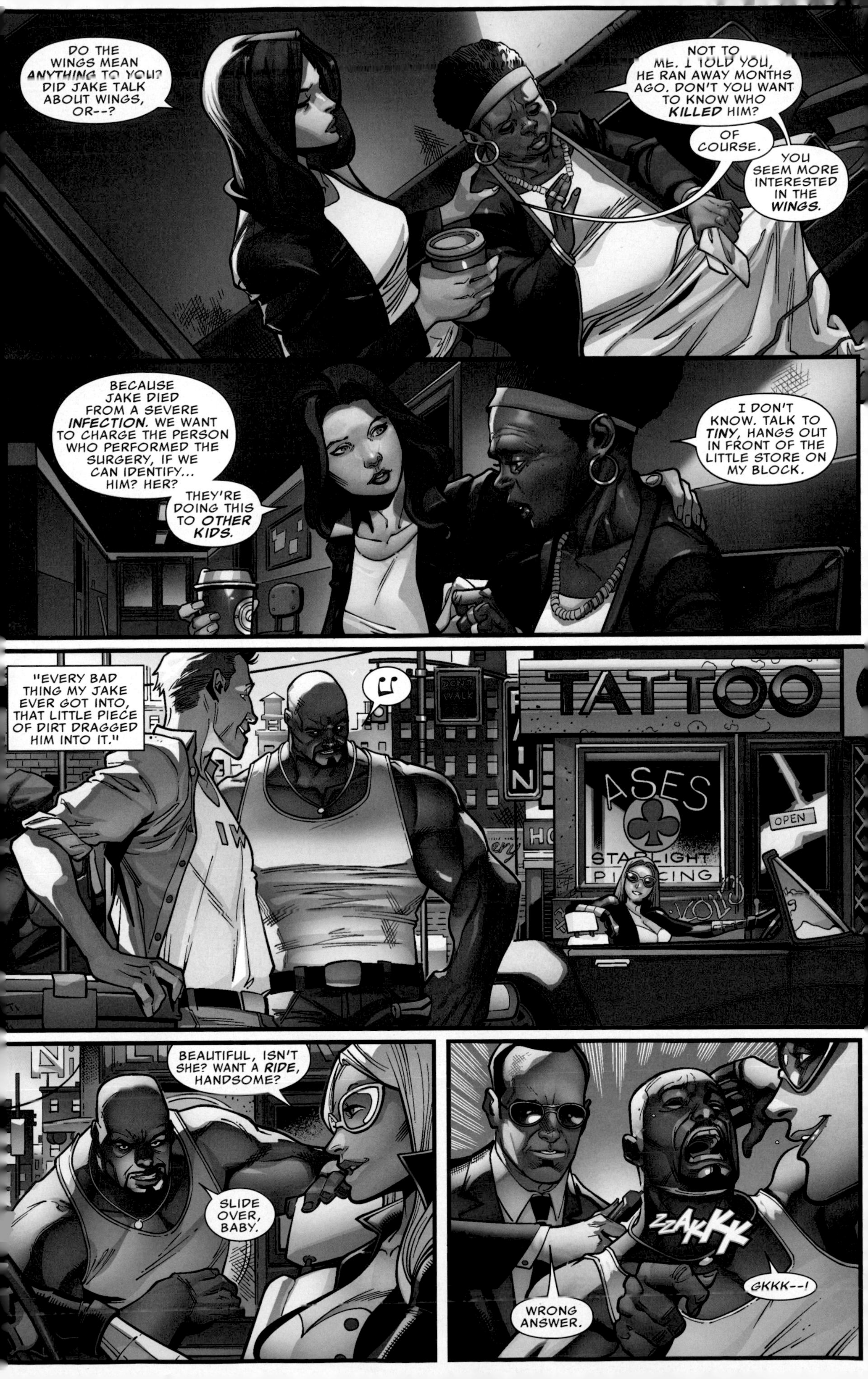

DO THE WINGS MEAN ANYTHING TO YOU? DID JAKE TALK ABOUT WINGS, OR--?
NOT TO ME. I TOLD YOU, HE RAN AWAY MONTHS AGO. DON'T YOU WANT TO KNOW WHO KILLED HIM?
OF COURSE.
YOU SEEM MORE INTERESTED IN THE WINGS.
BECAUSE JAKE DIED FROM A SEVERE INFECTION. WE WANT TO CHARGE THE PERSON WHO PERFORMED THE SURGERY, IF WE CAN IDENTIFY... HIM? HER?
THEY'RE DOING THIS TO OTHER KIDS.
I DON'T KNOW. TALK TO TINY, HANGS OUT IN FRONT OF THE LITTLE STORE ON MY BLOCK.
"EVERY BAD THING MY JAKE EVER GOT INTO, THAT LITTLE PIECE OF DIRT DRAGGED HIM INTO IT."
DON'T WALK
TATTOO
ASES
STARLIGHT PIERCING
OPEN
BEAUTIFUL, ISN'T SHE? WANT A RIDE, HANDSOME?
SLIDE OVER, BABY.
ZZAKKKK
WRONG ANSWER.
GKKK--!

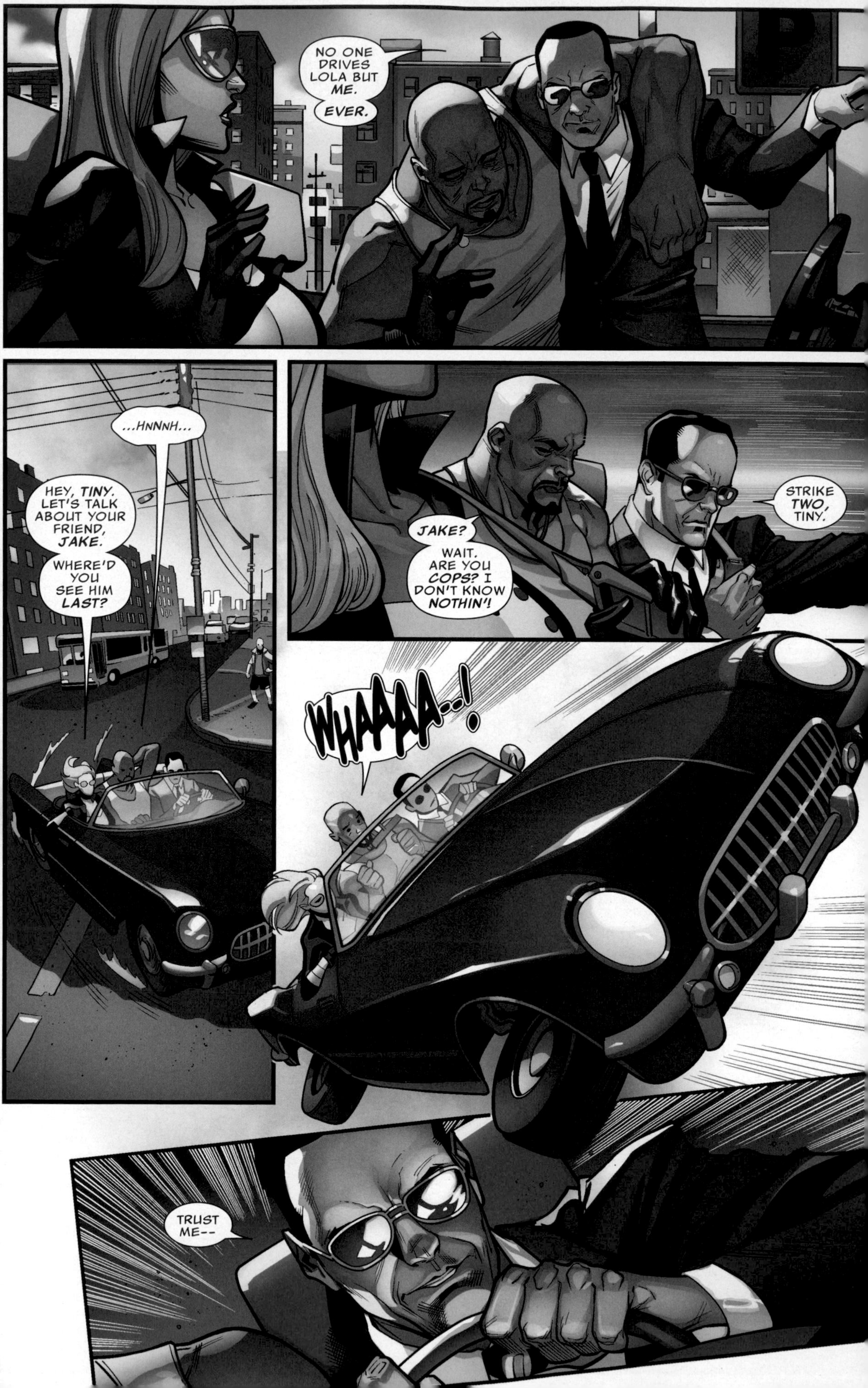

NO ONE DRIVES LOLA BUT ME.
EVER.
...HNNNH...
HEY, TINY. LET'S TALK ABOUT YOUR FRIEND, JAKE.
WHERE'D YOU SEE HIM LAST?
JAKE?
WAIT. ARE YOU COPS? I DON'T KNOW NOTHIN'!
STRIKE TWO, TINY.
WHAAAA--!
TRUST ME--

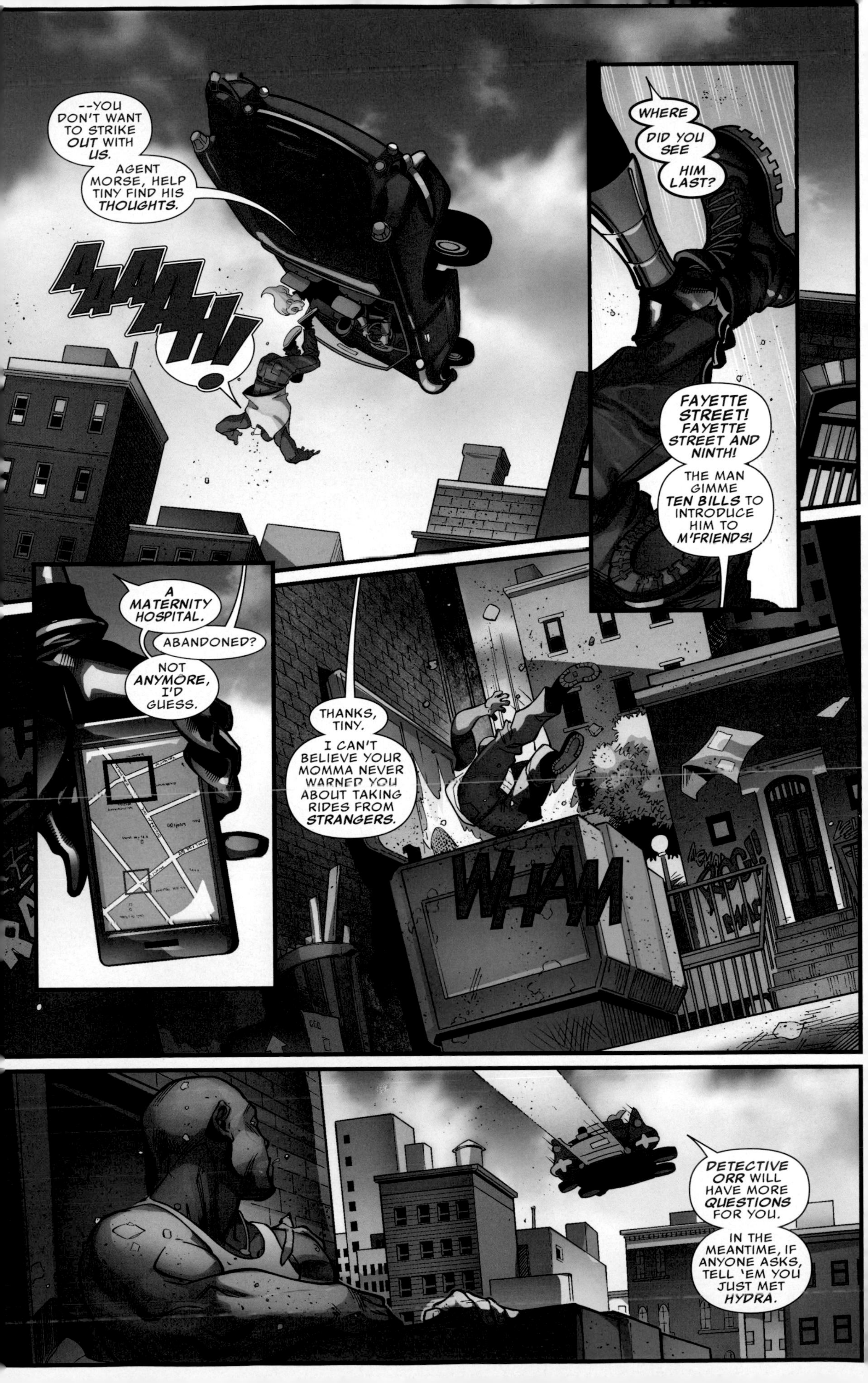
--YOU DON'T WANT TO STRIKE OUT WITH US.
AGENT MORSE, HELP TINY FIND HIS THOUGHTS.
AAAAHH!
WHERE DID YOU SEE HIM LAST?
FAYETTE STREET! FAYETTE STREET AND NINTH!
THE MAN GIMME TEN BILLS TO INTRODUCE HIM TO M'FRIENDS!
A MATERNITY HOSPITAL.
ABANDONED?
NOT ANYMORE, I'D GUESS.
THANKS, TINY.
I CAN'T BELIEVE YOUR MOMMA NEVER WARNED YOU ABOUT TAKING RIDES FROM STRANGERS.
WHAM
DETECTIVE ORR WILL HAVE MORE QUESTIONS FOR YOU.
IN THE MEANTIME, IF ANYONE ASKS, TELL 'EM YOU JUST MET HYDRA.

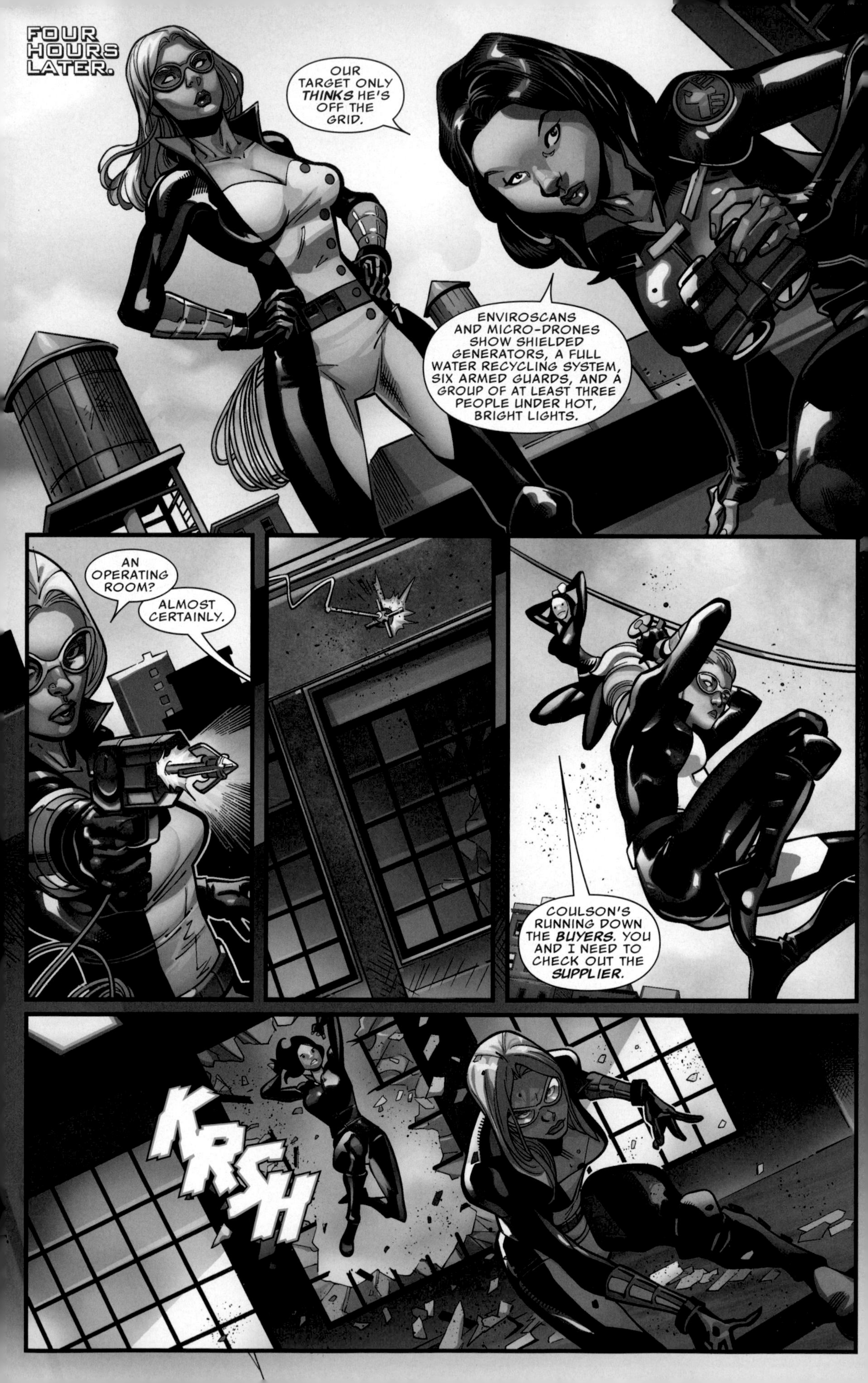
FOUR HOURS LATER.
OUR TARGET ONLY THINKS HE'S OFF THE GRID.
ENVIROSCANS AND MICRO-DRONES SHOW SHIELDED GENERATORS, A FULL WATER RECYCLING SYSTEM, SIX ARMED GUARDS, AND A GROUP OF AT LEAST THREE PEOPLE UNDER HOT, BRIGHT LIGHTS.
AN OPERATING ROOM?
ALMOST CERTAINLY.
COULSON'S RUNNING DOWN THE BUYERS. YOU AND I NEED TO CHECK OUT THE SUPPLIER.
KRSH

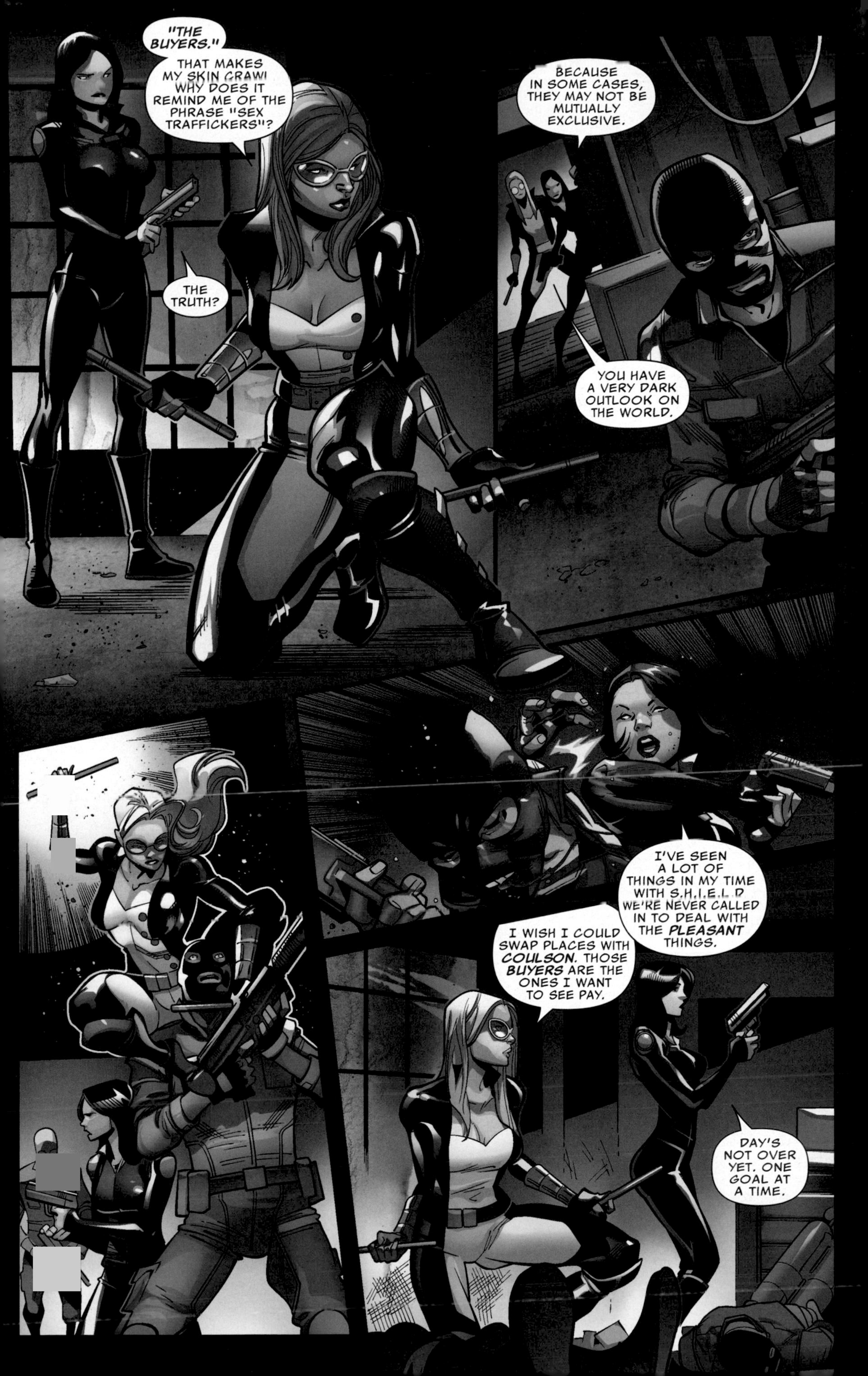
"THE BUYERS."
THAT MAKES MY SKIN CRAWL. WHY DOES IT REMIND ME OF THE PHRASE "SEX TRAFFICKERS"?
THE TRUTH?
BECAUSE IN SOME CASES, THEY MAY NOT BE MUTUALLY EXCLUSIVE.
YOU HAVE A VERY DARK OUTLOOK ON THE WORLD.
I'VE SEEN A LOT OF THINGS IN MY TIME WITH S.H.I.E.L.D. WE'RE NEVER CALLED IN TO DEAL WITH THE PLEASANT THINGS.
I WISH I COULD SWAP PLACES WITH COULSON. THOSE BUYERS ARE THE ONES I WANT TO SEE PAY.
DAY'S NOT OVER YET. ONE GOAL AT A TIME.

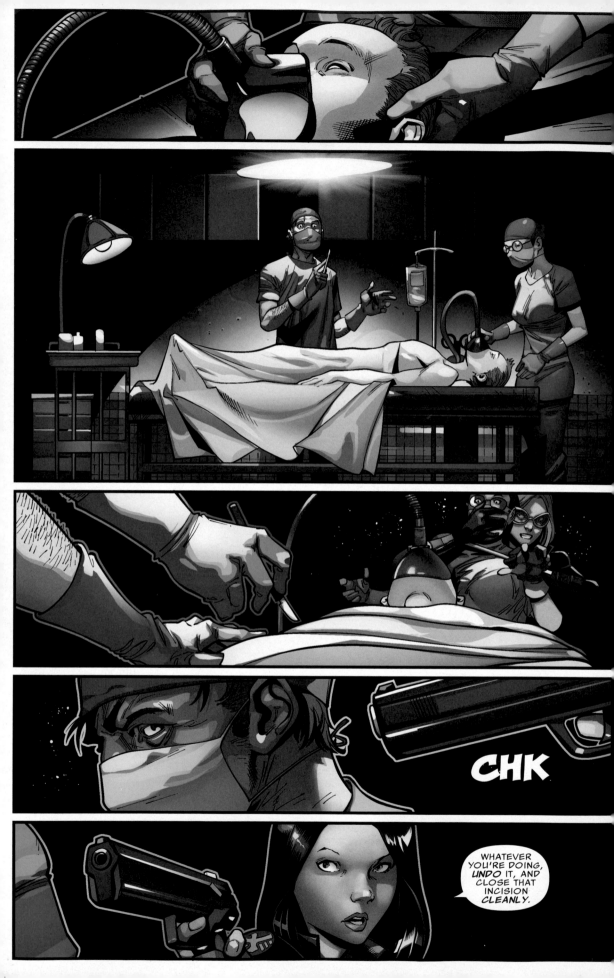

CHK

WHATEVER YOU'RE DOING, *UNDO* IT, AND CLOSE THAT INCISION *CLEANLY*.

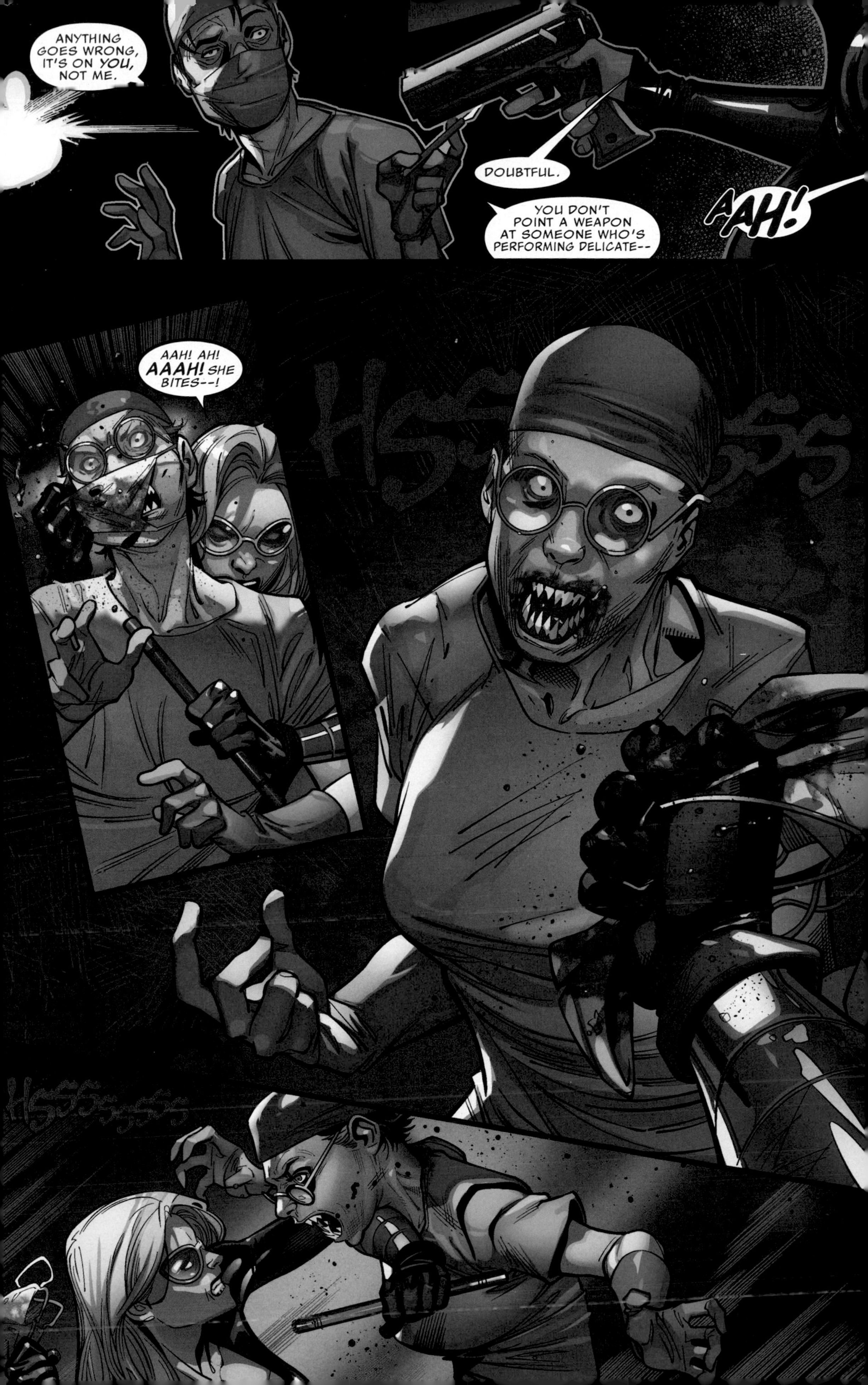

ANYTHING GOES WRONG, IT'S ON YOU, NOT ME.
DOUBTFUL.
YOU DON'T POINT A WEAPON AT SOMEONE WHO'S PERFORMING DELICATE--
AAH!
AAH! AH! AAAH! SHE BITES--!

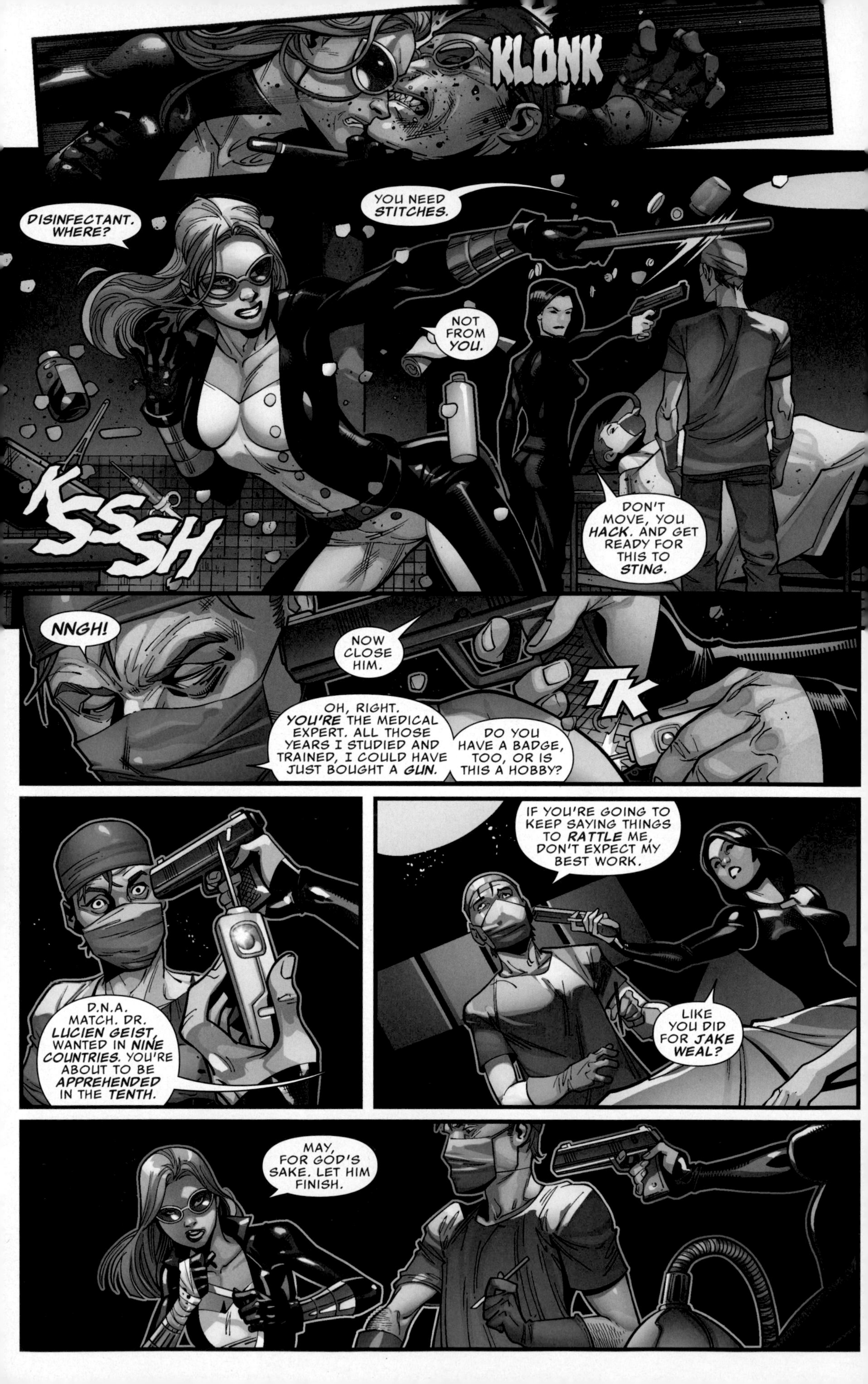
KLONK
DISINFECTANT. WHERE?
YOU NEED STITCHES.
NOT FROM YOU.
KSSSH
DON'T MOVE, YOU HACK. AND GET READY FOR THIS TO STING.
NNGH!
NOW CLOSE HIM.
TK
OH, RIGHT. YOU'RE THE MEDICAL EXPERT. ALL THOSE YEARS I STUDIED AND TRAINED, I COULD HAVE JUST BOUGHT A GUN.
DO YOU HAVE A BADGE, TOO, OR IS THIS A HOBBY?
D.N.A. MATCH. DR. LUCIEN GEIST, WANTED IN NINE COUNTRIES. YOU'RE ABOUT TO BE APPREHENDED IN THE TENTH.
IF YOU'RE GOING TO KEEP SAYING THINGS TO RATTLE ME, DON'T EXPECT MY BEST WORK.
LIKE YOU DID FOR JAKE WEAL?
MAY, FOR GOD'S SAKE. LET HIM FINISH.

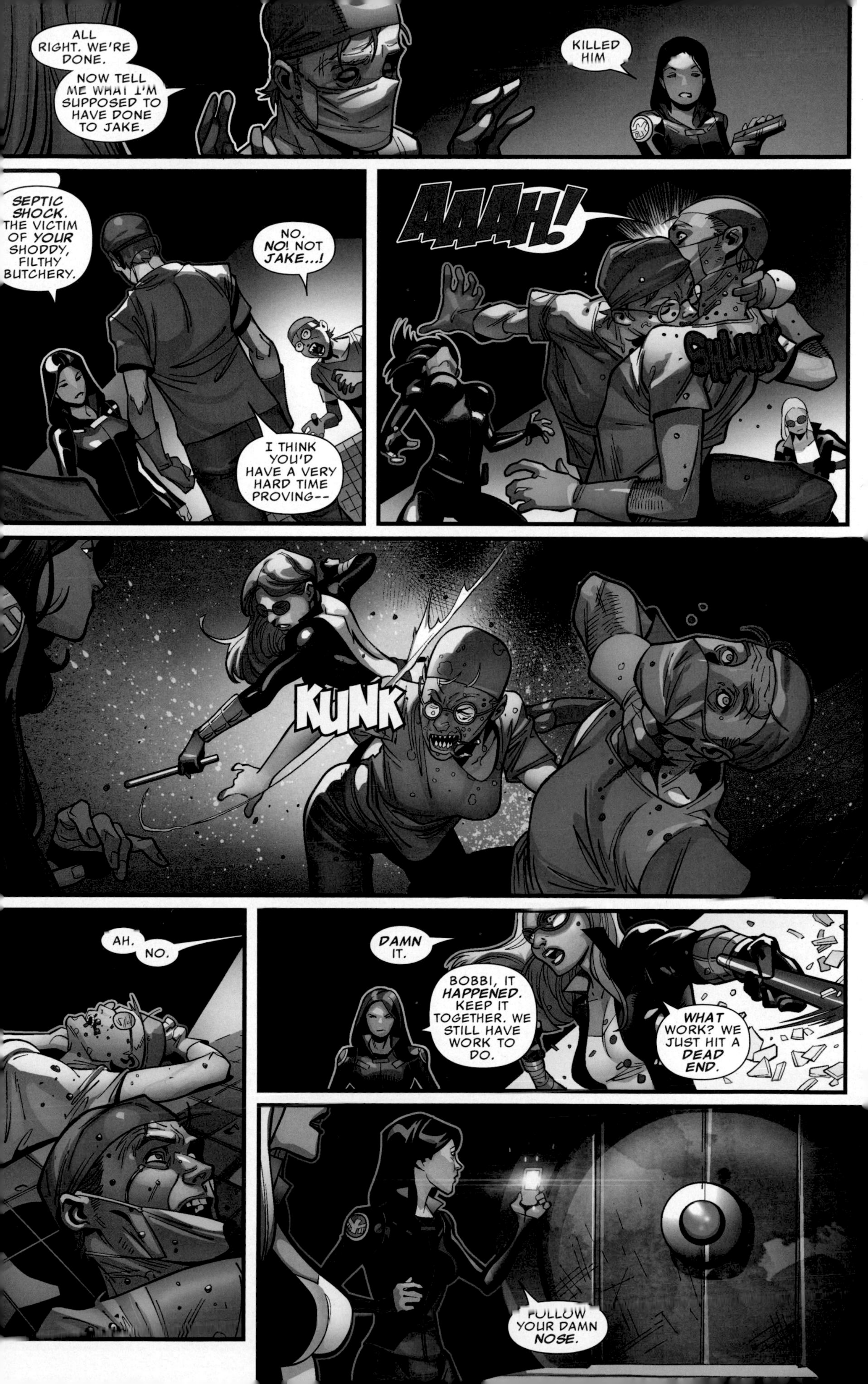
ALL RIGHT. WE'RE DONE.
NOW TELL ME WHAT I'M SUPPOSED TO HAVE DONE TO JAKE.
KILLED HIM
SEPTIC SHOCK. THE VICTIM OF YOUR SHODDY, FILTHY BUTCHERY.
NO. NO! NOT JAKE...!
I THINK YOU'D HAVE A VERY HARD TIME PROVING--
AAAAH!
SHLUUK
KUNK
AH. NO.
DAMN IT.
BOBBI, IT HAPPENED. KEEP IT TOGETHER. WE STILL HAVE WORK TO DO.
WHAT WORK? WE JUST HIT A DEAD END.
FOLLOW YOUR DAMN NOSE.

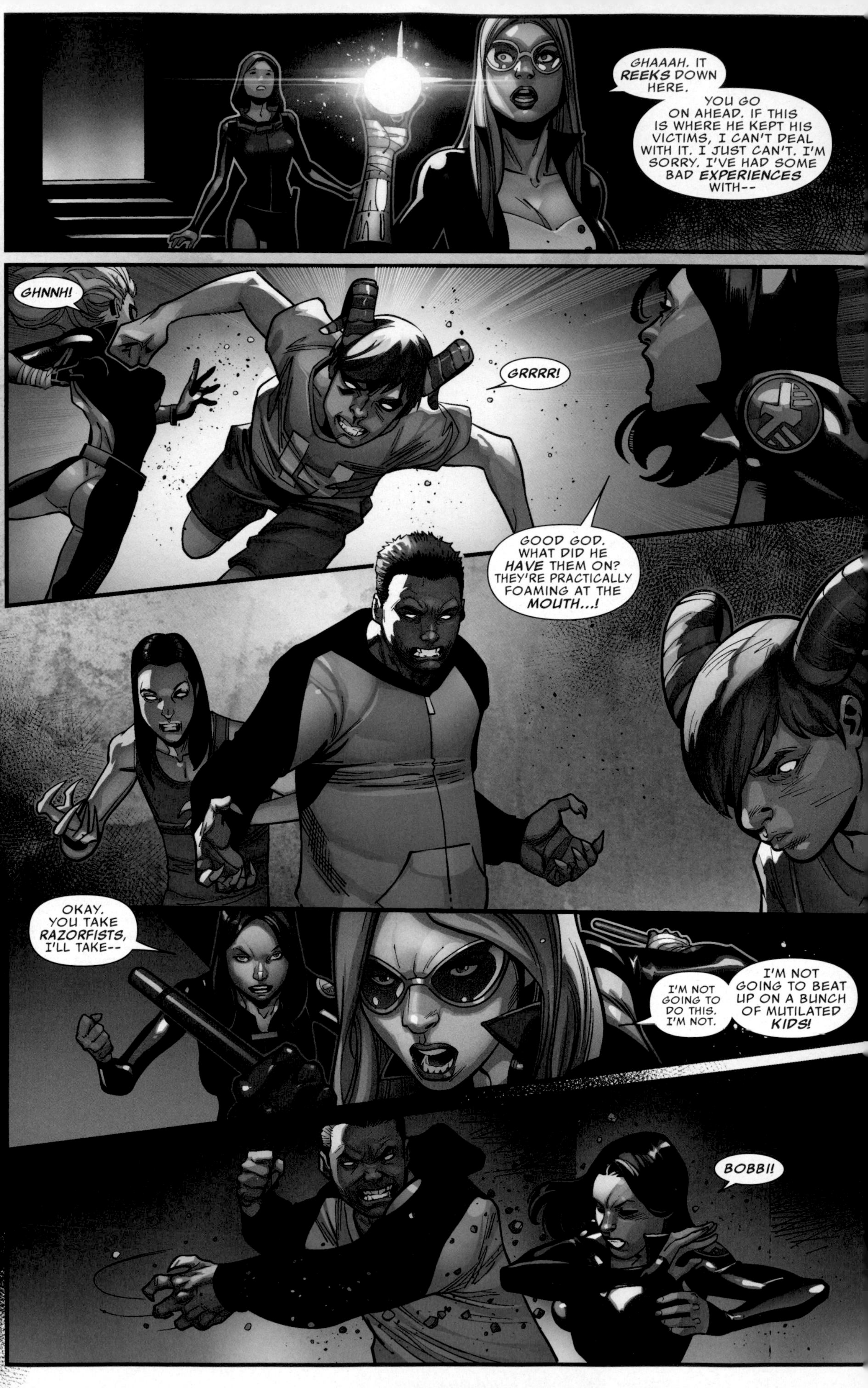
GHAAAH. IT REEKS DOWN HERE.
YOU GO ON AHEAD. IF THIS IS WHERE HE KEPT HIS VICTIMS, I CAN'T DEAL WITH IT. I JUST CAN'T. I'M SORRY. I'VE HAD SOME BAD EXPERIENCES WITH--
GHNNH!
GRRRR!
GOOD GOD. WHAT DID HE HAVE THEM ON? THEY'RE PRACTICALLY FOAMING AT THE MOUTH...!
OKAY. YOU TAKE RAZORFISTS, I'LL TAKE--
I'M NOT GOING TO DO THIS. I'M NOT.
I'M NOT GOING TO BEAT UP ON A BUNCH OF MUTILATED KIDS!
BOBBI!

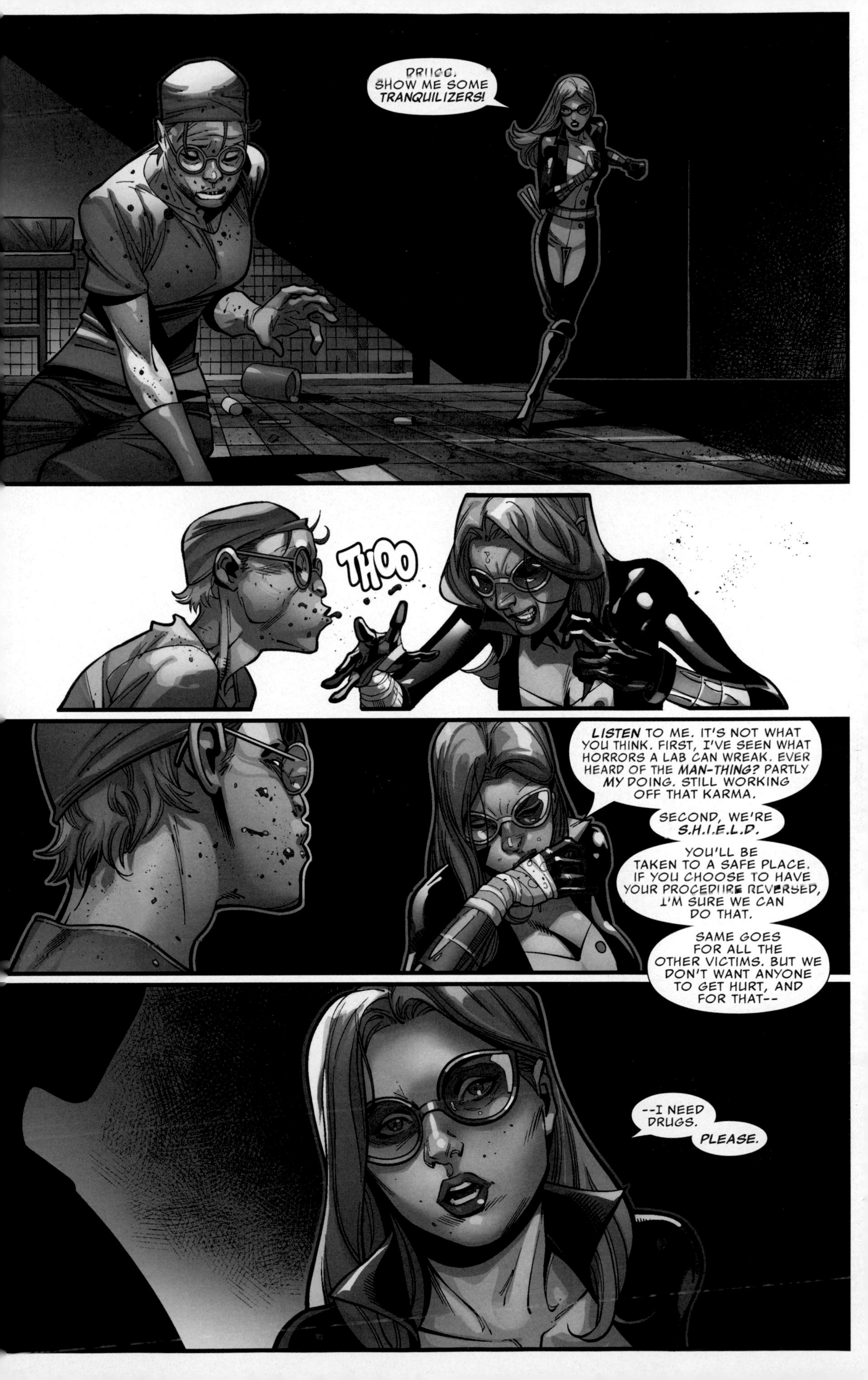
DRUGS. SHOW ME SOME TRANQUILIZERS!
THOO
LISTEN TO ME. IT'S NOT WHAT YOU THINK. FIRST, I'VE SEEN WHAT HORRORS A LAB CAN WREAK. EVER HEARD OF THE MAN-THING? PARTLY MY DOING. STILL WORKING OFF THAT KARMA.
SECOND, WE'RE S.H.I.E.L.D.
YOU'LL BE TAKEN TO A SAFE PLACE. IF YOU CHOOSE TO HAVE YOUR PROCEDURE REVERSED, I'M SURE WE CAN DO THAT.
SAME GOES FOR ALL THE OTHER VICTIMS. BUT WE DON'T WANT ANYONE TO GET HURT, AND FOR THAT--
--I NEED DRUGS. PLEASE.

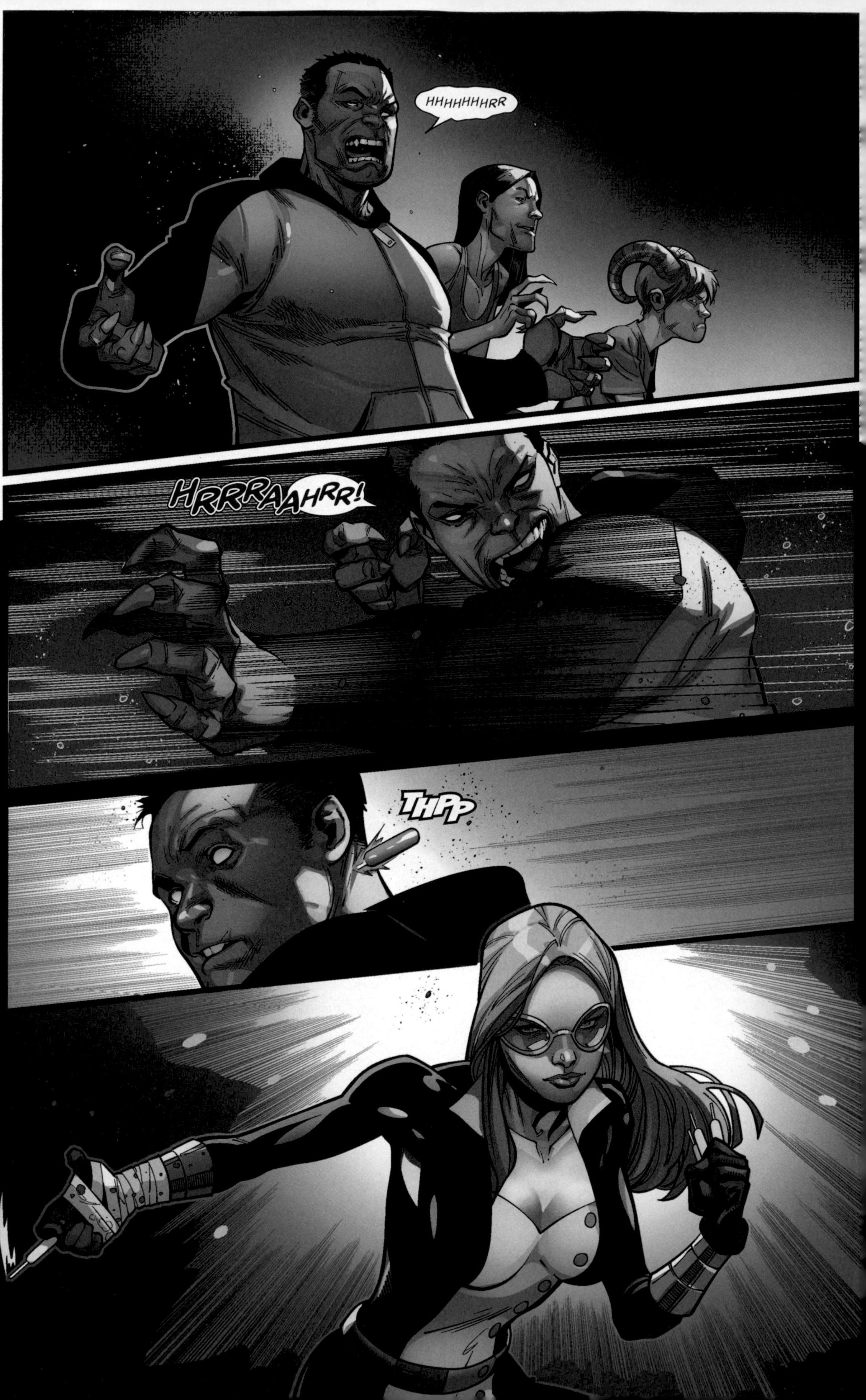
HHHHHHHRR
HRRRAAHRR!
THPP

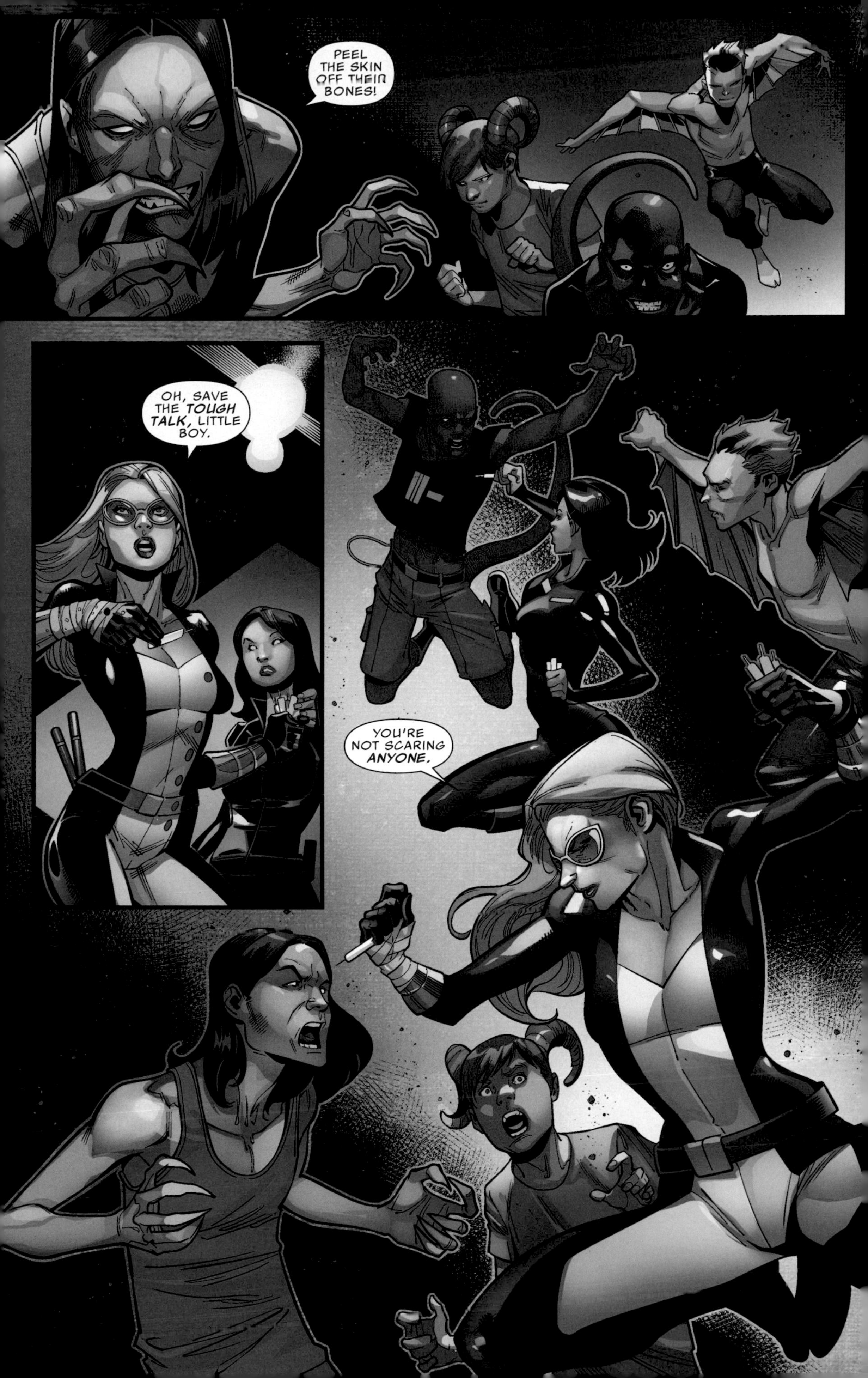
PEEL THE SKIN OFF THEIR BONES!
OH, SAVE THE TOUGH TALK, LITTLE BOY.
YOU'RE NOT SCARING ANYONE.

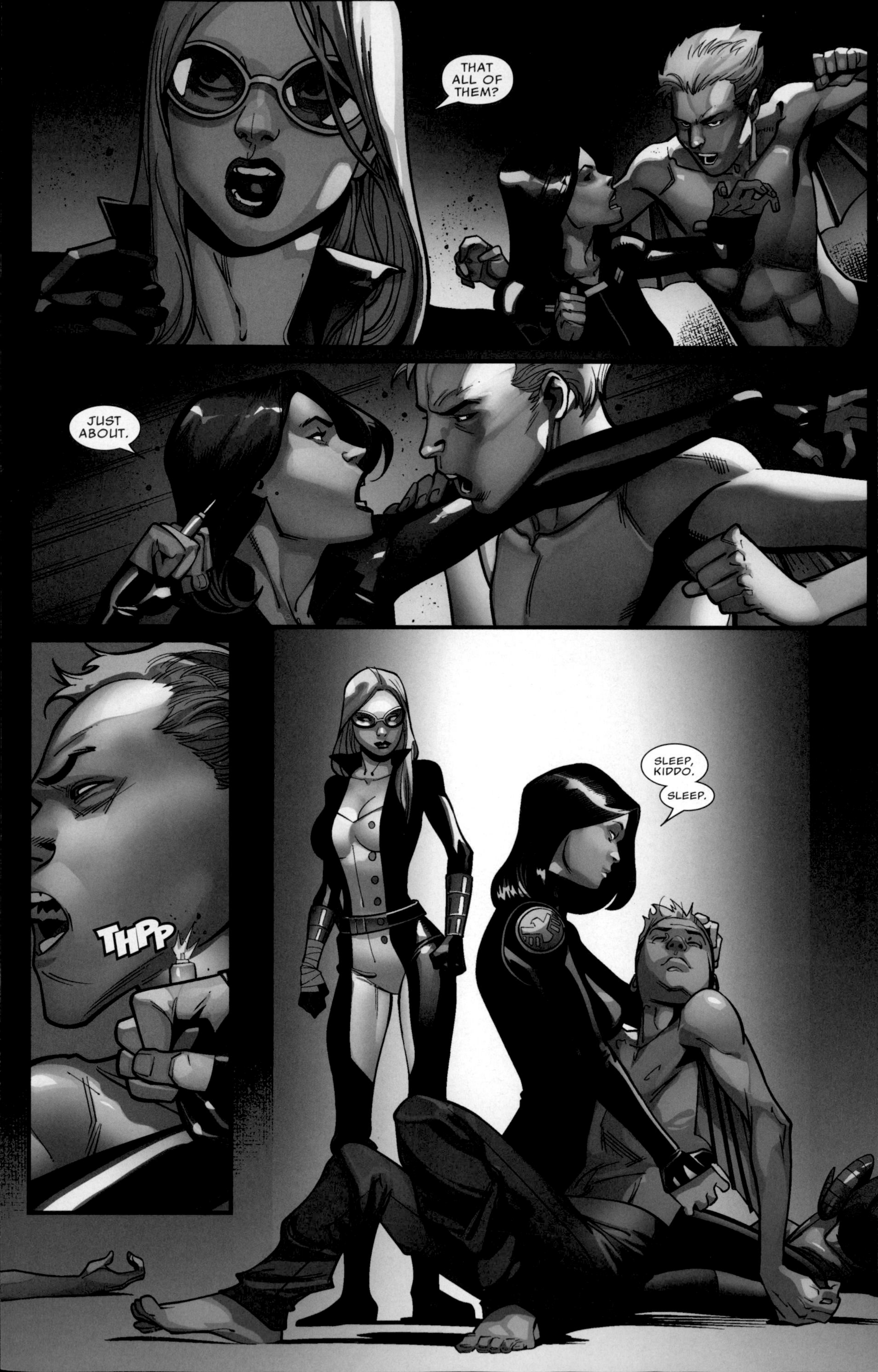
THAT ALL OF THEM?
JUST ABOUT.
THPP
SLEEP, KIDDO.
SLEEP.

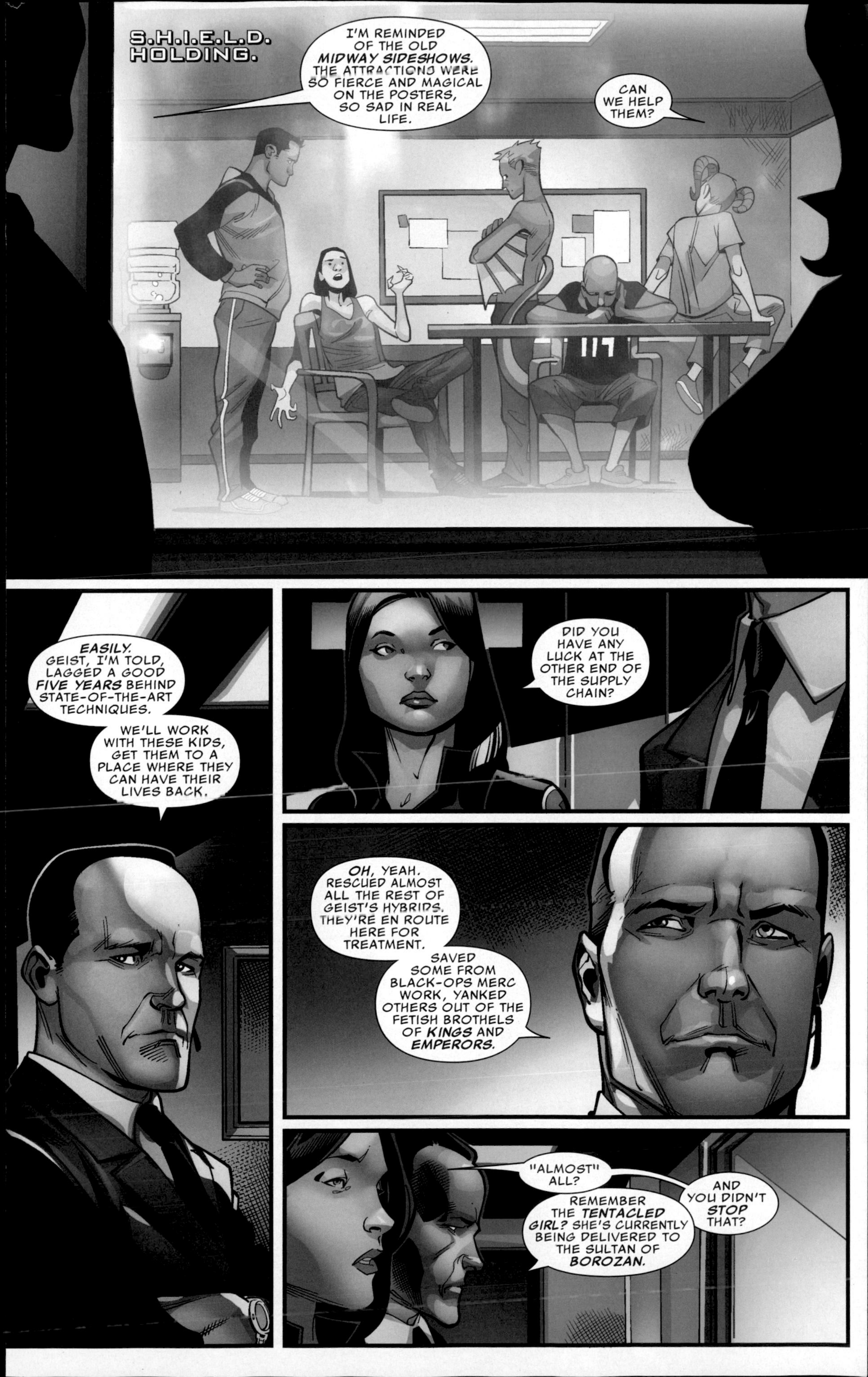
S.H.I.E.L.D. HOLDING.
I'M REMINDED OF THE OLD MIDWAY SIDESHOWS. THE ATTRACTIONS WERE SO FIERCE AND MAGICAL ON THE POSTERS, SO SAD IN REAL LIFE.
CAN WE HELP THEM?
EASILY. GEIST, I'M TOLD, LAGGED A GOOD FIVE YEARS BEHIND STATE-OF-THE-ART TECHNIQUES.
WE'LL WORK WITH THESE KIDS, GET THEM TO A PLACE WHERE THEY CAN HAVE THEIR LIVES BACK.
DID YOU HAVE ANY LUCK AT THE OTHER END OF THE SUPPLY CHAIN?
OH, YEAH. RESCUED ALMOST ALL THE REST OF GEIST'S HYBRIDS. THEY'RE EN ROUTE HERE FOR TREATMENT.
SAVED SOME FROM BLACK-OPS MERC WORK, YANKED OTHERS OUT OF THE FETISH BROTHELS OF KINGS AND EMPERORS.
"ALMOST" ALL?
REMEMBER THE TENTACLED GIRL? SHE'S CURRENTLY BEING DELIVERED TO THE SULTAN OF BOROZAN.
AND YOU DIDN'T STOP THAT?

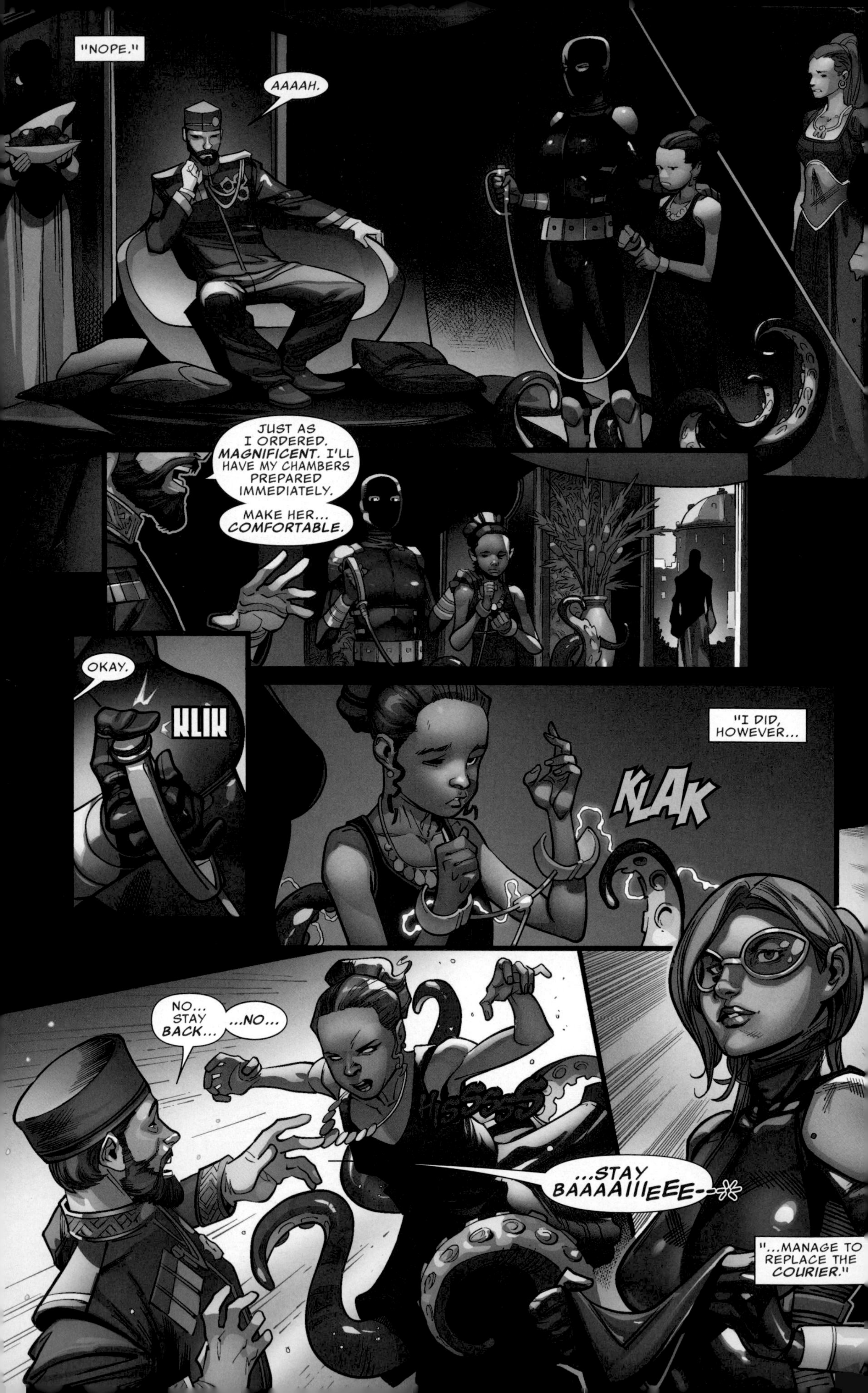
"NOPE."
AAAAH.
JUST AS I ORDERED. MAGNIFICENT. I'LL HAVE MY CHAMBERS PREPARED IMMEDIATELY.
MAKE HER... COMFORTABLE.
OKAY.
KLIK
"I DID, HOWEVER...
KLAK
NO... STAY BACK...
...NO...
HISSSSS
...STAY BAAAAIIIIEEE--
"...MANAGE TO REPLACE THE COURIER."

9.

ACTIVE MISSION:

THE MAN CALLED D·E·A·T·H·

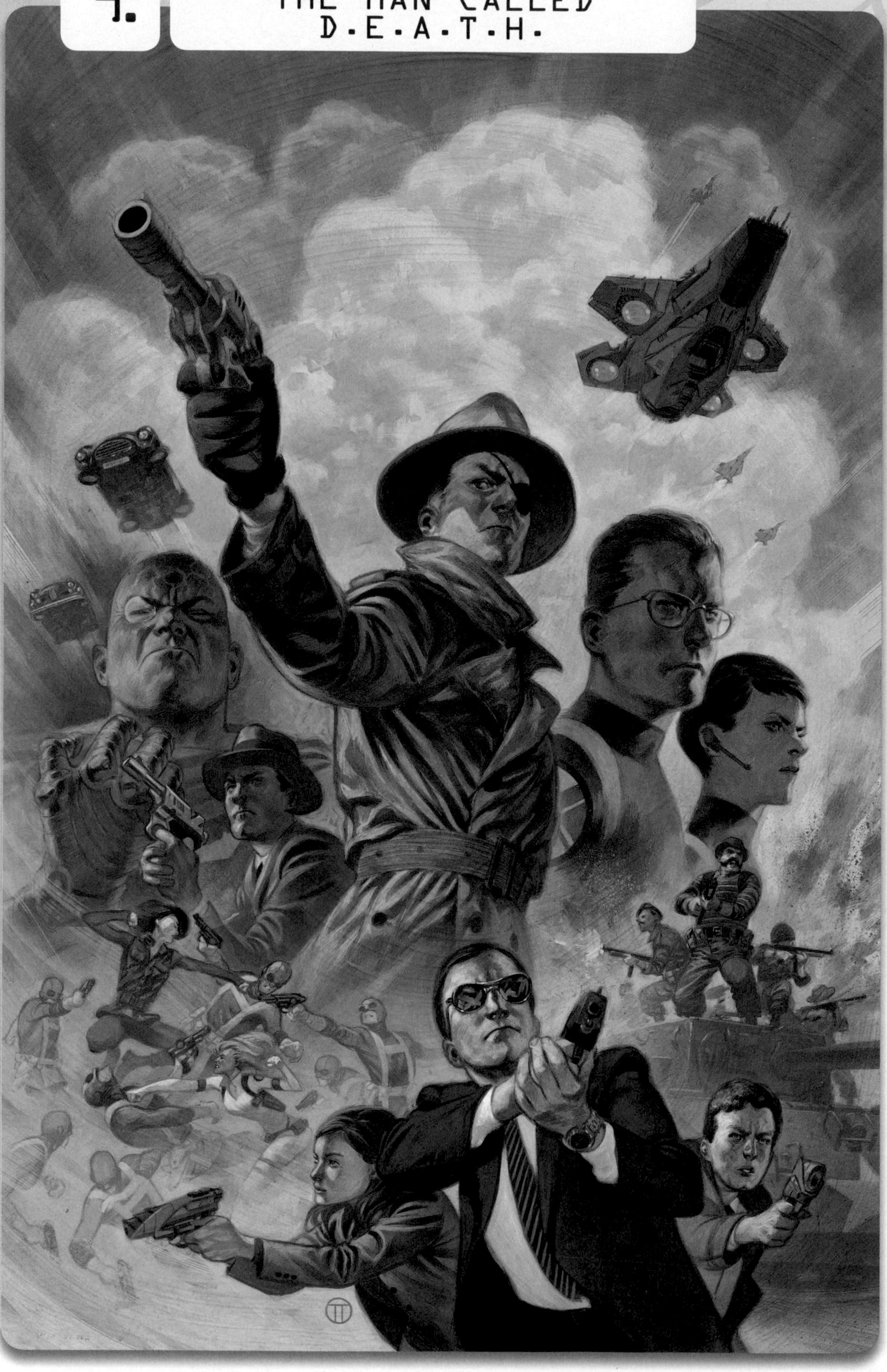

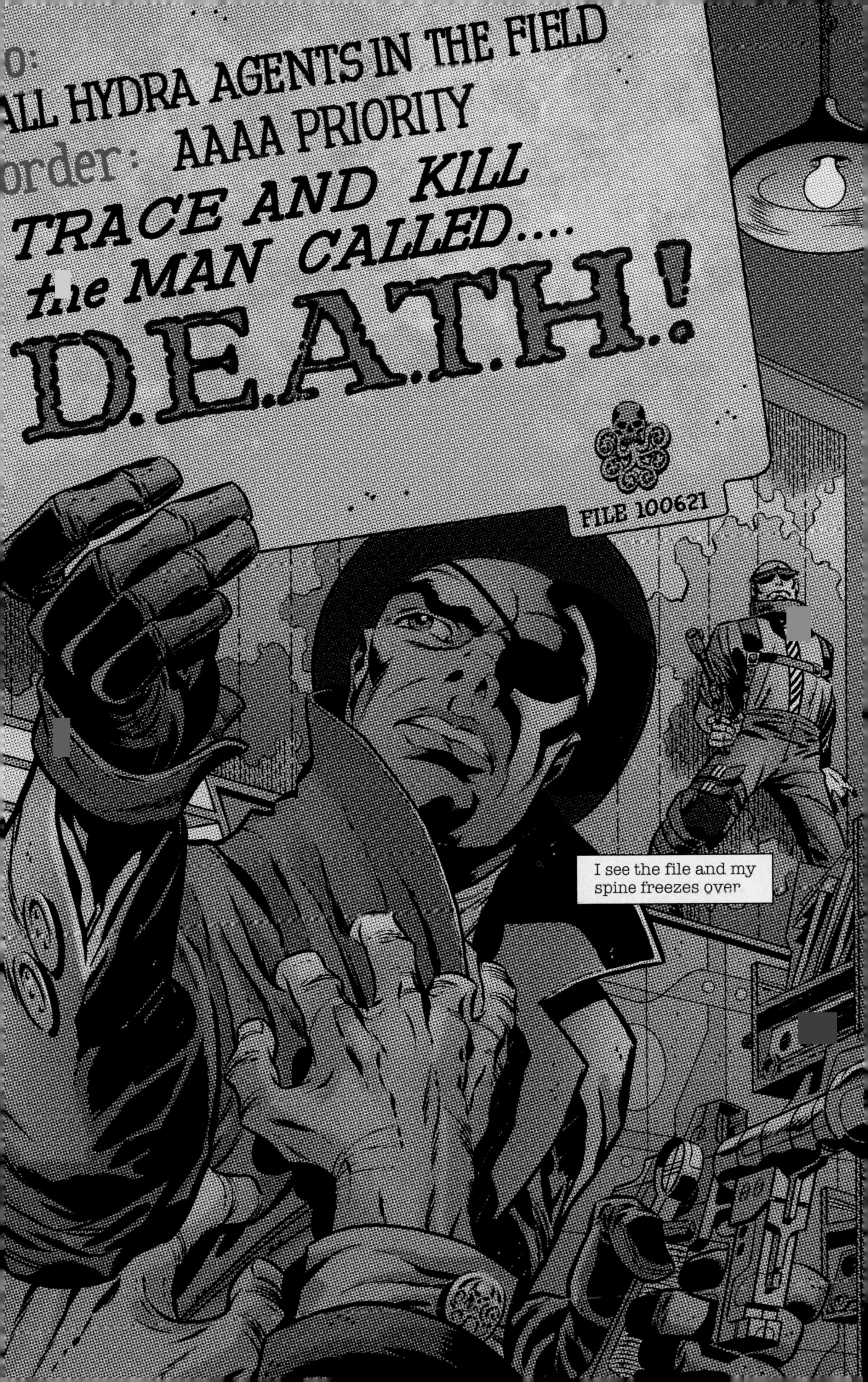
TO:
ALL HYDRA AGENTS IN THE FIELD
order: AAAA PRIORITY
TRACE AND KILL
the MAN CALLED....
D.E.A.T.H.!
FILE 100621
I see the file and my spine freezes over

Every once in a while, Dum Dum Dugan asks me what I want engraved on my tombstone. My answer's always the same: "I shoulda brought backup."

I thought this was a milk run. I didn't figure I'd be wandering into a full nest of Hydra goons.

And even though I'm topkick of the world's most powerful spy network--

--loaded with the sharpest surveillance and the craziest gadgets--my number could come up at any time. Hopefully, today's not the day.

I can't go to my grave without reading what's in this file. It holds a secret--the name of a man I can barely remember. The man who picked me for this nutty job.

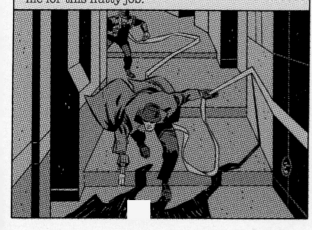

And his initials are D.E.A.T.H.

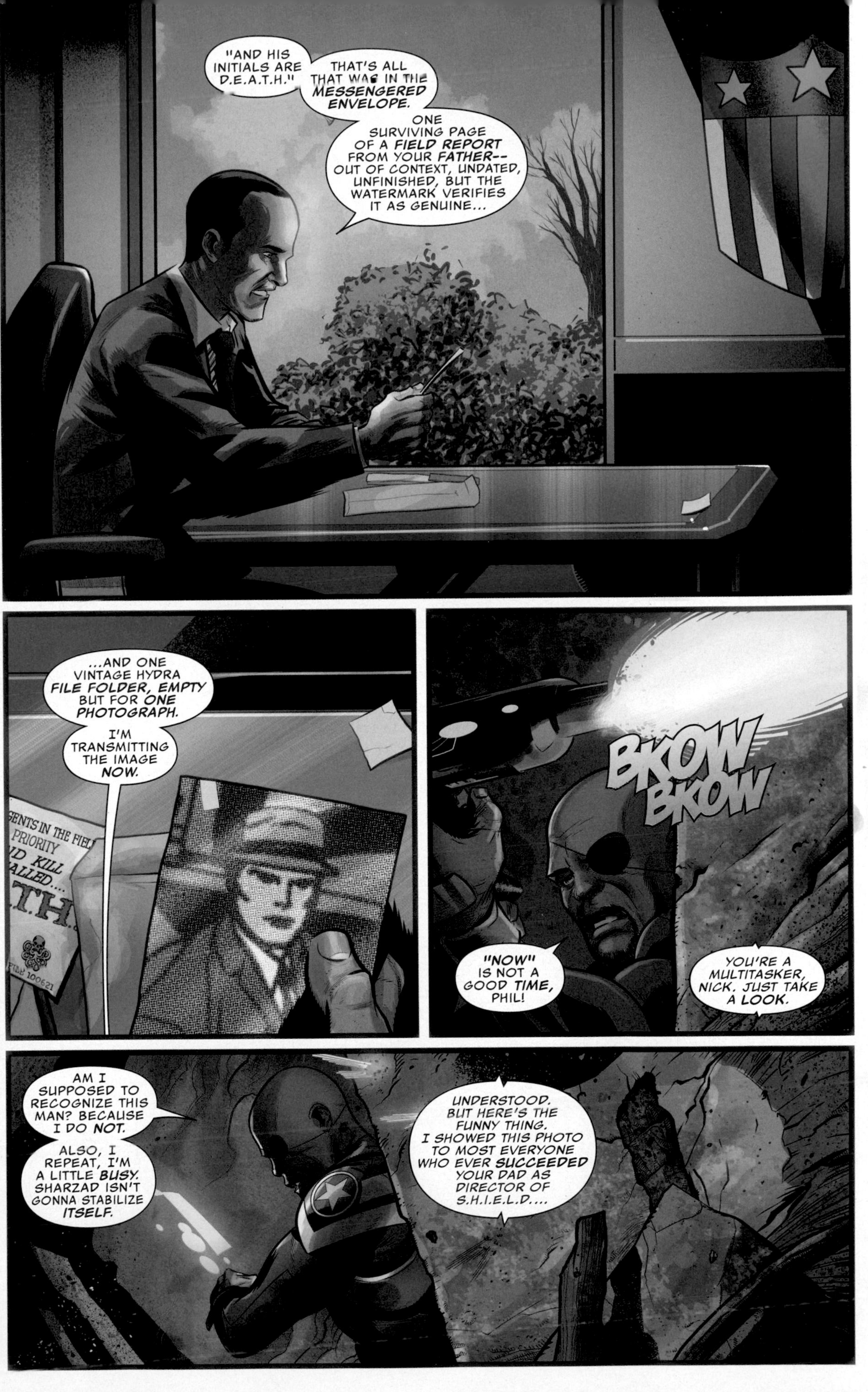
"AND HIS INITIALS ARE D.E.A.T.H."
THAT'S ALL THAT WAS IN THE MESSENGERED ENVELOPE.
ONE SURVIVING PAGE OF A FIELD REPORT FROM YOUR FATHER-- OUT OF CONTEXT, UNDATED, UNFINISHED, BUT THE WATERMARK VERIFIES IT AS GENUINE...
...AND ONE VINTAGE HYDRA FILE FOLDER, EMPTY BUT FOR ONE PHOTOGRAPH.
I'M TRANSMITTING THE IMAGE NOW.
BKOW BKOW
"NOW" IS NOT A GOOD TIME, PHIL!
YOU'RE A MULTITASKER, NICK. JUST TAKE A LOOK.
AM I SUPPOSED TO RECOGNIZE THIS MAN? BECAUSE I DO NOT.
ALSO, I REPEAT, I'M A LITTLE BUSY. SHARZAD ISN'T GONNA STABILIZE ITSELF.
UNDERSTOOD. BUT HERE'S THE FUNNY THING. I SHOWED THIS PHOTO TO MOST EVERYONE WHO EVER SUCCEEDED YOUR DAD AS DIRECTOR OF S.H.I.E.L.D....

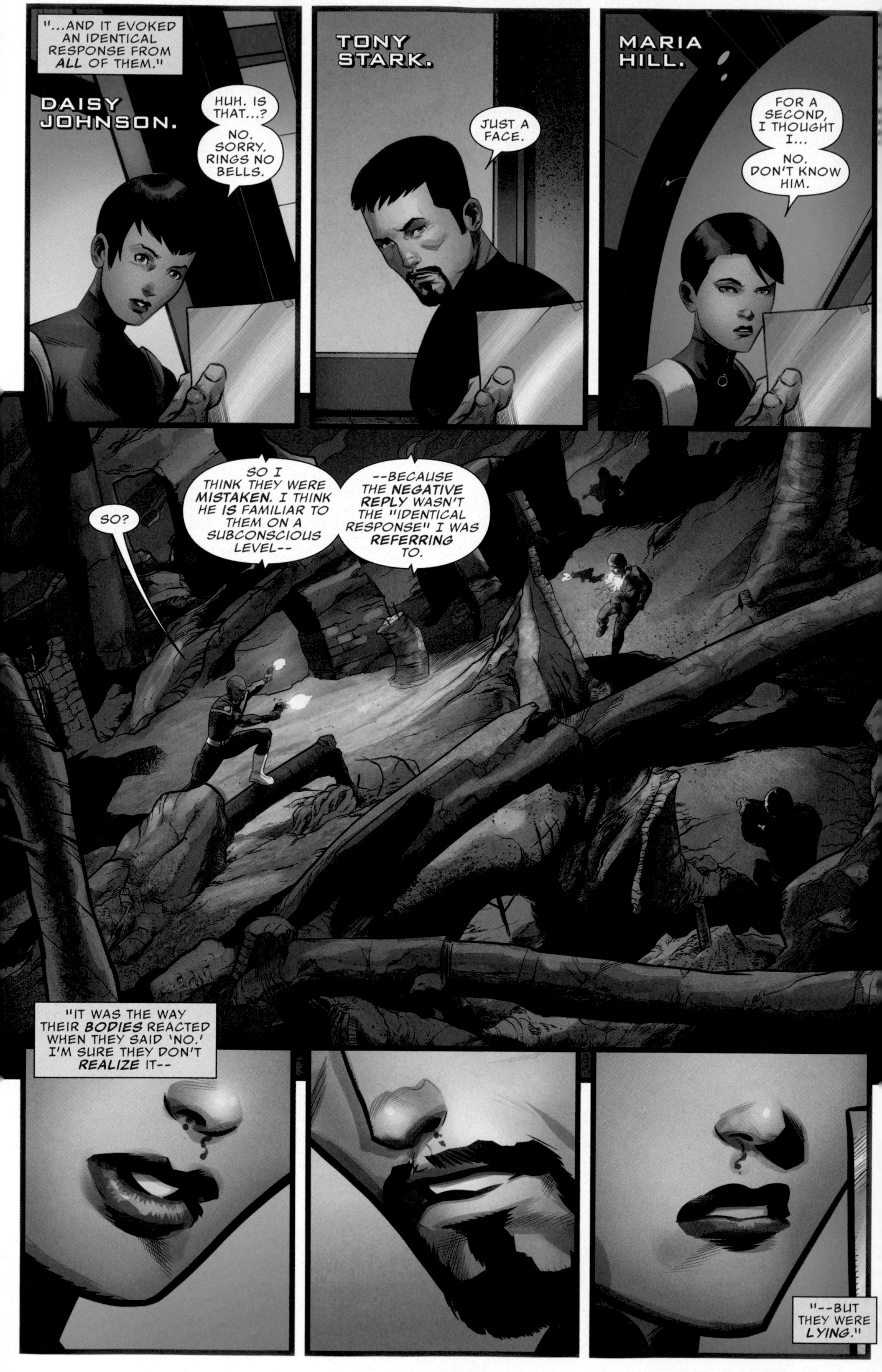
"...AND IT EVOKED AN IDENTICAL RESPONSE FROM ALL OF THEM."
DAISY JOHNSON.
HUH. IS THAT...?
NO. SORRY. RINGS NO BELLS.
TONY STARK.
JUST A FACE.
MARIA HILL.
FOR A SECOND, I THOUGHT I...
NO. DON'T KNOW HIM.
SO?
SO I THINK THEY WERE MISTAKEN. I THINK HE IS FAMILIAR TO THEM ON A SUBCONSCIOUS LEVEL--
--BECAUSE THE NEGATIVE REPLY WASN'T THE "IDENTICAL RESPONSE" I WAS REFERRING TO.
"IT WAS THE WAY THEIR BODIES REACTED WHEN THEY SAID 'NO.' I'M SURE THEY DON'T REALIZE IT--
"--BUT THEY WERE LYING."

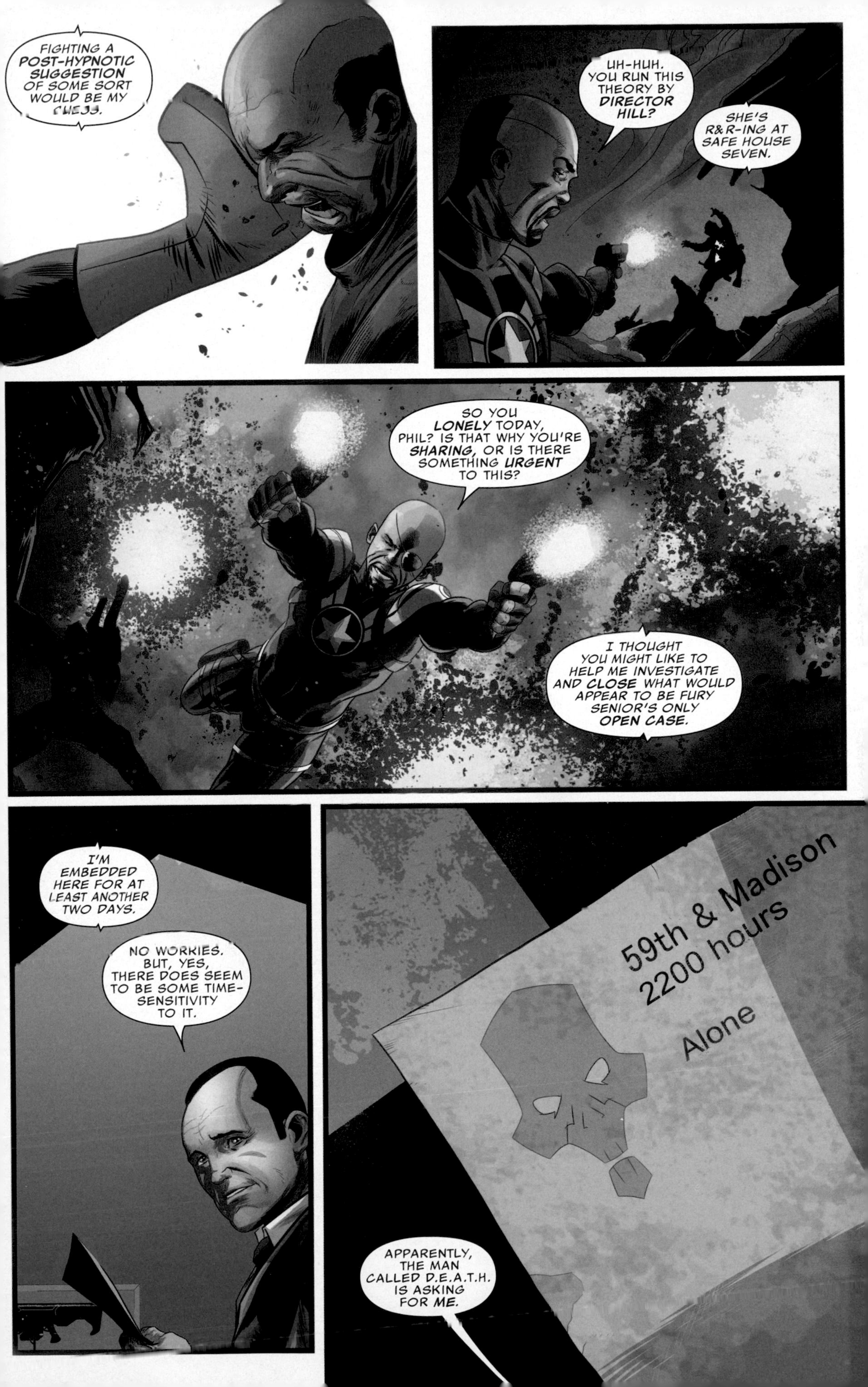
FIGHTING A POST-HYPNOTIC SUGGESTION OF SOME SORT WOULD BE MY GUESS.
UH-HUH. YOU RUN THIS THEORY BY DIRECTOR HILL?
SHE'S R&R-ING AT SAFE HOUSE SEVEN.
SO YOU LONELY TODAY, PHIL? IS THAT WHY YOU'RE SHARING, OR IS THERE SOMETHING URGENT TO THIS?
I THOUGHT YOU MIGHT LIKE TO HELP ME INVESTIGATE AND CLOSE WHAT WOULD APPEAR TO BE FURY SENIOR'S ONLY OPEN CASE.
I'M EMBEDDED HERE FOR AT LEAST ANOTHER TWO DAYS.
NO WORRIES. BUT, YES, THERE DOES SEEM TO BE SOME TIME-SENSITIVITY TO IT.
59th & Madison
2200 hours
Alone
APPARENTLY, THE MAN CALLED D.E.A.T.H. IS ASKING FOR ME.

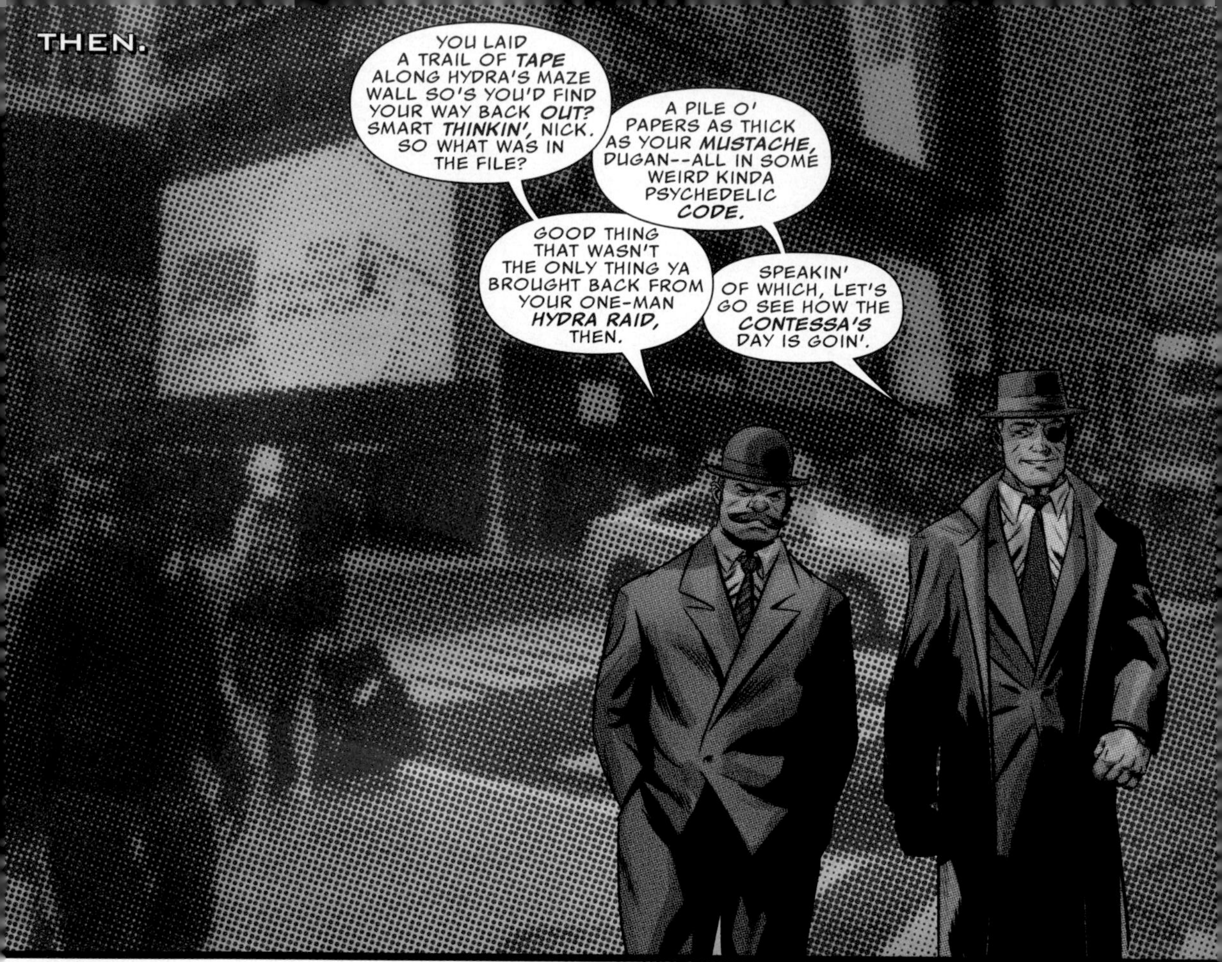
THEN.
YOU LAID A TRAIL OF TAPE ALONG HYDRA'S MAZE WALL SO'S YOU'D FIND YOUR WAY BACK OUT? SMART THINKIN', NICK. SO WHAT WAS IN THE FILE?
A PILE O' PAPERS AS THICK AS YOUR MUSTACHE, DUGAN--ALL IN SOME WEIRD KINDA PSYCHEDELIC CODE.
GOOD THING THAT WASN'T THE ONLY THING YA BROUGHT BACK FROM YOUR ONE-MAN HYDRA RAID, THEN.
SPEAKIN' OF WHICH, LET'S GO SEE HOW THE CONTESSA'S DAY IS GOIN'.

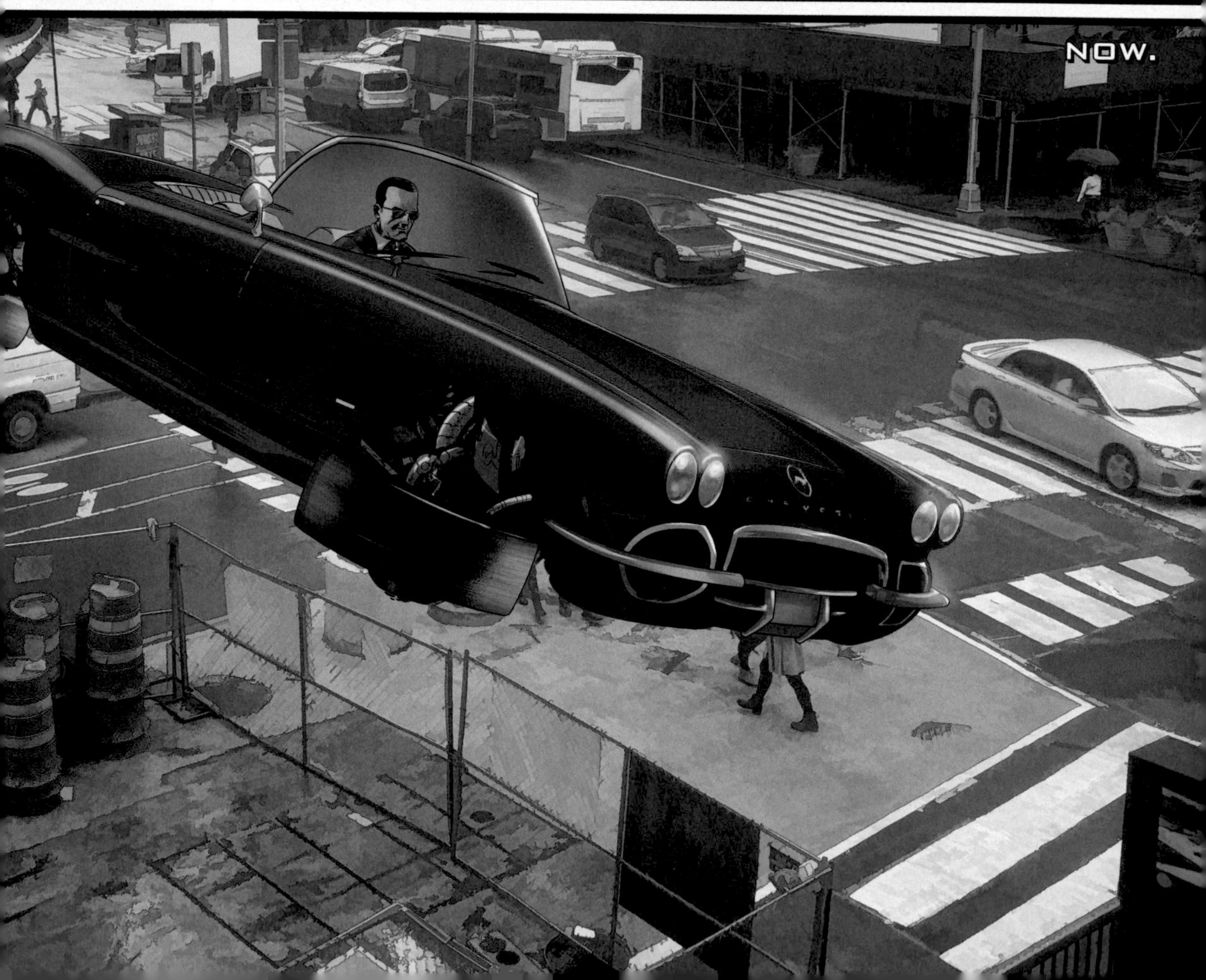
NOW.

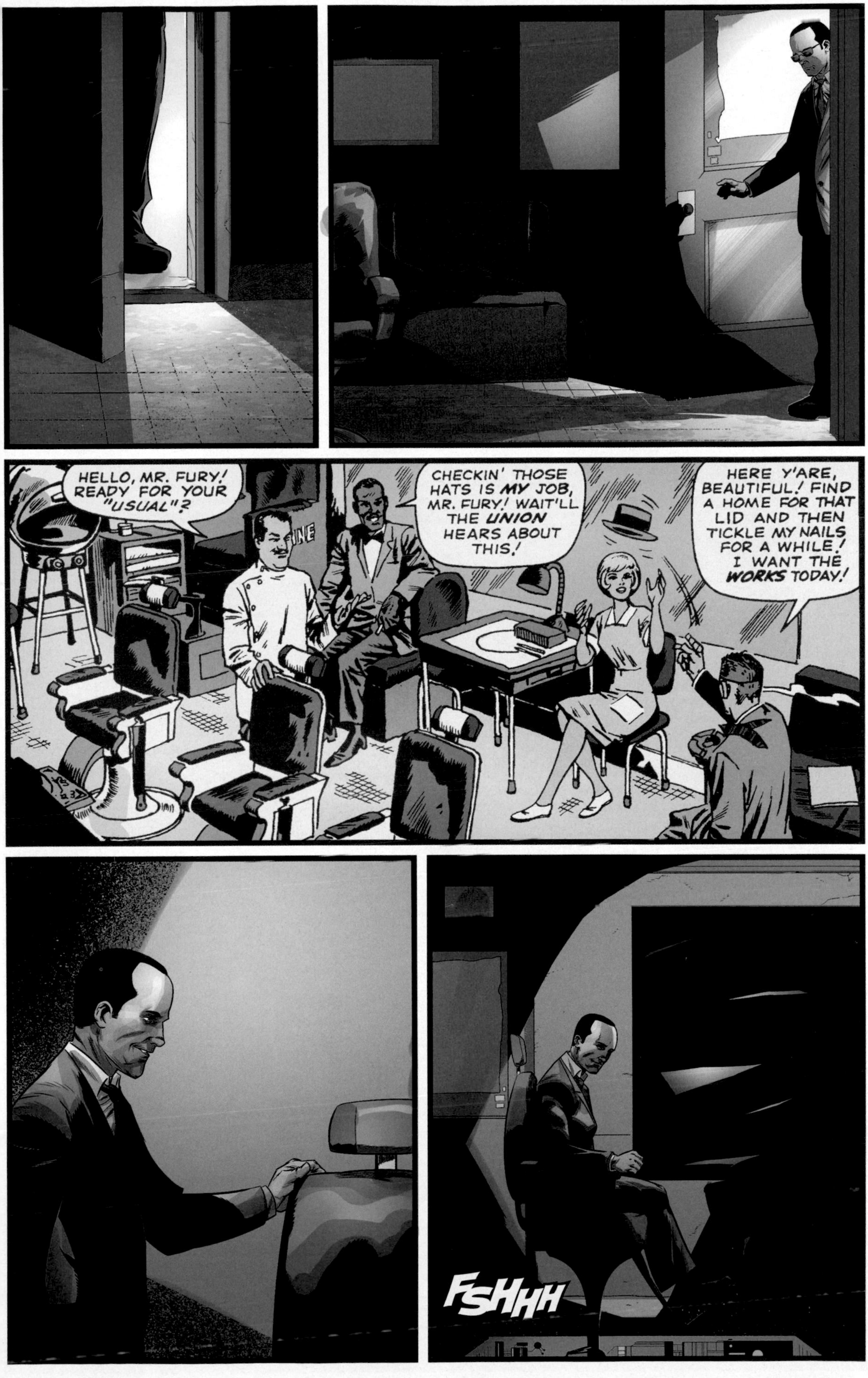
HELLO, MR. FURY! READY FOR YOUR "USUAL"?
CHECKIN' THOSE HATS IS MY JOB, MR. FURY! WAIT'LL THE UNION HEARS ABOUT THIS!
HERE Y'ARE, BEAUTIFUL! FIND A HOME FOR THAT LID AND THEN TICKLE MY NAILS FOR A WHILE! I WANT THE WORKS TODAY!
FSHHH

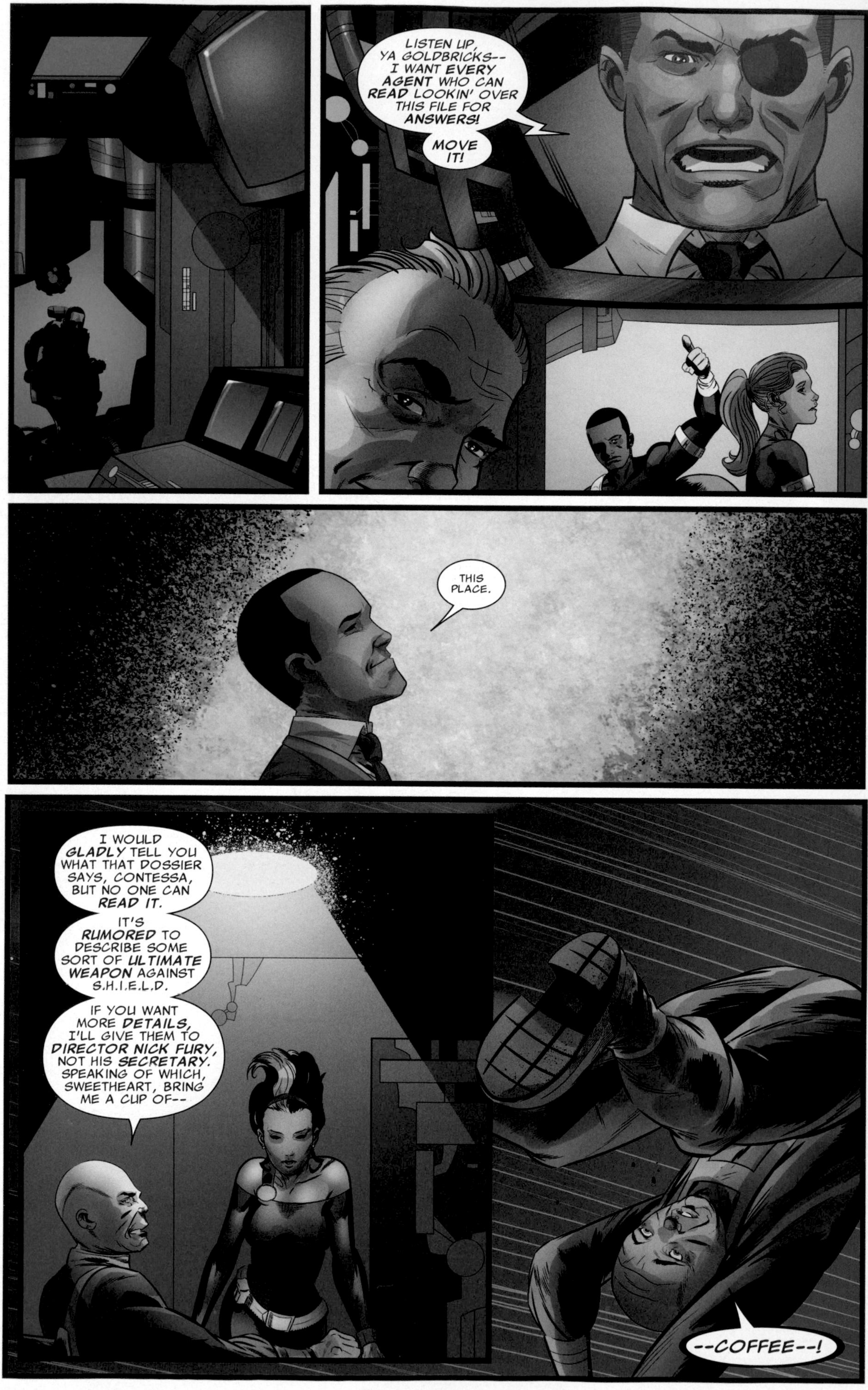
LISTEN UP, YA GOLDBRICKS-- I WANT EVERY AGENT WHO CAN READ LOOKIN' OVER THIS FILE FOR ANSWERS!
MOVE IT!
THIS PLACE.
I WOULD GLADLY TELL YOU WHAT THAT DOSSIER SAYS, CONTESSA, BUT NO ONE CAN READ IT.
IT'S RUMORED TO DESCRIBE SOME SORT OF ULTIMATE WEAPON AGAINST S.H.I.E.L.D.
IF YOU WANT MORE DETAILS, I'LL GIVE THEM TO DIRECTOR NICK FURY, NOT HIS SECRETARY. SPEAKING OF WHICH, SWEETHEART, BRING ME A CUP OF--
--COFFEE--!

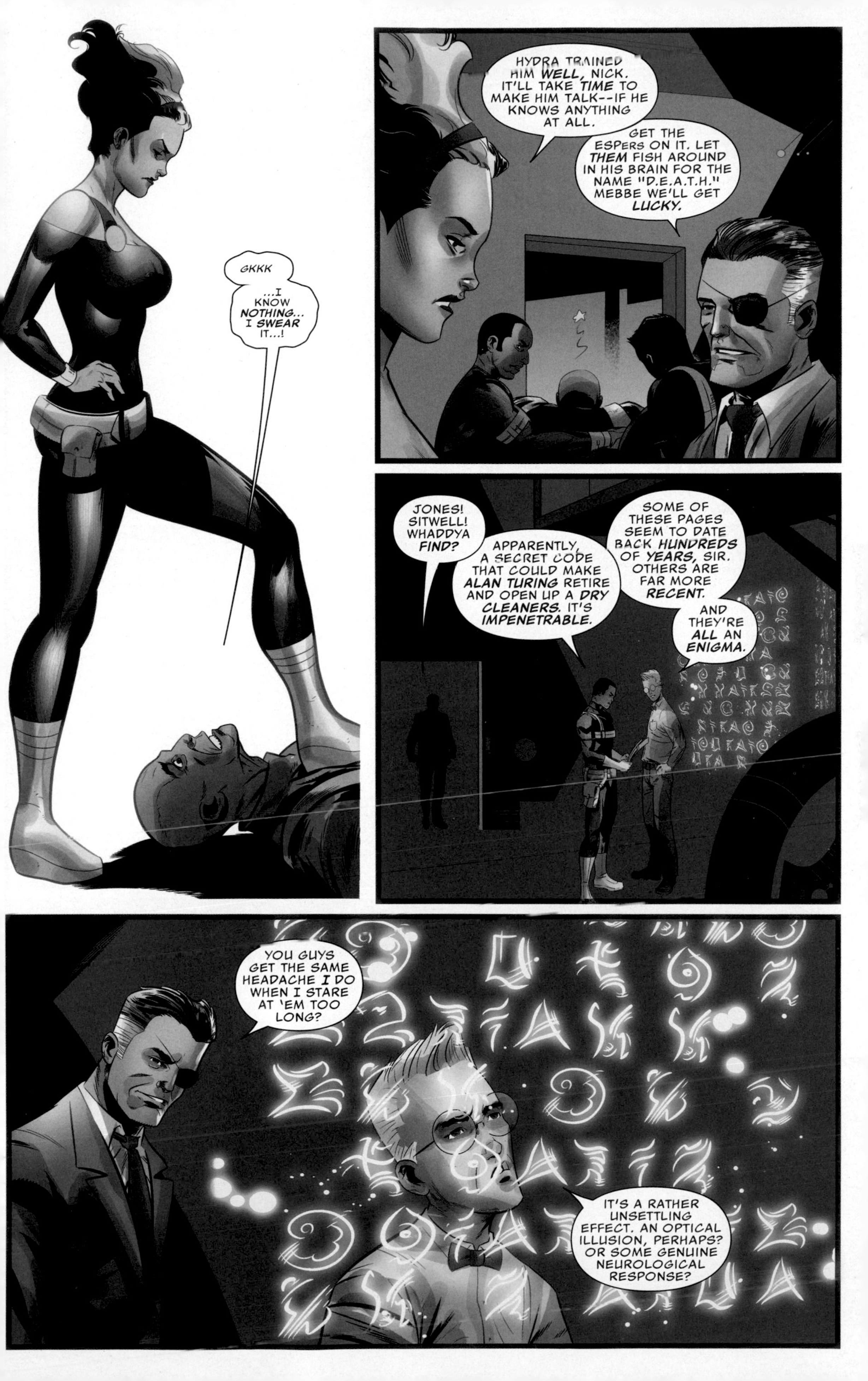
GKKK
...I KNOW NOTHING... I SWEAR IT...!
HYDRA TRAINED HIM WELL, NICK. IT'LL TAKE TIME TO MAKE HIM TALK--IF HE KNOWS ANYTHING AT ALL.
GET THE ESPers ON IT. LET THEM FISH AROUND IN HIS BRAIN FOR THE NAME "D.E.A.T.H." MEBBE WE'LL GET LUCKY.
JONES! SITWELL! WHADDYA FIND?
APPARENTLY, A SECRET CODE THAT COULD MAKE ALAN TURING RETIRE AND OPEN UP A DRY CLEANERS. IT'S IMPENETRABLE.
SOME OF THESE PAGES SEEM TO DATE BACK HUNDREDS OF YEARS, SIR. OTHERS ARE FAR MORE RECENT.
AND THEY'RE ALL AN ENIGMA.
YOU GUYS GET THE SAME HEADACHE I DO WHEN I STARE AT 'EM TOO LONG?
IT'S A RATHER UNSETTLING EFFECT. AN OPTICAL ILLUSION, PERHAPS? OR SOME GENUINE NEUROLOGICAL RESPONSE?

YOU'RE THE *EGGHEAD*, SITWELL. YOU DOPE IT OUT.

ANYBODY NEEDS ME, TELL 'EM I'M IN CONFERENCE WITH AGENTS *JIM BEAM* AND *JOHNNIE WALKER*.

FCHOK

NICHOLAS FURY
DIRECTOR

BILE X-RAY

FWPP

FWPP FWPP

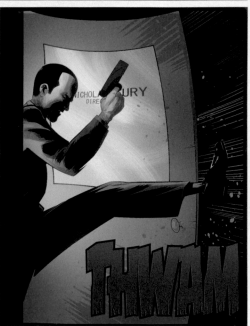

NICHOLAS FURY
DIRECTOR

THWAM

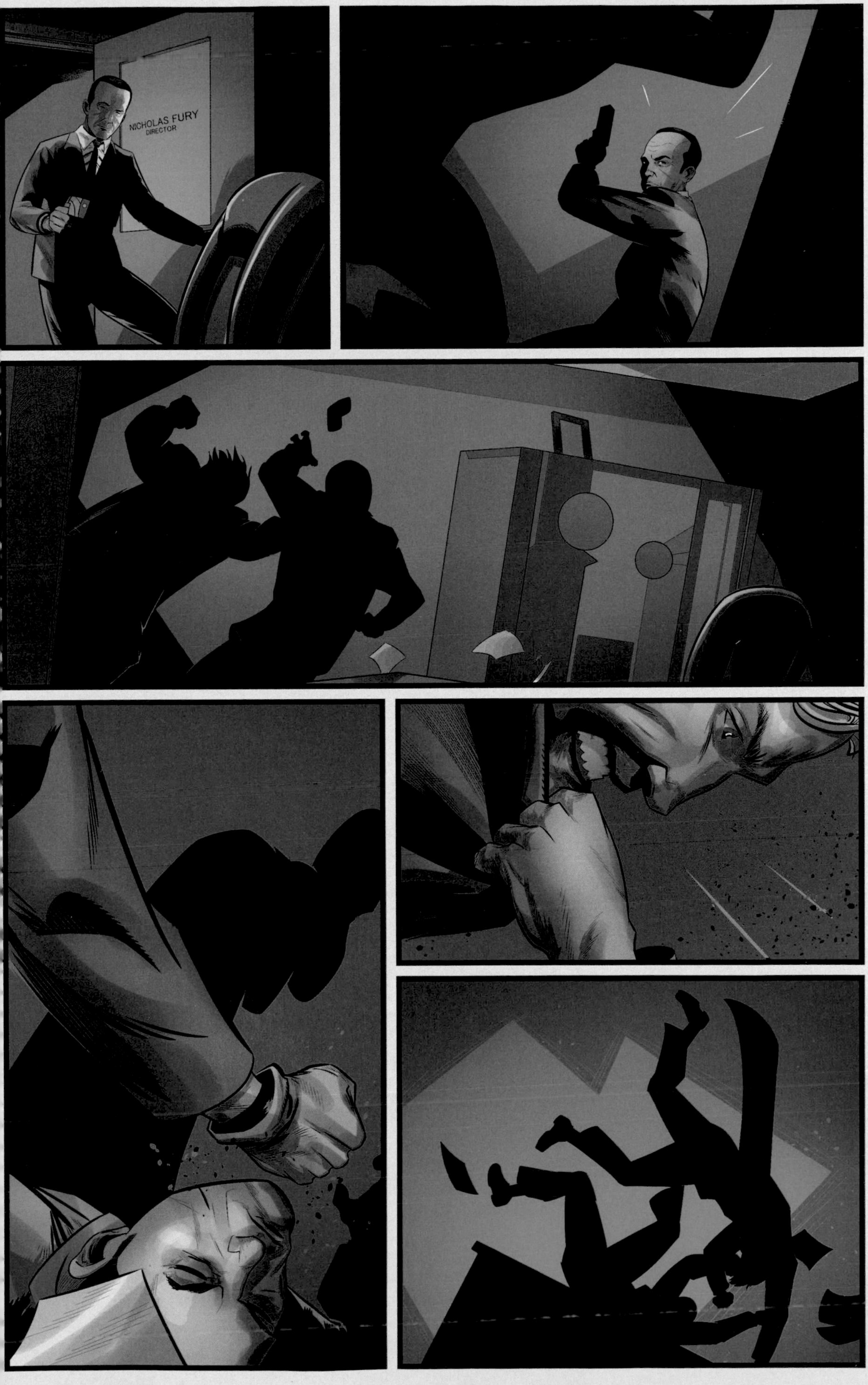
NICHOLAS FURY
DIRECTOR

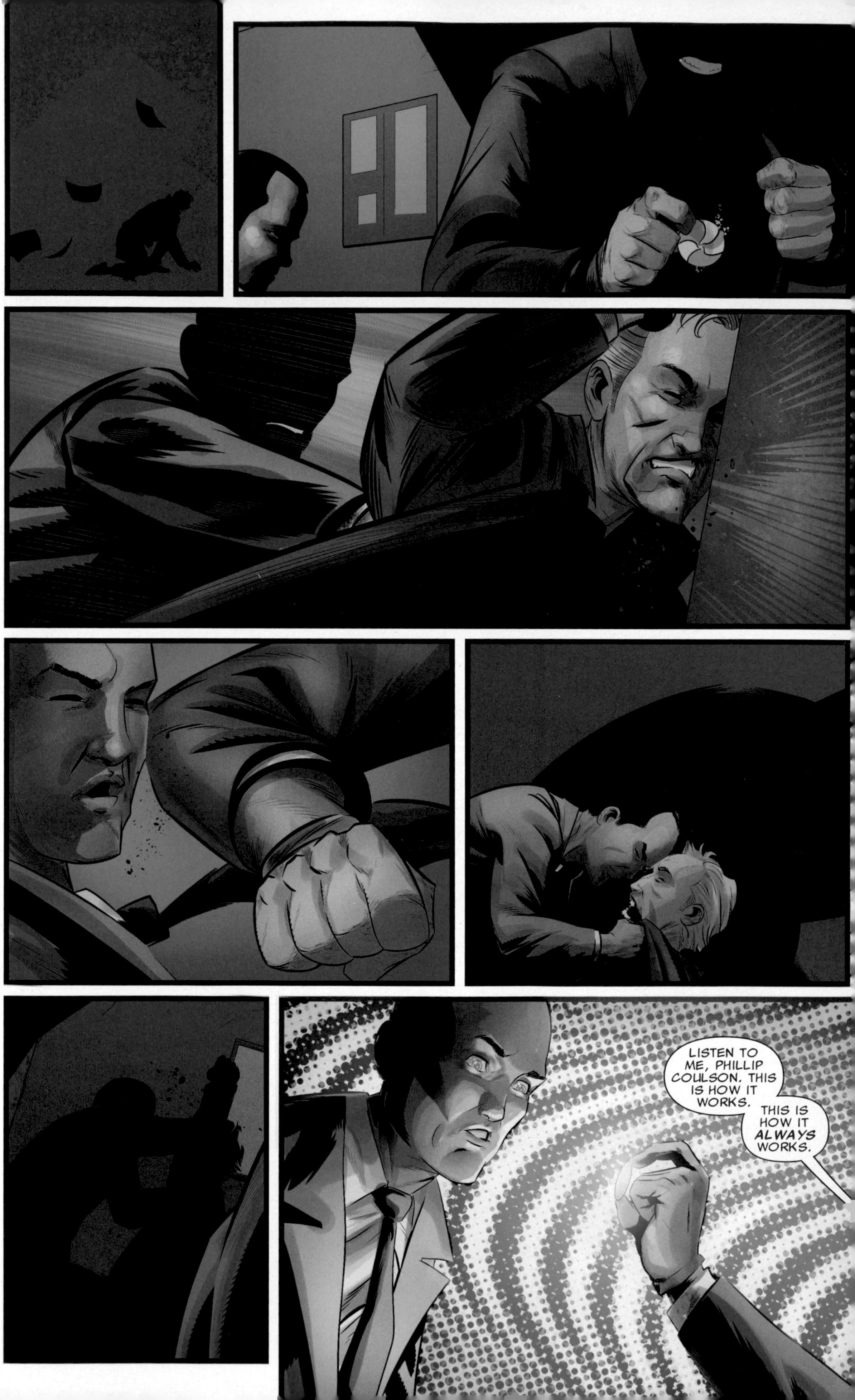
LISTEN TO ME, PHILLIP COULSON. THIS IS HOW IT WORKS.
THIS IS HOW IT *ALWAYS* WORKS.

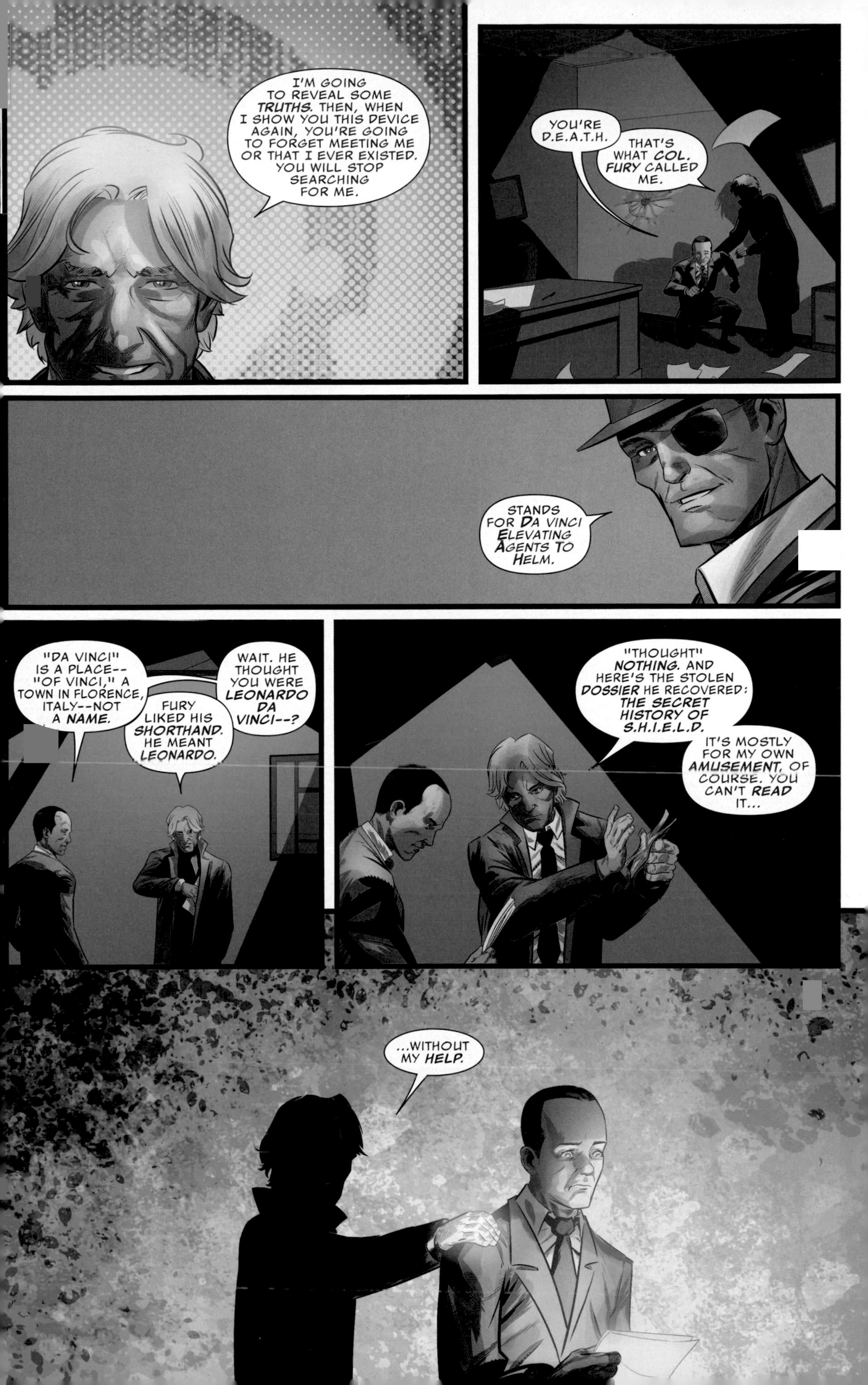
I'M GOING TO REVEAL SOME TRUTHS. THEN, WHEN I SHOW YOU THIS DEVICE AGAIN, YOU'RE GOING TO FORGET MEETING ME OR THAT I EVER EXISTED. YOU WILL STOP SEARCHING FOR ME.
YOU'RE D.E.A.T.H.
THAT'S WHAT COL. FURY CALLED ME.
STANDS FOR DA VINCI ELEVATING AGENTS TO HELM.
"DA VINCI" IS A PLACE-- "OF VINCI," A TOWN IN FLORENCE, ITALY--NOT A NAME.
FURY LIKED HIS SHORTHAND. HE MEANT LEONARDO.
WAIT. HE THOUGHT YOU WERE LEONARDO DA VINCI--?
"THOUGHT" NOTHING. AND HERE'S THE STOLEN DOSSIER HE RECOVERED: THE SECRET HISTORY OF S.H.I.E.L.D.
IT'S MOSTLY FOR MY OWN AMUSEMENT, OF COURSE. YOU CAN'T READ IT...
...WITHOUT MY HELP.

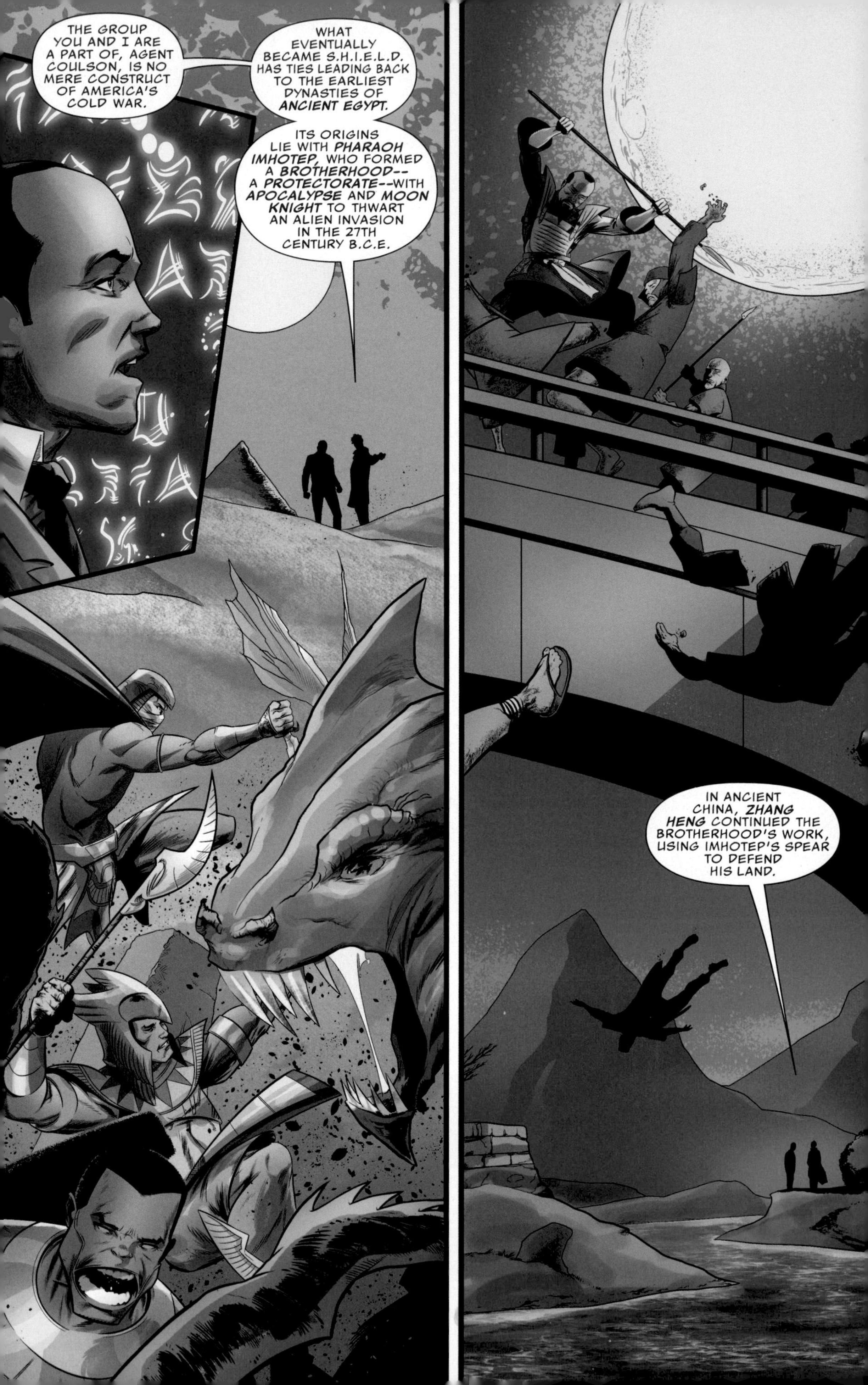
THE GROUP YOU AND I ARE A PART OF, AGENT COULSON, IS NO MERE CONSTRUCT OF AMERICA'S COLD WAR.
WHAT EVENTUALLY BECAME S.H.I.E.L.D. HAS TIES LEADING BACK TO THE EARLIEST DYNASTIES OF ANCIENT EGYPT.
ITS ORIGINS LIE WITH PHARAOH IMHOTEP, WHO FORMED A BROTHERHOOD-- A PROTECTORATE--WITH APOCALYPSE AND MOON KNIGHT TO THWART AN ALIEN INVASION IN THE 27TH CENTURY B.C.E.
IN ANCIENT CHINA, ZHANG HENG CONTINUED THE BROTHERHOOD'S WORK, USING IMHOTEP'S SPEAR TO DEFEND HIS LAND.

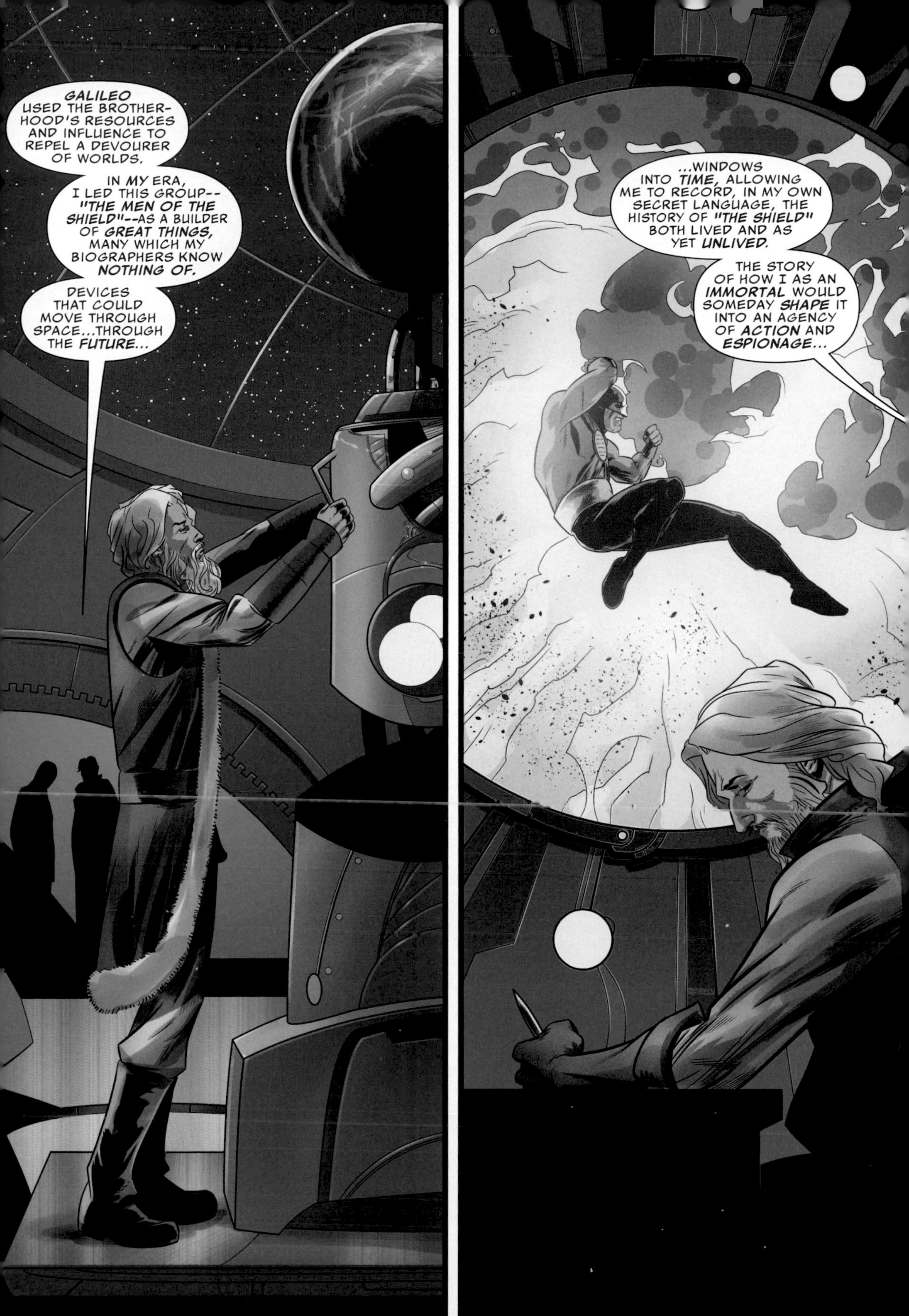
GALILEO USED THE BROTHERHOOD'S RESOURCES AND INFLUENCE TO REPEL A DEVOURER OF WORLDS.
IN MY ERA, I LED THIS GROUP--"THE MEN OF THE SHIELD"--AS A BUILDER OF GREAT THINGS, MANY WHICH MY BIOGRAPHERS KNOW NOTHING OF.
DEVICES THAT COULD MOVE THROUGH SPACE...THROUGH THE FUTURE...
...WINDOWS INTO TIME, ALLOWING ME TO RECORD, IN MY OWN SECRET LANGUAGE, THE HISTORY OF "THE SHIELD" BOTH LIVED AND AS YET UNLIVED.
THE STORY OF HOW I AS AN IMMORTAL WOULD SOMEDAY SHAPE IT INTO AN AGENCY OF ACTION AND ESPIONAGE...

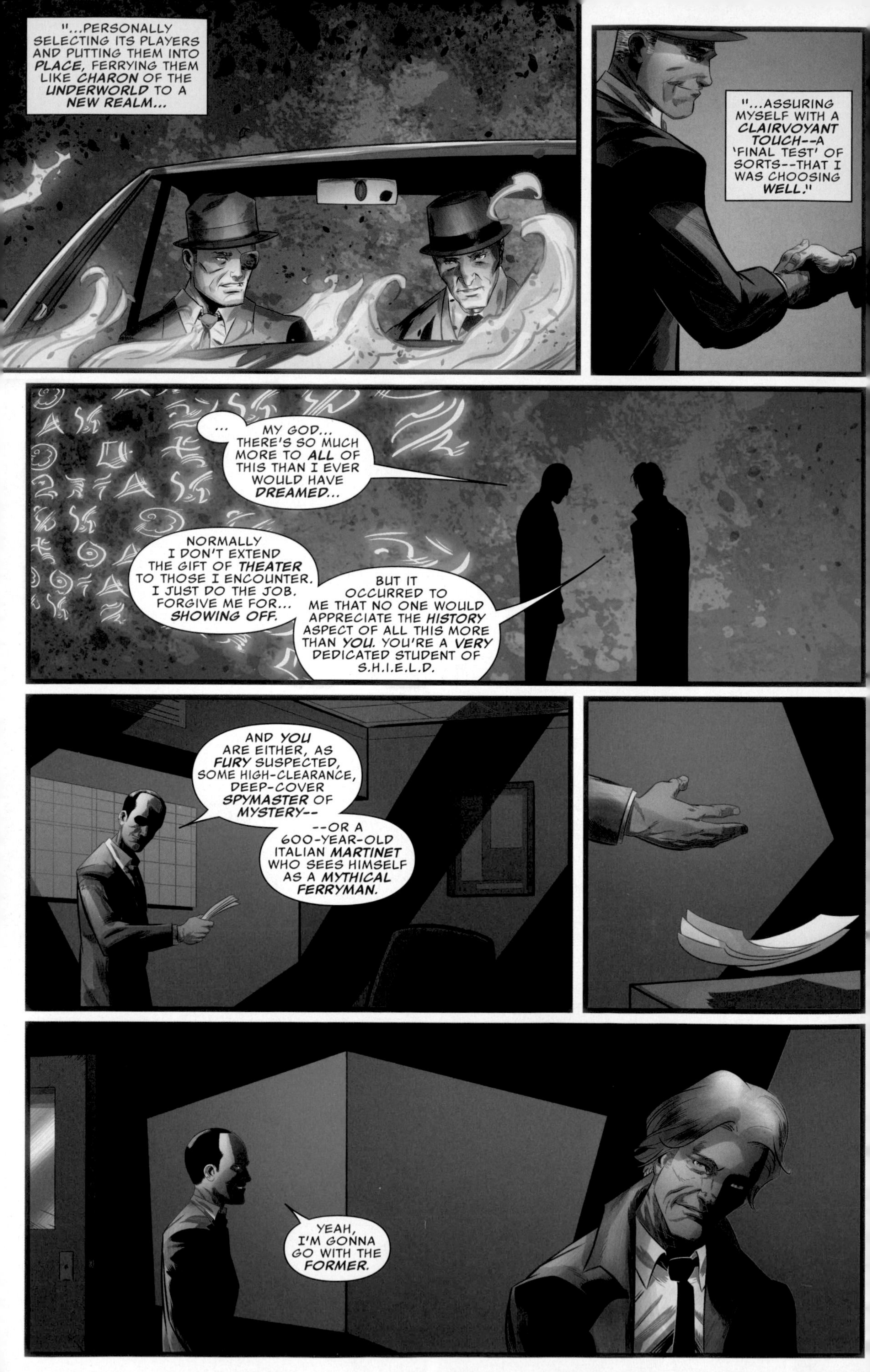
"...PERSONALLY SELECTING ITS PLAYERS AND PUTTING THEM INTO PLACE, FERRYING THEM LIKE CHARON OF THE UNDERWORLD TO A NEW REALM...
"...ASSURING MYSELF WITH A CLAIRVOYANT TOUCH--A 'FINAL TEST' OF SORTS--THAT I WAS CHOOSING WELL."
... MY GOD... THERE'S SO MUCH MORE TO ALL OF THIS THAN I EVER WOULD HAVE DREAMED...
NORMALLY I DON'T EXTEND THE GIFT OF THEATER TO THOSE I ENCOUNTER. I JUST DO THE JOB. FORGIVE ME FOR... SHOWING OFF.
BUT IT OCCURRED TO ME THAT NO ONE WOULD APPRECIATE THE HISTORY ASPECT OF ALL THIS MORE THAN YOU. YOU'RE A VERY DEDICATED STUDENT OF S.H.I.E.L.D.
AND YOU ARE EITHER, AS FURY SUSPECTED, SOME HIGH-CLEARANCE, DEEP-COVER SPYMASTER OF MYSTERY--
--OR A 600-YEAR-OLD ITALIAN MARTINET WHO SEES HIMSELF AS A MYTHICAL FERRYMAN.
YEAH, I'M GONNA GO WITH THE FORMER.

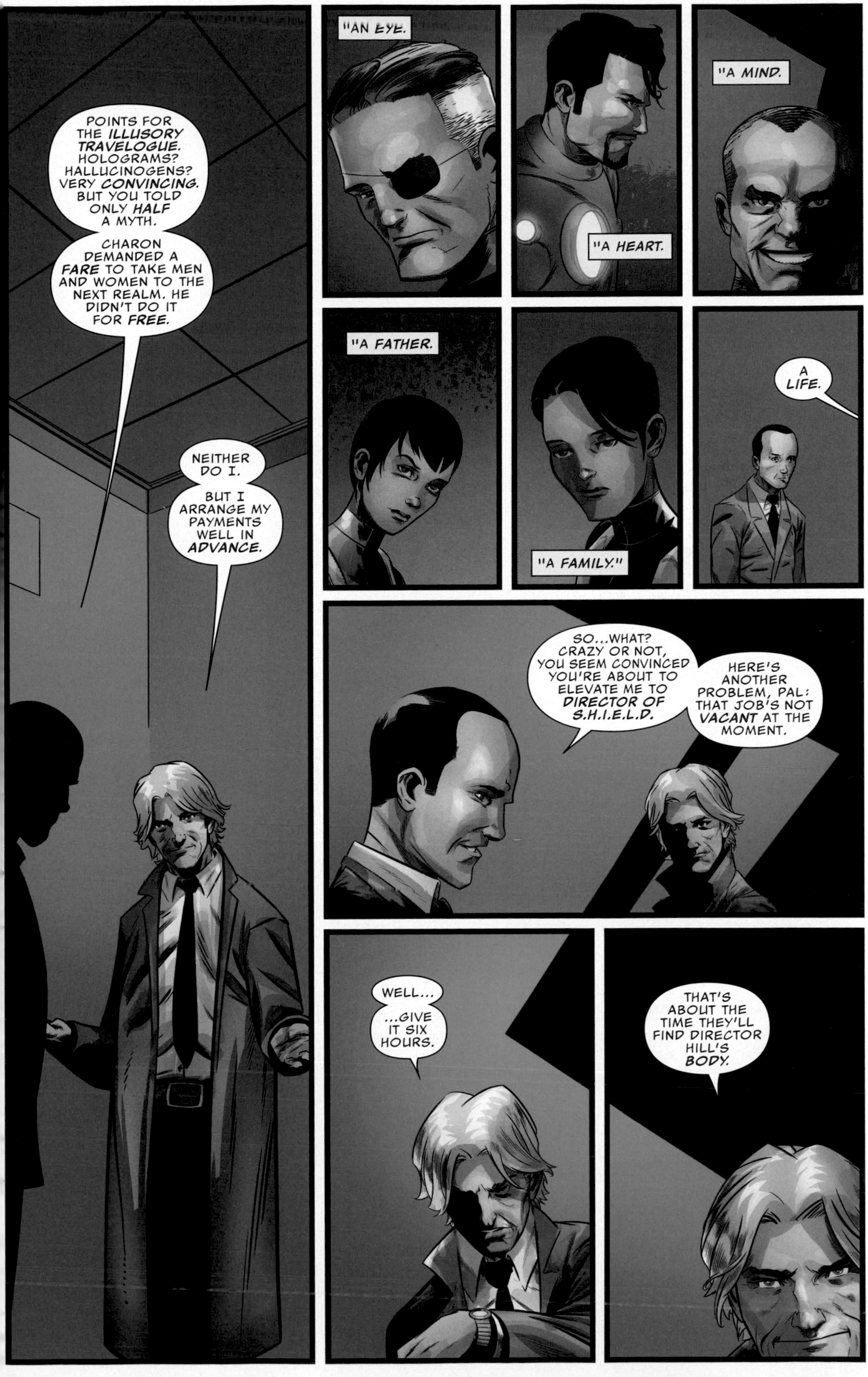
POINTS FOR THE ILLUSORY TRAVELOGUE. HOLOGRAMS? HALLUCINOGENS? VERY CONVINCING. BUT YOU TOLD ONLY HALF A MYTH.
CHARON DEMANDED A FARE TO TAKE MEN AND WOMEN TO THE NEXT REALM. HE DIDN'T DO IT FOR FREE.
NEITHER DO I.
BUT I ARRANGE MY PAYMENTS WELL IN ADVANCE.
"AN EYE.
"A HEART.
"A MIND.
"A FATHER.
"A FAMILY."
A LIFE.
SO...WHAT? CRAZY OR NOT, YOU SEEM CONVINCED YOU'RE ABOUT TO ELEVATE ME TO DIRECTOR OF S.H.I.E.L.D.
HERE'S ANOTHER PROBLEM, PAL: THAT JOB'S NOT VACANT AT THE MOMENT.
WELL...
...GIVE IT SIX HOURS.
THAT'S ABOUT THE TIME THEY'LL FIND DIRECTOR HILL'S BODY.

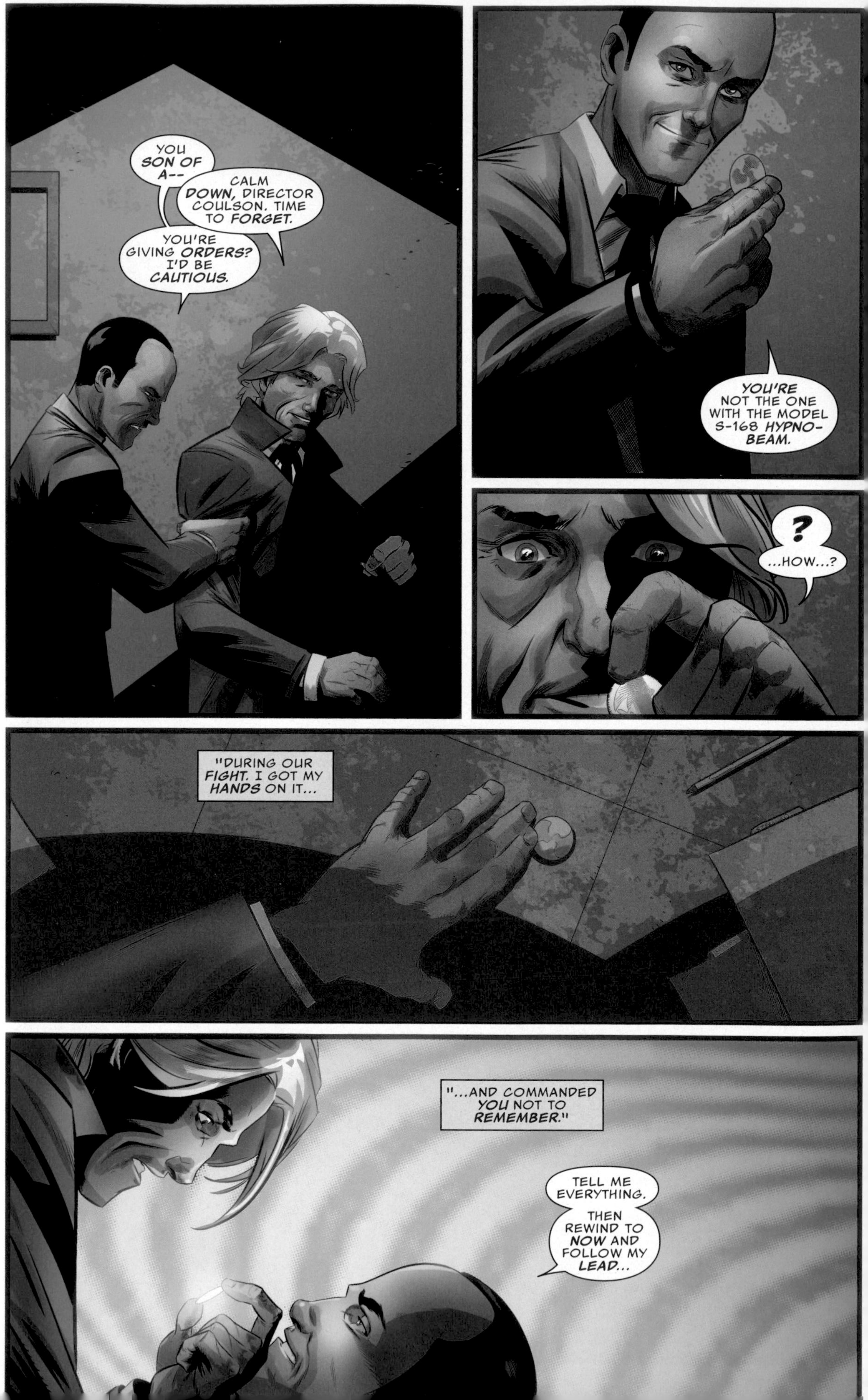
YOU SON OF A--
CALM DOWN, DIRECTOR COULSON. TIME TO FORGET.
YOU'RE GIVING ORDERS? I'D BE CAUTIOUS.
YOU'RE NOT THE ONE WITH THE MODEL S-168 HYPNO-BEAM.
?
...HOW...?
"DURING OUR FIGHT, I GOT MY HANDS ON IT...
"...AND COMMANDED YOU NOT TO REMEMBER."
TELL ME EVERYTHING.
THEN REWIND TO NOW AND FOLLOW MY LEAD...

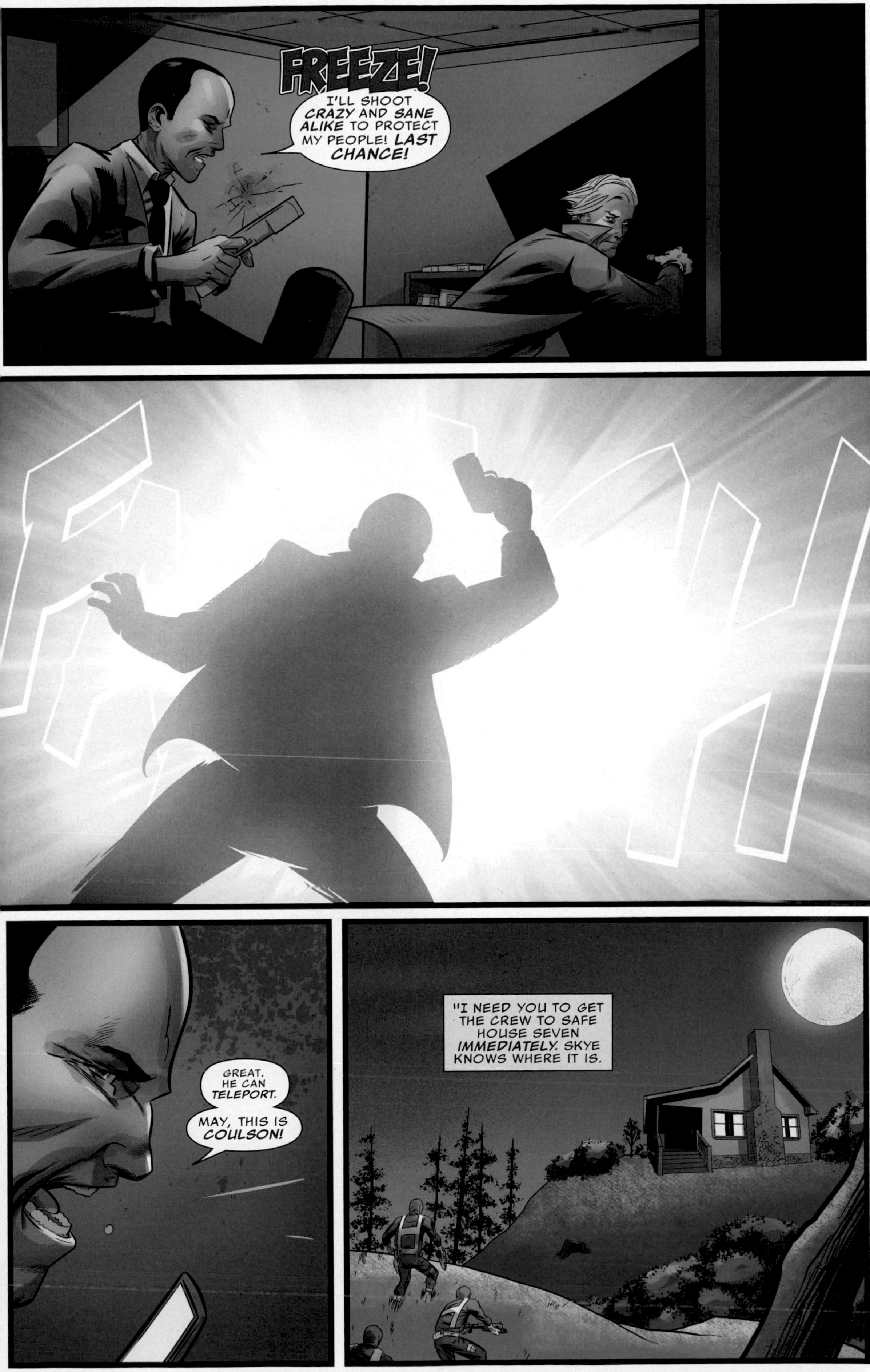
FREEZE!
I'LL SHOOT CRAZY AND SANE ALIKE TO PROTECT MY PEOPLE! LAST CHANCE!
GREAT. HE CAN TELEPORT.
MAY, THIS IS COULSON!
"I NEED YOU TO GET THE CREW TO SAFE HOUSE SEVEN IMMEDIATELY. SKYE KNOWS WHERE IT IS.

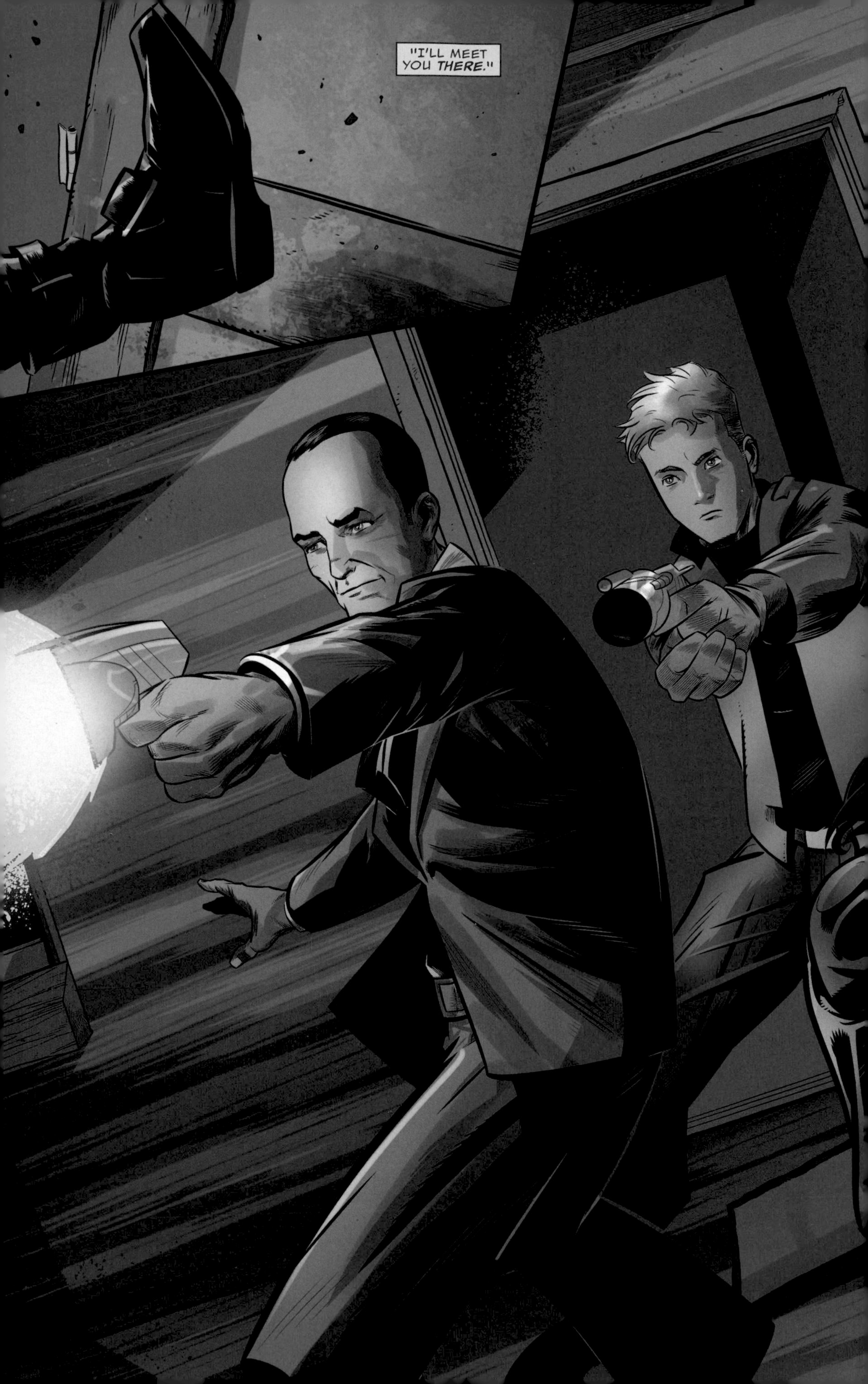
"I'LL MEET YOU THERE."

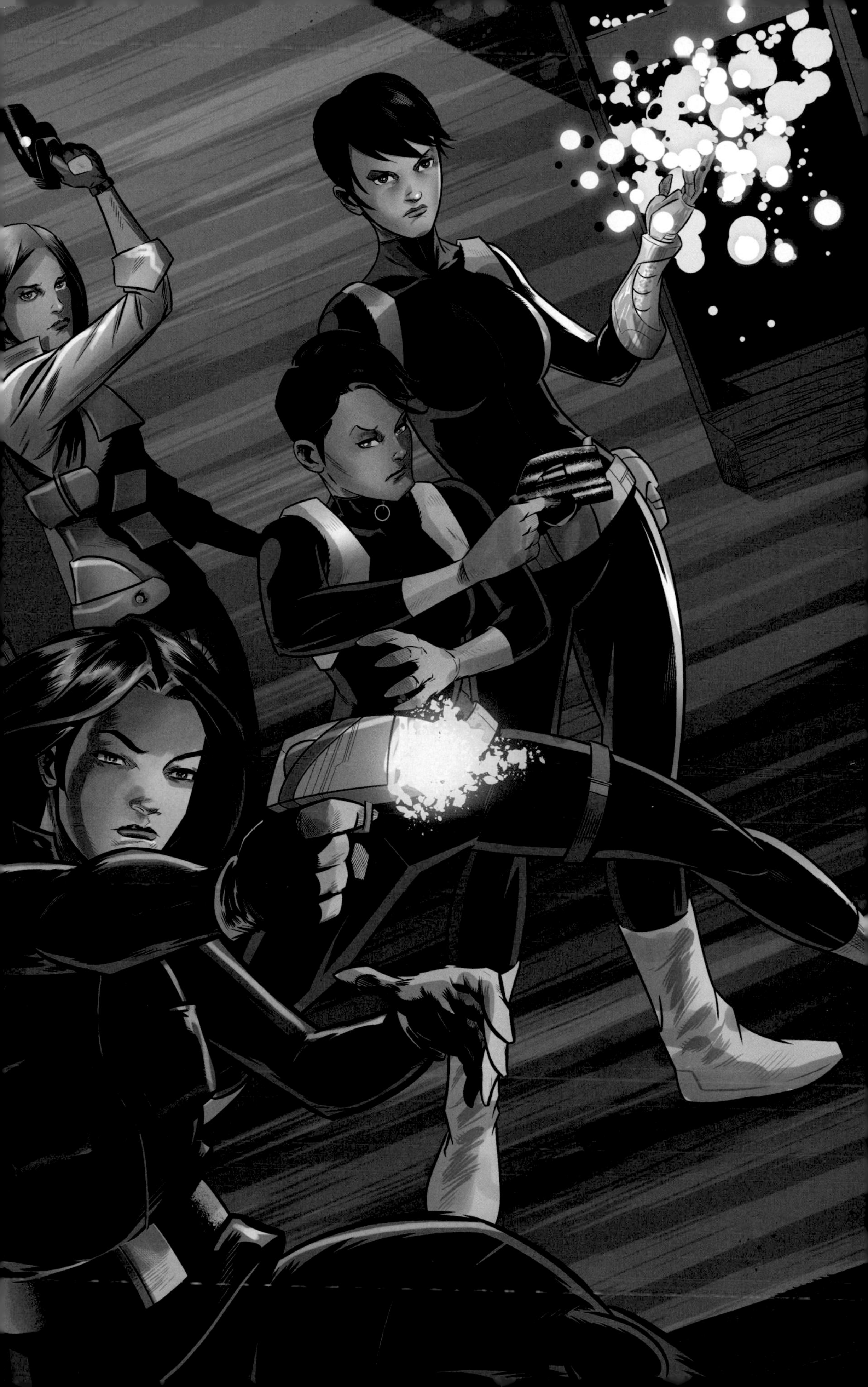

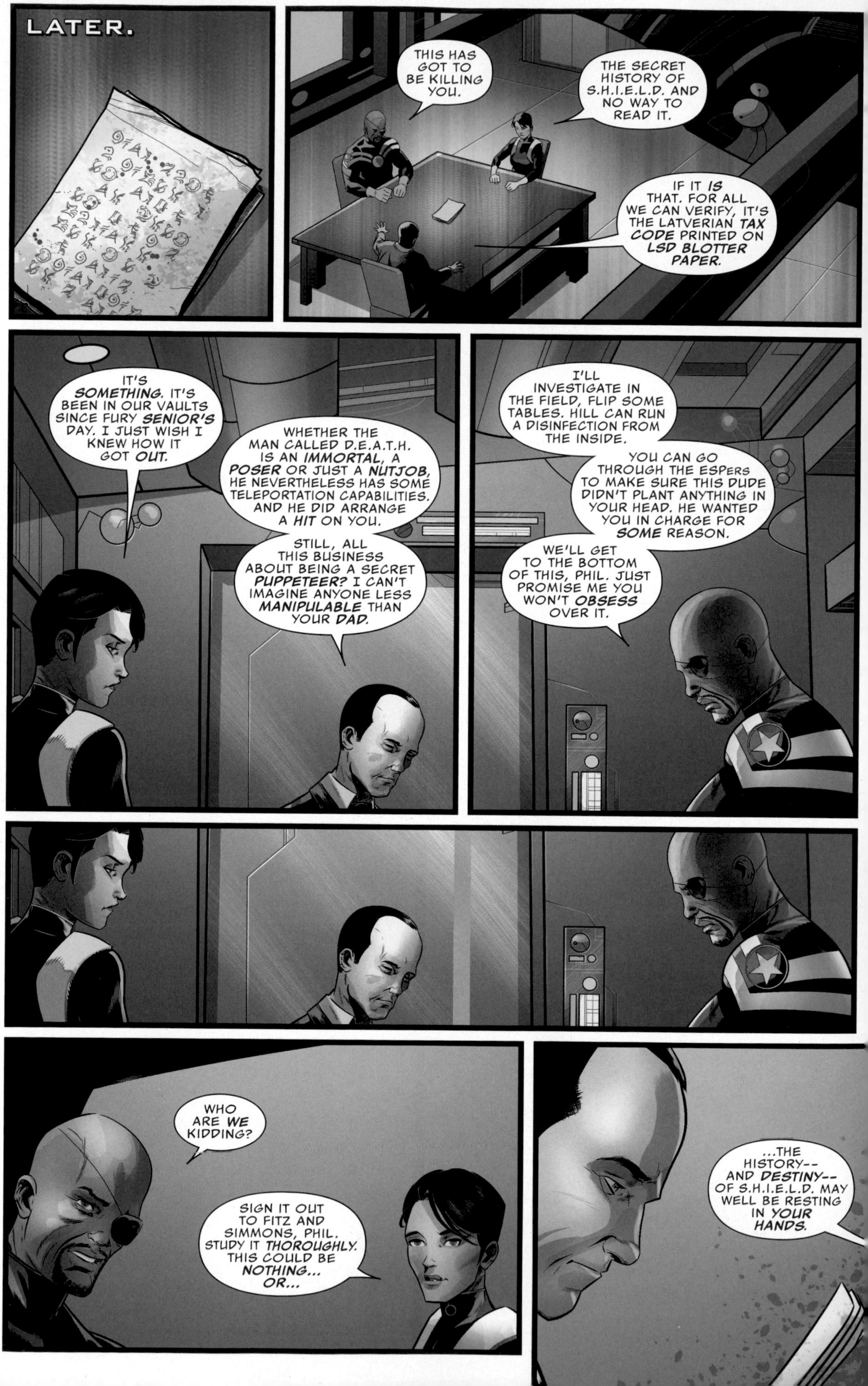
LATER.
THIS HAS GOT TO BE KILLING YOU.
THE SECRET HISTORY OF S.H.I.E.L.D. AND NO WAY TO READ IT.
IF IT IS THAT. FOR ALL WE CAN VERIFY, IT'S THE LATVERIAN TAX CODE PRINTED ON LSD BLOTTER PAPER.
IT'S SOMETHING. IT'S BEEN IN OUR VAULTS SINCE FURY SENIOR'S DAY. I JUST WISH I KNEW HOW IT GOT OUT.
WHETHER THE MAN CALLED D.E.A.T.H. IS AN IMMORTAL, A POSER OR JUST A NUTJOB, HE NEVERTHELESS HAS SOME TELEPORTATION CAPABILITIES. AND HE DID ARRANGE A HIT ON YOU.
STILL, ALL THIS BUSINESS ABOUT BEING A SECRET PUPPETEER? I CAN'T IMAGINE ANYONE LESS MANIPULABLE THAN YOUR DAD.
I'LL INVESTIGATE IN THE FIELD, FLIP SOME TABLES. HILL CAN RUN A DISINFECTION FROM THE INSIDE.
YOU CAN GO THROUGH THE ESPERS TO MAKE SURE THIS DUDE DIDN'T PLANT ANYTHING IN YOUR HEAD. HE WANTED YOU IN CHARGE FOR SOME REASON.
WE'LL GET TO THE BOTTOM OF THIS, PHIL. JUST PROMISE ME YOU WON'T OBSESS OVER IT.
WHO ARE WE KIDDING?
SIGN IT OUT TO FITZ AND SIMMONS, PHIL. STUDY IT THOROUGHLY. THIS COULD BE NOTHING... OR...
...THE HISTORY-- AND DESTINY-- OF S.H.I.E.L.D. MAY WELL BE RESTING IN YOUR HANDS.

10.

ACTIVE MISSION:

THE DUCK CALLED H•O•W•A•R•D•

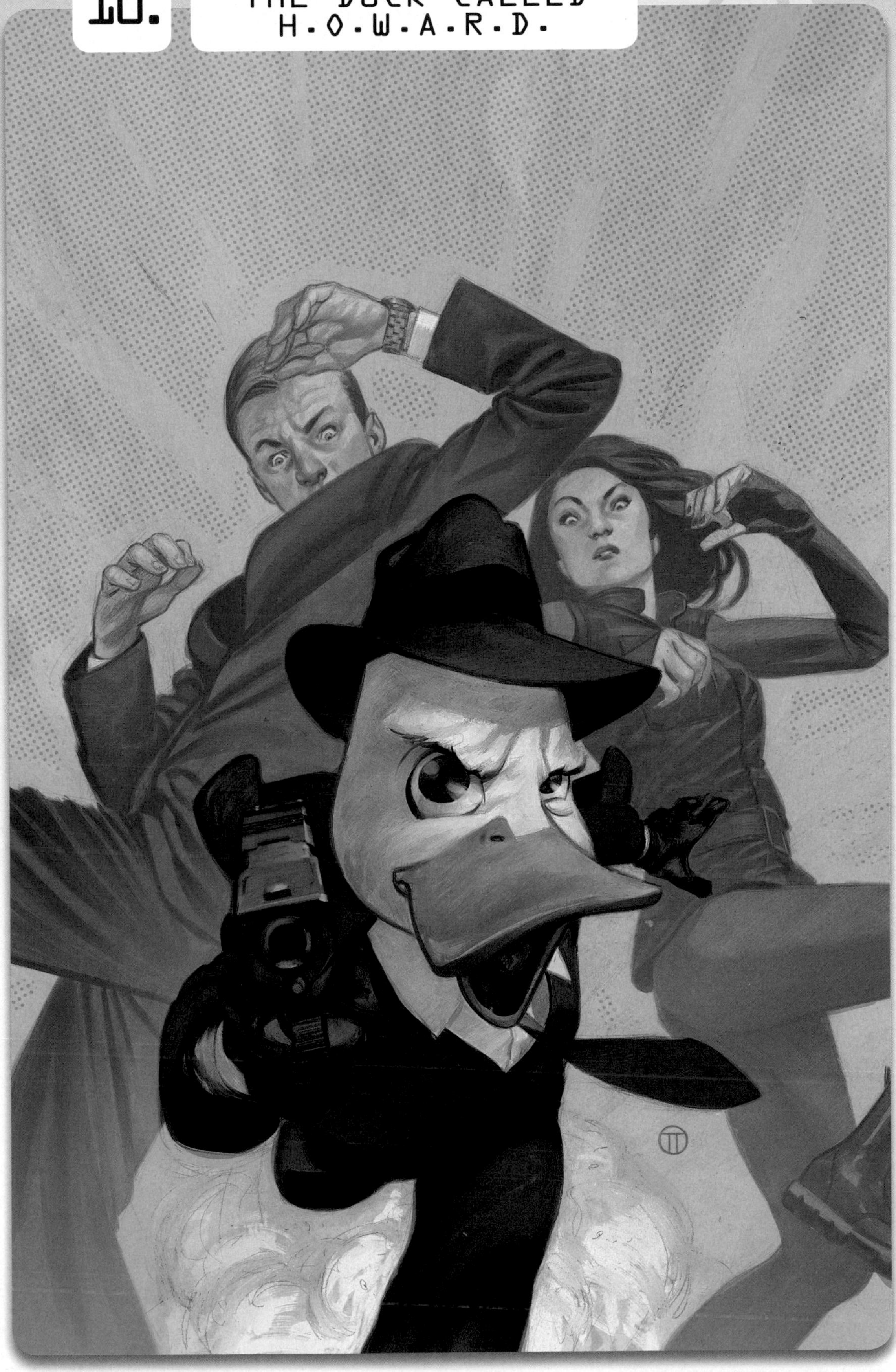

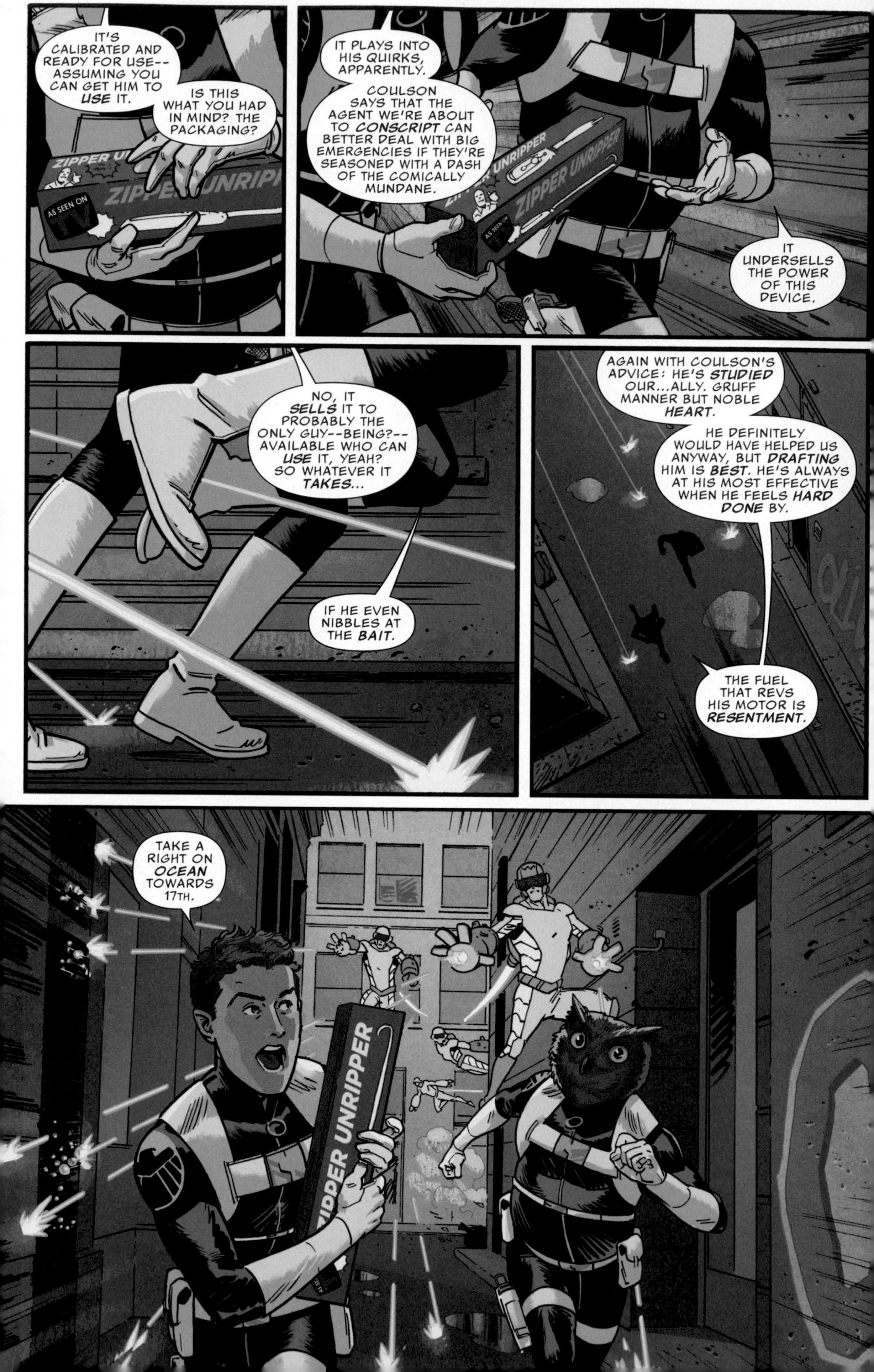
IT'S CALIBRATED AND READY FOR USE--ASSUMING YOU CAN GET HIM TO USE IT.
IS THIS WHAT YOU HAD IN MIND? THE PACKAGING?
ZIPPER UNRIPPER
AS SEEN ON TV
IT PLAYS INTO HIS QUIRKS, APPARENTLY.
COULSON SAYS THAT THE AGENT WE'RE ABOUT TO CONSCRIPT CAN BETTER DEAL WITH BIG EMERGENCIES IF THEY'RE SEASONED WITH A DASH OF THE COMICALLY MUNDANE.
IT UNDERSELLS THE POWER OF THIS DEVICE.
NO, IT SELLS IT TO PROBABLY THE ONLY GUY--BEING?--AVAILABLE WHO CAN USE IT, YEAH? SO WHATEVER IT TAKES...
IF HE EVEN NIBBLES AT THE BAIT.
AGAIN WITH COULSON'S ADVICE: HE'S STUDIED OUR...ALLY. GRUFF MANNER BUT NOBLE HEART.
HE DEFINITELY WOULD HAVE HELPED US ANYWAY, BUT DRAFTING HIM IS BEST. HE'S ALWAYS AT HIS MOST EFFECTIVE WHEN HE FEELS HARD DONE BY.
THE FUEL THAT REVS HIS MOTOR IS RESENTMENT.
TAKE A RIGHT ON OCEAN TOWARDS 17TH.
ZIPPER UNRIPPER

"THAT'S WHERE I'M HAVING HIM *MEET US.*"

THANKS, COULSON!

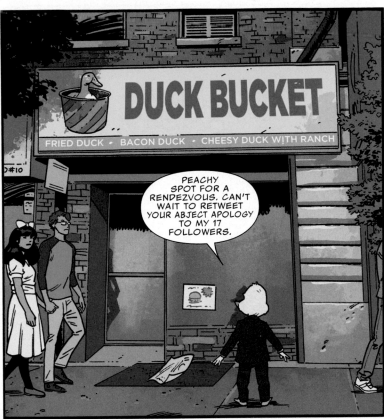

DUCK BUCKET

FRIED DUCK · BACON DUCK · CHEESY DUCK WITH RANCH

PEACHY SPOT FOR A RENDEZVOUS. CAN'T WAIT TO RETWEET YOUR ABJECT APOLOGY TO MY 17 FOLLOWERS.

YOU'RE A DU-- A DU--

I KNOW! AWKWARD, AIN'T IT?

DU-- DU--DU-- DU--

--*UCK!* I'M A DUCK. AND *YOU* JUST STUMBLED A HALF DOZEN TIMES OVER A ONE-SYLLABLE WORD. IS IT *GUILT* I'M SENSING?

LOOK, IF IT'S *VUH-VUH-VENGEANCE* YOU WANT--

RELAX, KID. MY RESEMBLANCE TO THE LUCKLESS SLOBS ON YOUR KIDDIE MENU IS ONLY *FEATHER-DEEP.* I'M ERE-HAY FOR I.E.L.D.-*S.H.A.Y.,* GET IT?

S.H.I.E.L.D....?

DUCK BUCKET Ranch DRESSING

GEEZ. I DIDN'T KNOW IT WAS POSSIBLE FOR YOU TO PLAY *DUMBER.* AND DON'T TRY TO TELL ME THE *SECRET ENTRANCE* IS THROUGH THE *FRYER BASKET.* I'M NOT FALLING FOR--

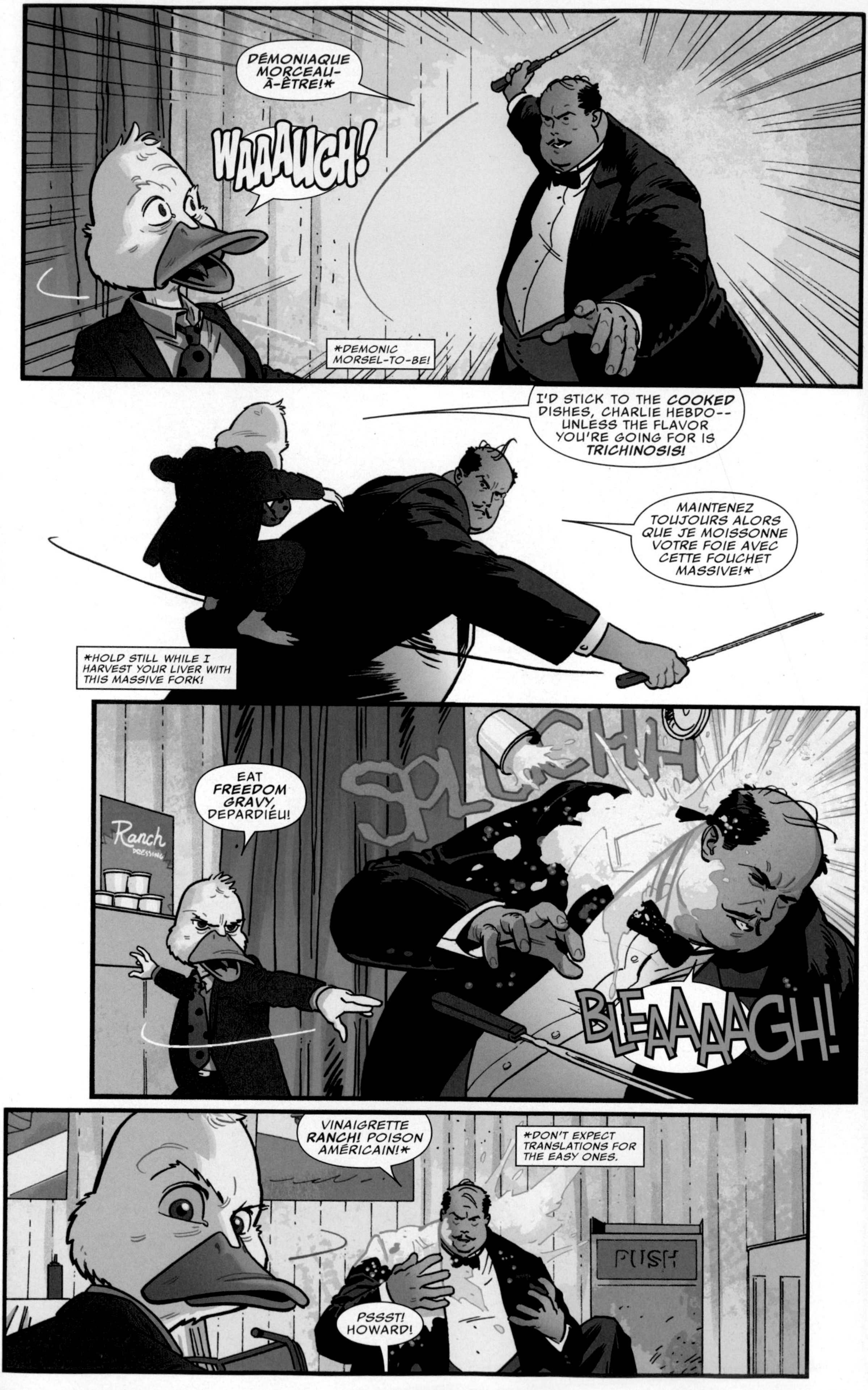
DÉMONIAQUE MORCEAU-À-ÊTRE!*
WAAAUGH!
*DEMONIC MORSEL-TO-BE!
I'D STICK TO THE COOKED DISHES, CHARLIE HEBDO-- UNLESS THE FLAVOR YOU'RE GOING FOR IS TRICHINOSIS!
MAINTENEZ TOUJOURS ALORS QUE JE MOISSONNE VOTRE FOIE AVEC CETTE FOUCHET MASSIVE!*
*HOLD STILL WHILE I HARVEST YOUR LIVER WITH THIS MASSIVE FORK!
EAT FREEDOM GRAVY, DEPARDIEU!
Ranch DRESSING
SPLOOSH
BLEAAAAAGH!
VINAIGRETTE RANCH! POISON AMÉRICAIN!*
*DON'T EXPECT TRANSLATIONS FOR THE EASY ONES.
PUSH
PSSST! HOWARD!

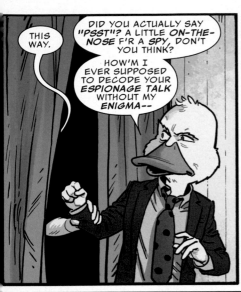

THIS WAY.

DID YOU ACTUALLY SAY "PSST"? A LITTLE ON-THE-NOSE F'R A SPY, DON'T YOU THINK?

HOW'M I EVER SUPPOSED TO DECODE YOUR ESPIONAGE TALK WITHOUT MY ENIGMA--

NOW!

--MACHINE--?

HOWARD, YOU'RE LATE.

AND YOU ARE COULSONLESS. WHO ARE YOU? AND OF ALL THE S.H.I.E.L.D. SATELLITE OFFICES IN ALL OF BROOKLYN, YOU SUMMON ME TO THE ONE GUARANTEED TO OFFEND?

"OFFEND" HOW?

IT'S A DUCK RESTAURANT!

AH. OKAY. IT'S NOT A DUCK RESTAURANT.

I WAS JUST OUT THERE!

ONE LARGE DUCK AND A DIET GRAPE, PLEASE.

WHUH?

SEE?

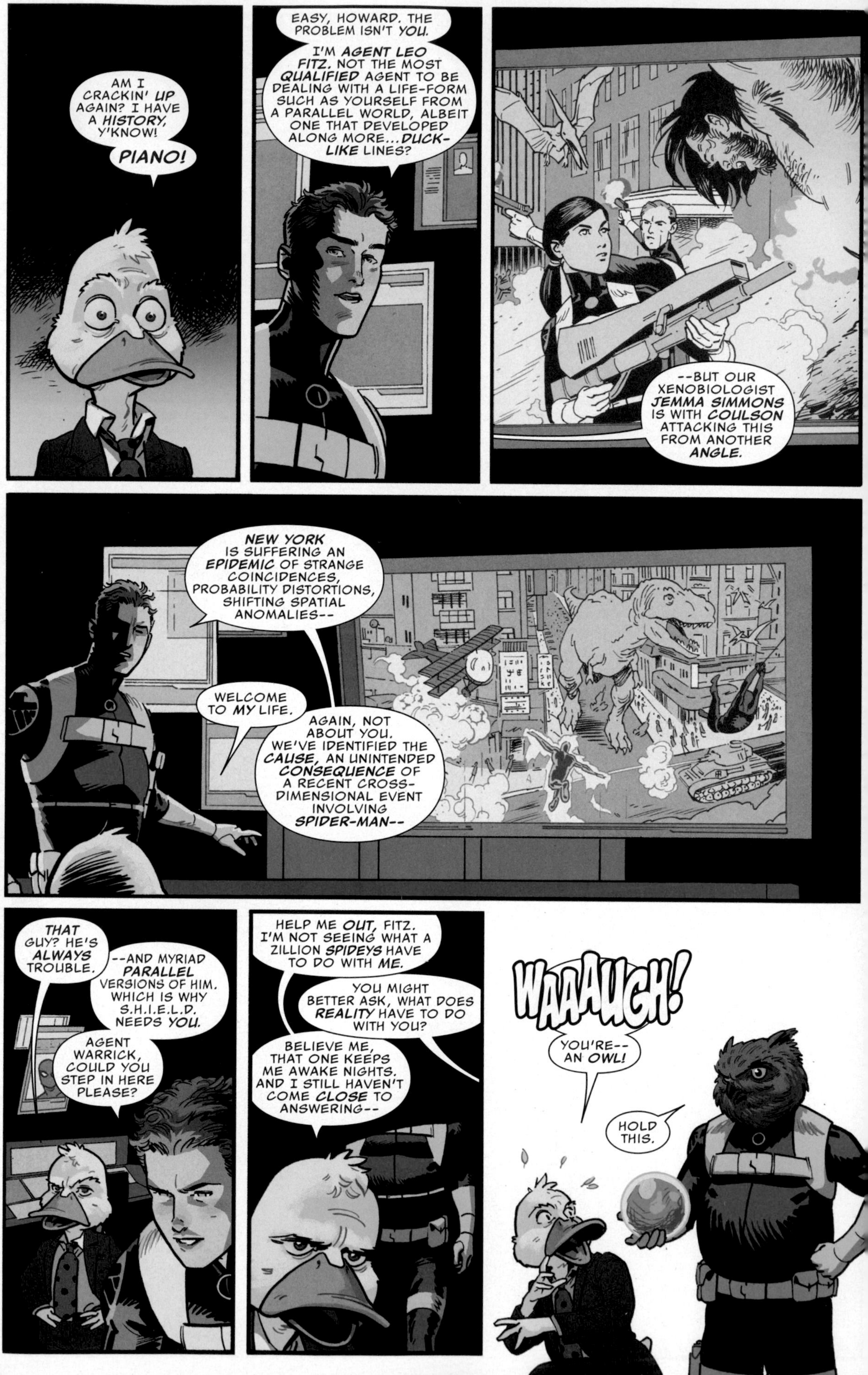
AM I CRACKIN' UP AGAIN? I HAVE A HISTORY, Y'KNOW!
PIANO!
EASY, HOWARD. THE PROBLEM ISN'T YOU.
I'M AGENT LEO FITZ. NOT THE MOST QUALIFIED AGENT TO BE DEALING WITH A LIFE-FORM SUCH AS YOURSELF FROM A PARALLEL WORLD, ALBEIT ONE THAT DEVELOPED ALONG MORE...DUCK-LIKE LINES?
--BUT OUR XENOBIOLOGIST JEMMA SIMMONS IS WITH COULSON ATTACKING THIS FROM ANOTHER ANGLE.
NEW YORK IS SUFFERING AN EPIDEMIC OF STRANGE COINCIDENCES, PROBABILITY DISTORTIONS, SHIFTING SPATIAL ANOMALIES--
WELCOME TO MY LIFE.
AGAIN, NOT ABOUT YOU. WE'VE IDENTIFIED THE CAUSE, AN UNINTENDED CONSEQUENCE OF A RECENT CROSS-DIMENSIONAL EVENT INVOLVING SPIDER-MAN--
THAT GUY? HE'S ALWAYS TROUBLE.
--AND MYRIAD PARALLEL VERSIONS OF HIM. WHICH IS WHY S.H.I.E.L.D. NEEDS YOU.
AGENT WARRICK, COULD YOU STEP IN HERE PLEASE?
HELP ME OUT, FITZ. I'M NOT SEEING WHAT A ZILLION SPIDEYS HAVE TO DO WITH ME.
YOU MIGHT BETTER ASK, WHAT DOES REALITY HAVE TO DO WITH YOU?
BELIEVE ME, THAT ONE KEEPS ME AWAKE NIGHTS. AND I STILL HAVEN'T COME CLOSE TO ANSWERING--
WAAAUGH!
YOU'RE-- AN OWL!
HOLD THIS.

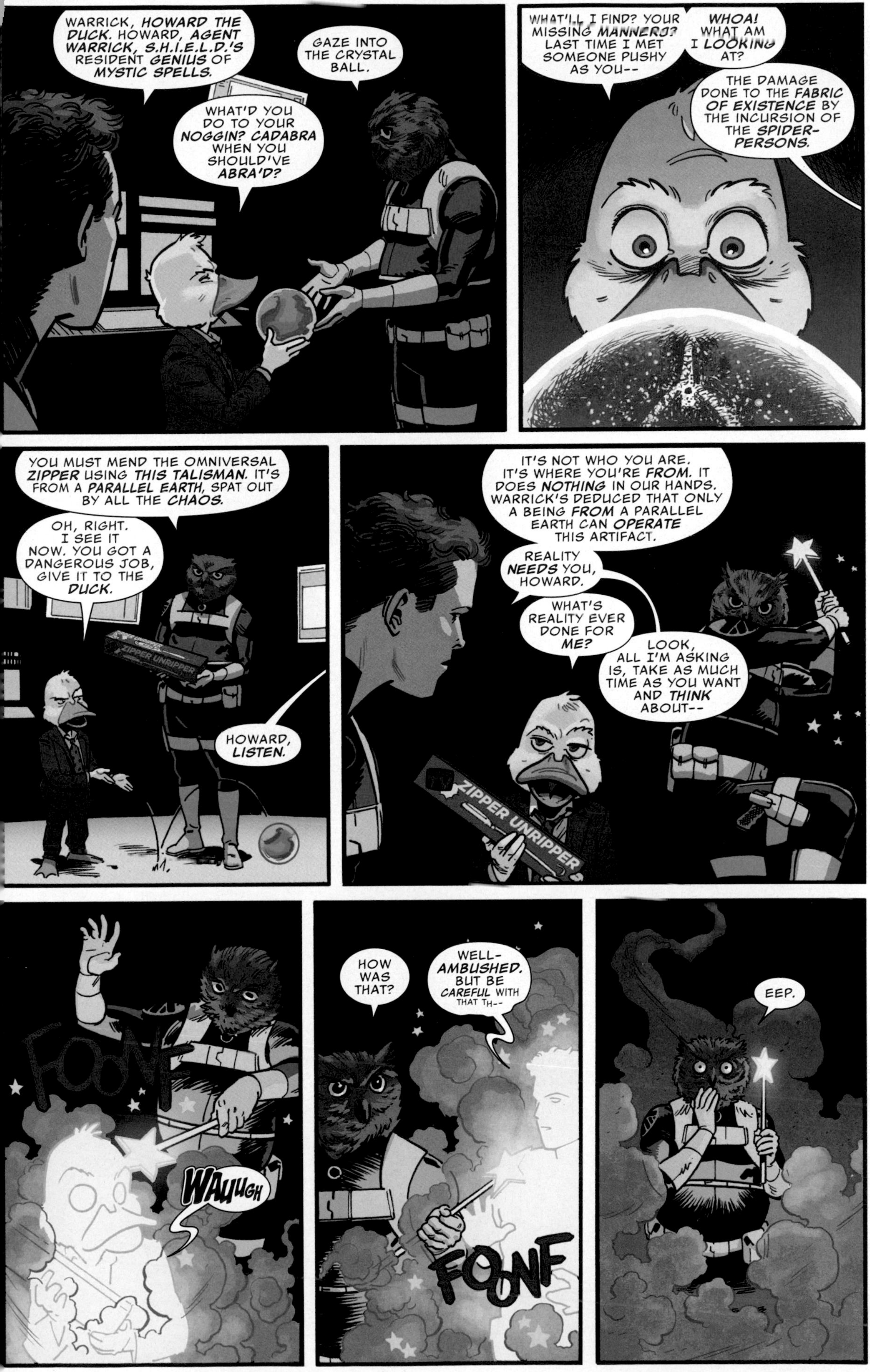
WARRICK, HOWARD THE DUCK. HOWARD, AGENT WARRICK, S.H.I.E.L.D.'S RESIDENT GENIUS OF MYSTIC SPELLS.
GAZE INTO THE CRYSTAL BALL.
WHAT'D YOU DO TO YOUR NOGGIN? CADABRA WHEN YOU SHOULD'VE ABRA'D?
WHAT'LL I FIND? YOUR MISSING MANNERS? LAST TIME I MET SOMEONE PUSHY AS YOU--
WHOA! WHAT AM I LOOKING AT?
THE DAMAGE DONE TO THE FABRIC OF EXISTENCE BY THE INCURSION OF THE SPIDER-PERSONS.
YOU MUST MEND THE OMNIVERSAL ZIPPER USING THIS TALISMAN. IT'S FROM A PARALLEL EARTH, SPAT OUT BY ALL THE CHAOS.
OH, RIGHT. I SEE IT NOW. YOU GOT A DANGEROUS JOB, GIVE IT TO THE DUCK.
ZIPPER UNRIPPER
HOWARD, LISTEN.
IT'S NOT WHO YOU ARE. IT'S WHERE YOU'RE FROM. IT DOES NOTHING IN OUR HANDS. WARRICK'S DEDUCED THAT ONLY A BEING FROM A PARALLEL EARTH CAN OPERATE THIS ARTIFACT.
REALITY NEEDS YOU, HOWARD.
WHAT'S REALITY EVER DONE FOR ME?
LOOK, ALL I'M ASKING IS, TAKE AS MUCH TIME AS YOU WANT AND THINK ABOUT--
ZIPPER UNRIPPER
FOOMF
WAUUGH
HOW WAS THAT?
WELL-AMBUSHED. BUT BE CAREFUL WITH THAT TH--
FOOMF
EEP.

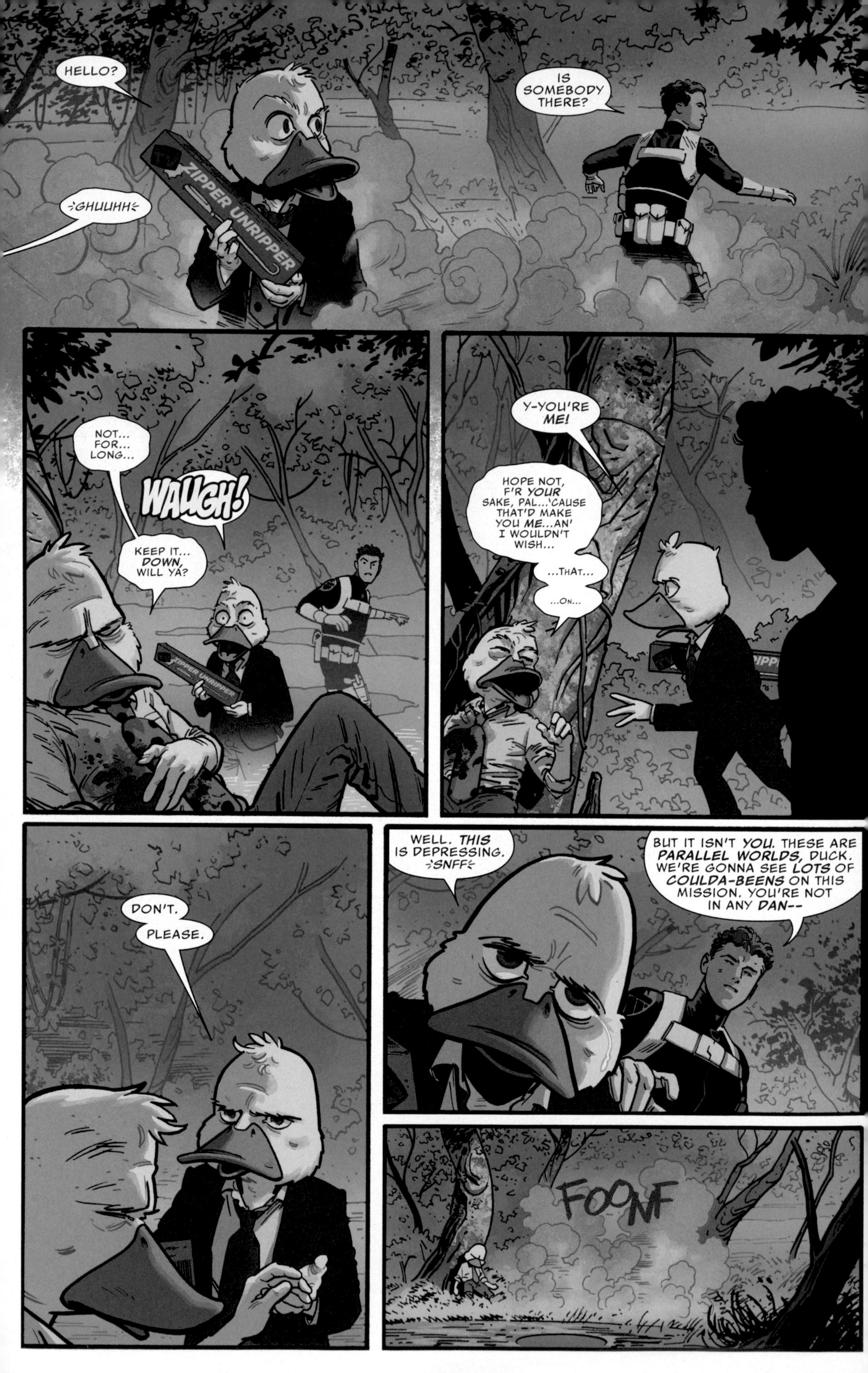
HELLO?
IS SOMEBODY THERE?
ZIPPER UNRIPPER
GHUUHH
NOT... FOR... LONG...
WAUGH!
KEEP IT... DOWN, WILL YA?
ZIPPER UNRIPPER
Y-YOU'RE ME!
HOPE NOT, F'R YOUR SAKE, PAL...'CAUSE THAT'D MAKE YOU ME...AN' I WOULDN'T WISH...
...THAT...
...ON...
DON'T.
PLEASE.
WELL. THIS IS DEPRESSING. SNFF
BUT IT ISN'T YOU. THESE ARE PARALLEL WORLDS, DUCK. WE'RE GONNA SEE LOTS OF COULDA-BEENS ON THIS MISSION. YOU'RE NOT IN ANY DAN--
FOOMF

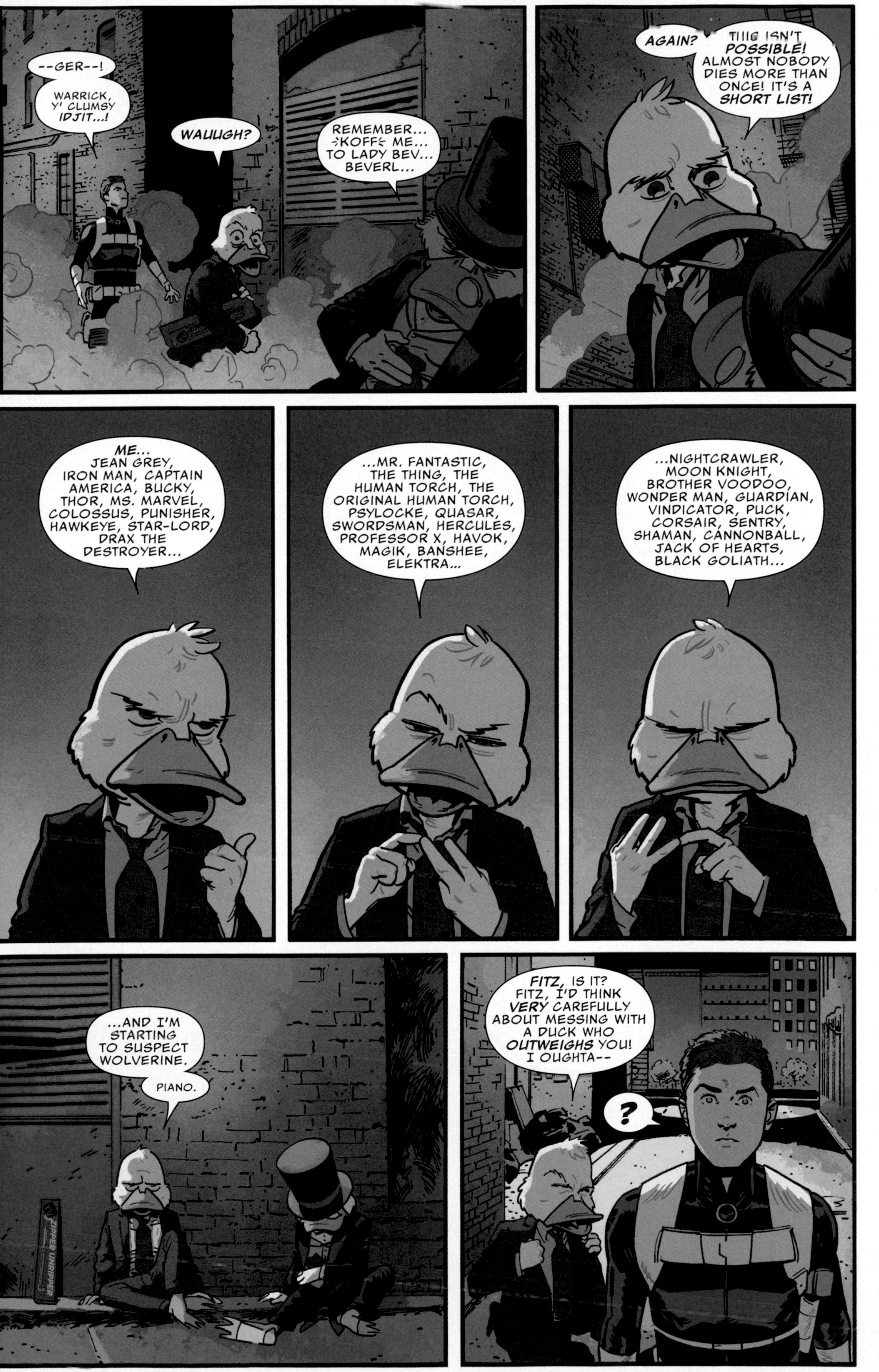
--GER--!
WARRICK, Y' CLUMSY IDJIT...!
WAUUGH?
REMEMBER... *KOFF* ME... TO LADY BEV... BEVERL...
AGAIN?
THIS ISN'T POSSIBLE! ALMOST NOBODY DIES MORE THAN ONCE! IT'S A SHORT LIST!
ME... JEAN GREY, IRON MAN, CAPTAIN AMERICA, BUCKY, THOR, MS. MARVEL, COLOSSUS, PUNISHER, HAWKEYE, STAR-LORD, DRAX THE DESTROYER...
...MR. FANTASTIC, THE THING, THE HUMAN TORCH, THE ORIGINAL HUMAN TORCH, PSYLOCKE, QUASAR, SWORDSMAN, HERCULES, PROFESSOR X, HAVOK, MAGIK, BANSHEE, ELEKTRA...
...NIGHTCRAWLER, MOON KNIGHT, BROTHER VOODOO, WONDER MAN, GUARDIAN, VINDICATOR, PUCK, CORSAIR, SENTRY, SHAMAN, CANNONBALL, JACK OF HEARTS, BLACK GOLIATH...
...AND I'M STARTING TO SUSPECT WOLVERINE.
PIANO.
ZIPPER UNRIPPER
FITZ, IS IT? FITZ, I'D THINK VERY CAREFULLY ABOUT MESSING WITH A DUCK WHO OUTWEIGHS YOU! I OUGHTA--
?

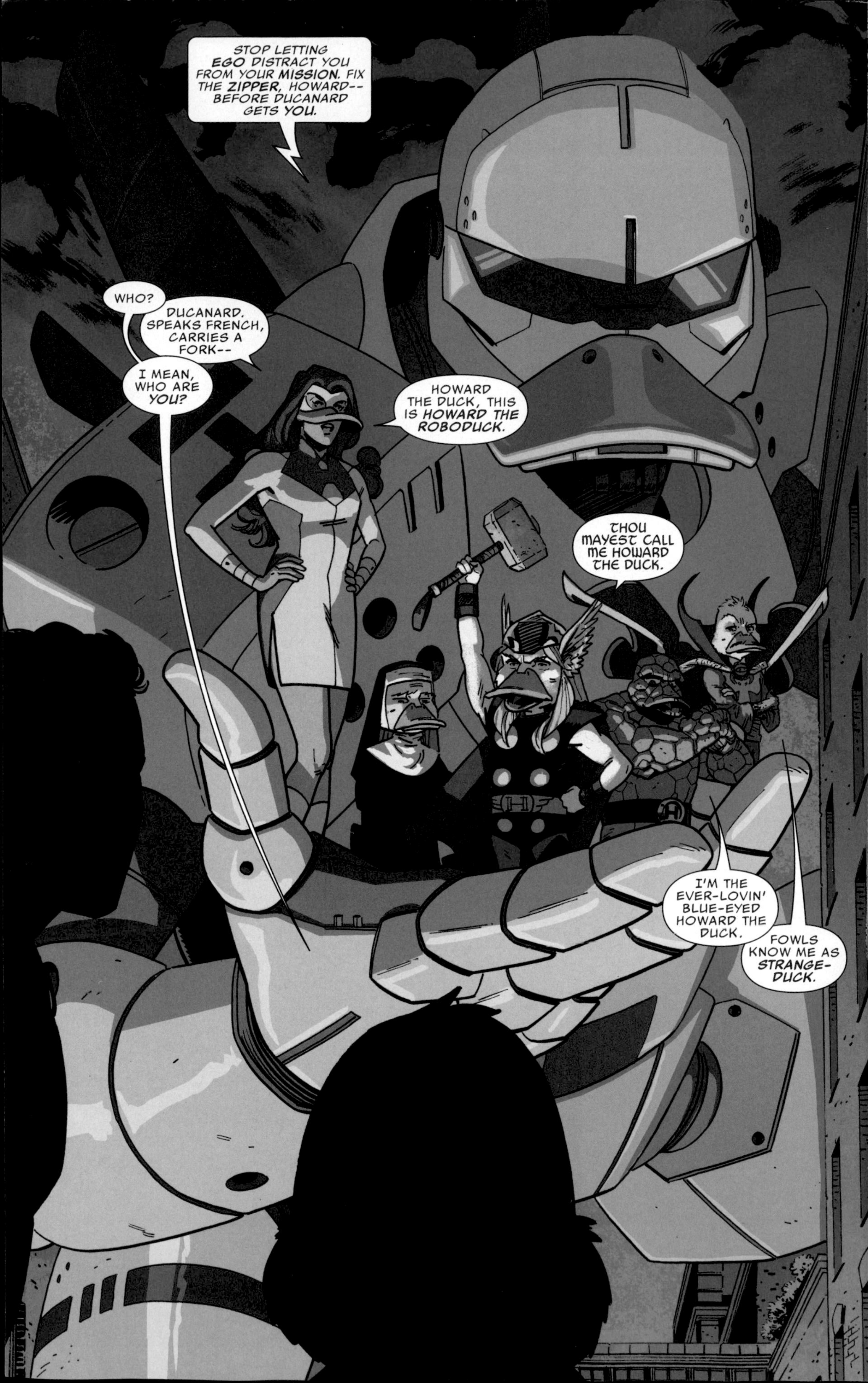
STOP LETTING EGO DISTRACT YOU FROM YOUR MISSION. FIX THE ZIPPER, HOWARD-- BEFORE DUCANARD GETS YOU.
WHO?
DUCANARD. SPEAKS FRENCH, CARRIES A FORK--
I MEAN, WHO ARE YOU?
HOWARD THE DUCK, THIS IS HOWARD THE ROBODUCK.
THOU MAYEST CALL ME HOWARD THE DUCK.
I'M THE EVER-LOVIN' BLUE-EYED HOWARD THE DUCK.
FOWLS KNOW ME AS STRANGE-DUCK.

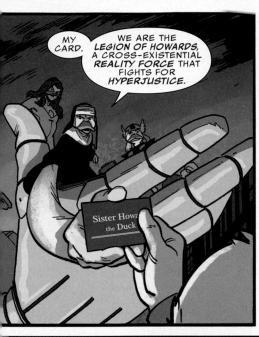

MY CARD.

WE ARE THE **LEGION OF HOWARDS**, A CROSS-EXISTENTIAL **REALITY FORCE** THAT FIGHTS FOR **HYPERJUSTICE.**

Sister Howa[rd] the Duck

ALMOST **CONVINCING**, "SISTER HOWARD," EXCEPT FOR ONE **DETAIL:** HOW COME I WAS NEVER INVITED INTO YOUR LITTLE COFFEE KLATCH?

FIX THE ZIPPER, HOWARD. **STRANGEDUCK** TELLS US THOU HAST THE TOOL. SAVE ALL OF OUR UNIVERSES BEFORE THE MORTAL WITH THE FORK COMETH TO CLAIM THY--

OW.

CHUTT

DUCKY!

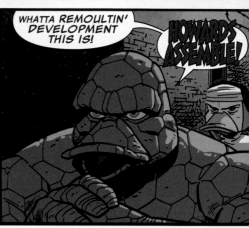

WHATTA REMOULTIN' DEVELOPMENT THIS IS!

HOWARDS ASSEMBLE!

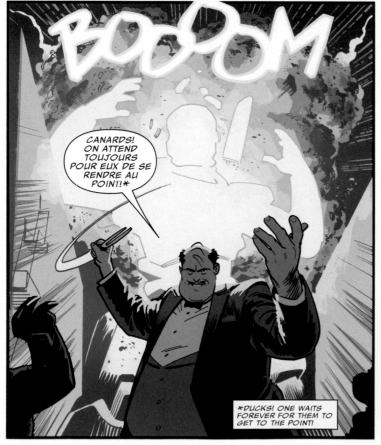

BOOOOM

CANARDS! ON ATTEND TOUJOURS POUR EUX DE SE RENDRE AU POINT!*

*DUCKS! ONE WAITS FOREVER FOR THEM TO GET TO THE POINT!

MAIS ICI, CE EST MON POINT! PAS D'ATTENTE!*

*BUT HERE IS MY POINT! NO WAITING!

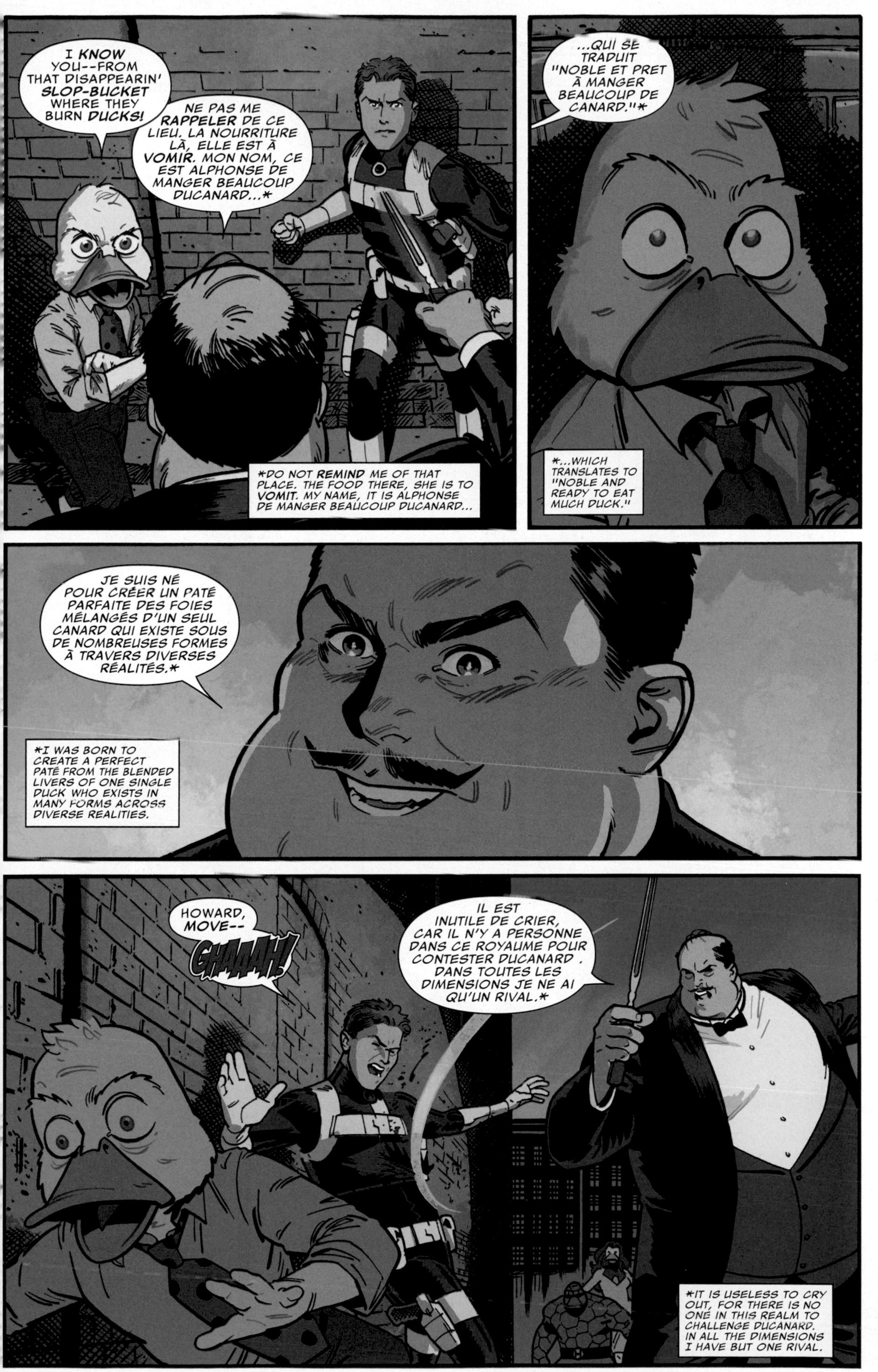
I KNOW YOU--FROM THAT DISAPPEARIN' SLOP-BUCKET WHERE THEY BURN DUCKS!
NE PAS ME RAPPELER DE CE LIEU. LA NOURRITURE LÀ, ELLE EST À VOMIR. MON NOM, CE EST ALPHONSE DE MANGER BEAUCOUP DUCANARD...*
*DO NOT REMIND ME OF THAT PLACE. THE FOOD THERE, SHE IS TO VOMIT. MY NAME, IT IS ALPHONSE DE MANGER BEAUCOUP DUCANARD...
...QUI SE TRADUIT "NOBLE ET PRET À MANGER BEAUCOUP DE CANARD."*
*...WHICH TRANSLATES TO "NOBLE AND READY TO EAT MUCH DUCK."
JE SUIS NÉ POUR CRÉER UN PATÉ PARFAITE DES FOIES MÉLANGÉS D'UN SEUL CANARD QUI EXISTE SOUS DE NOMBREUSES FORMES À TRAVERS DIVERSES RÉALITÉS.*
*I WAS BORN TO CREATE A PERFECT PATÉ FROM THE BLENDED LIVERS OF ONE SINGLE DUCK WHO EXISTS IN MANY FORMS ACROSS DIVERSE REALITIES.
HOWARD, MOVE--
GHAAAH!
IL EST INUTILE DE CRIER, CAR IL N'Y A PERSONNE DANS CE ROYAUME POUR CONTESTER DUCANARD . DANS TOUTES LES DIMENSIONS JE NE AI QU'UN RIVAL.*
*IT IS USELESS TO CRY OUT, FOR THERE IS NO ONE IN THIS REALM TO CHALLENGE DUCANARD. IN ALL THE DIMENSIONS I HAVE BUT ONE RIVAL.

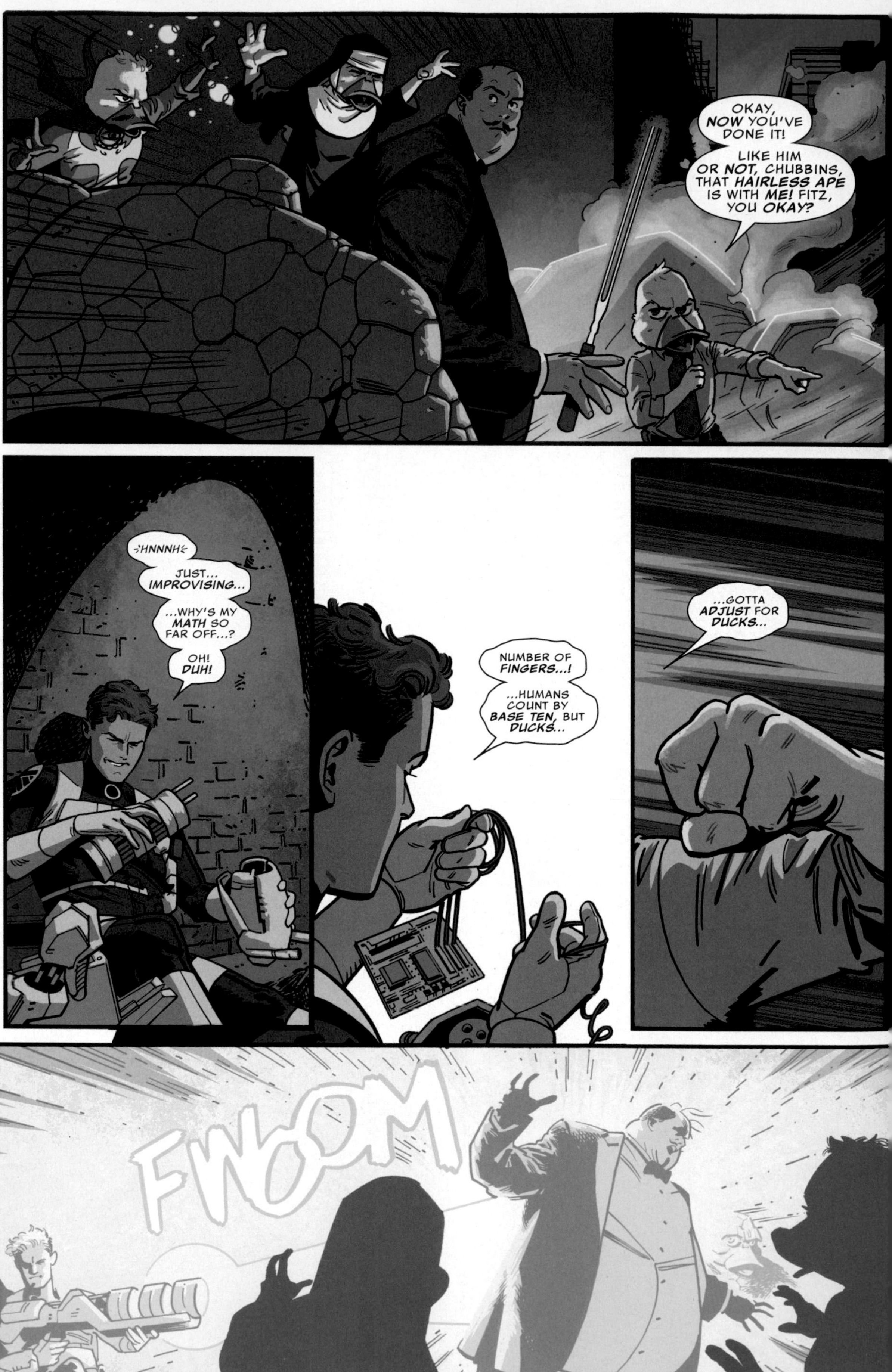

OKAY, NOW YOU'VE DONE IT!
LIKE HIM OR NOT, CHUBBINS, THAT HAIRLESS APE IS WITH ME! FITZ, YOU OKAY?
HNNNH
JUST... IMPROVISING...
...WHY'S MY MATH SO FAR OFF...?
OH! DUH!
NUMBER OF FINGERS...!
...HUMANS COUNT BY BASE TEN, BUT DUCKS...
...GOTTA ADJUST FOR DUCKS...
FWOOM

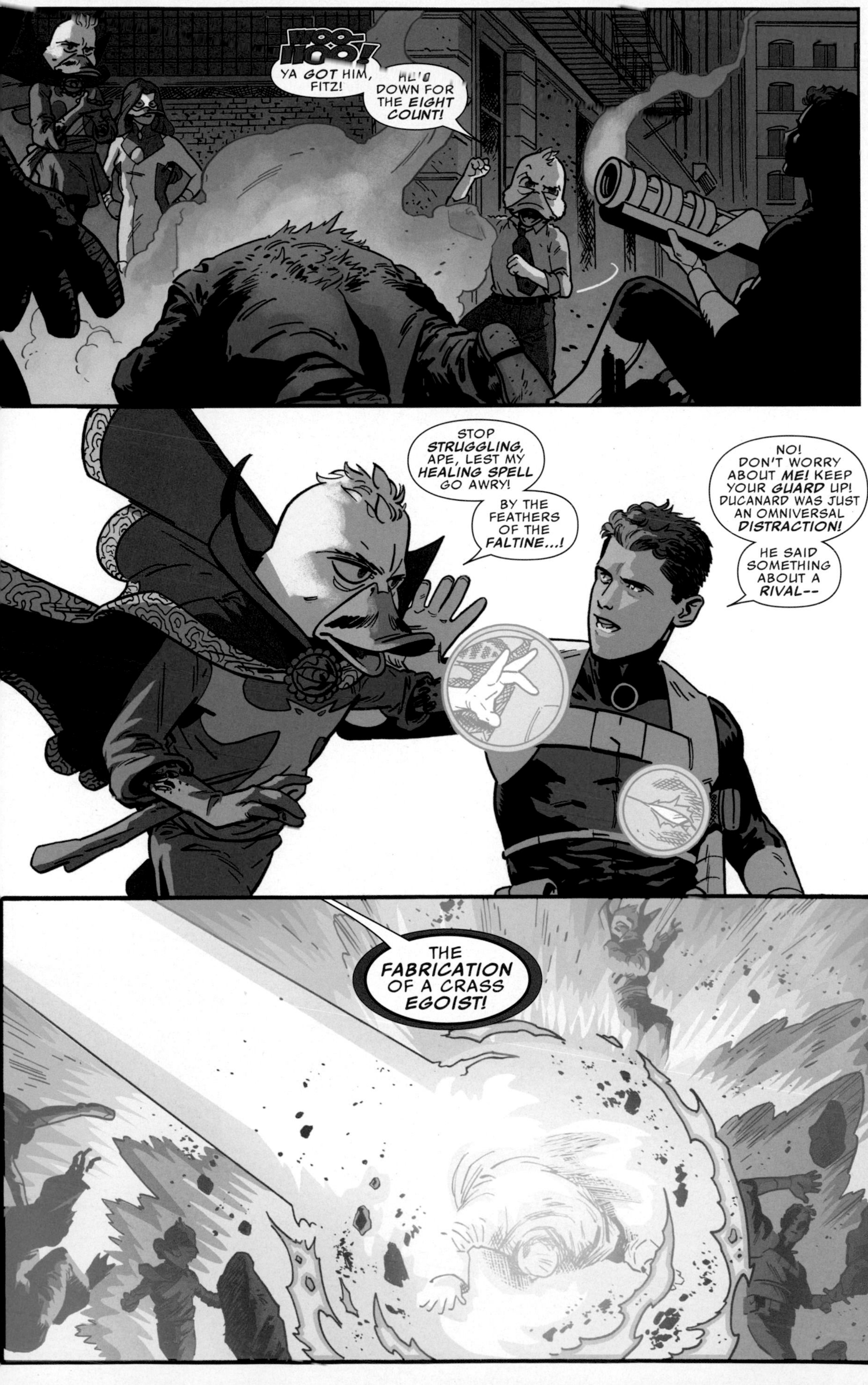
WOO-HOO!
YA GOT HIM, FITZ!
HE'D DOWN FOR THE EIGHT COUNT!
STOP STRUGGLING, APE, LEST MY HEALING SPELL GO AWRY!
BY THE FEATHERS OF THE FALTINE...!
NO! DON'T WORRY ABOUT ME! KEEP YOUR GUARD UP! DUCANARD WAS JUST AN OMNIVERSAL DISTRACTION!
HE SAID SOMETHING ABOUT A RIVAL--
THE FABRICATION OF A CRASS EGOIST!

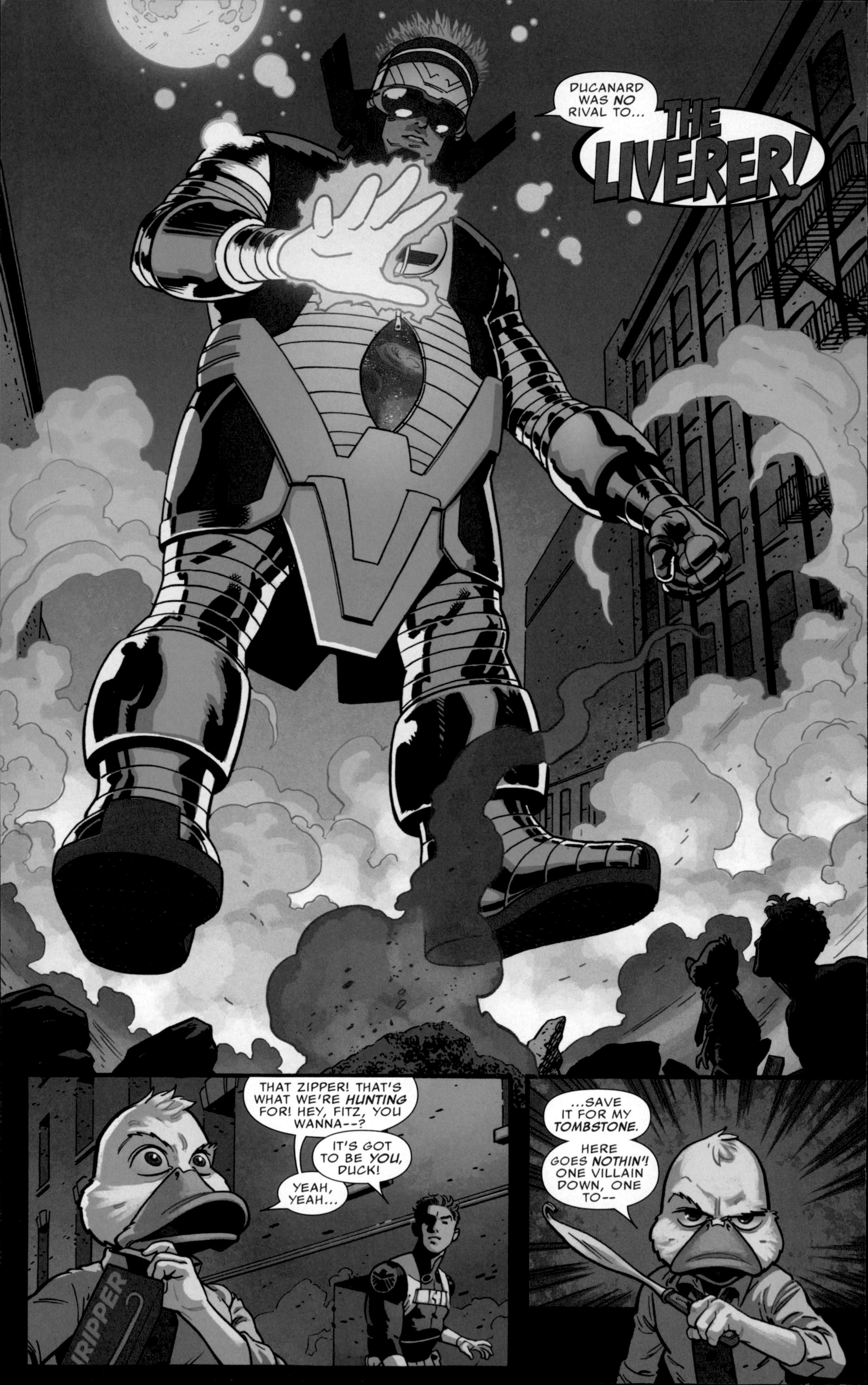
DUCANARD WAS NO RIVAL TO...
THE LIVERER!
THAT ZIPPER! THAT'S WHAT WE'RE HUNTING FOR! HEY, FITZ, YOU WANNA--?
IT'S GOT TO BE YOU, DUCK!
YEAH, YEAH...
RIPPER
...SAVE IT FOR MY TOMBSTONE.
HERE GOES NOTHIN'! ONE VILLAIN DOWN, ONE TO--

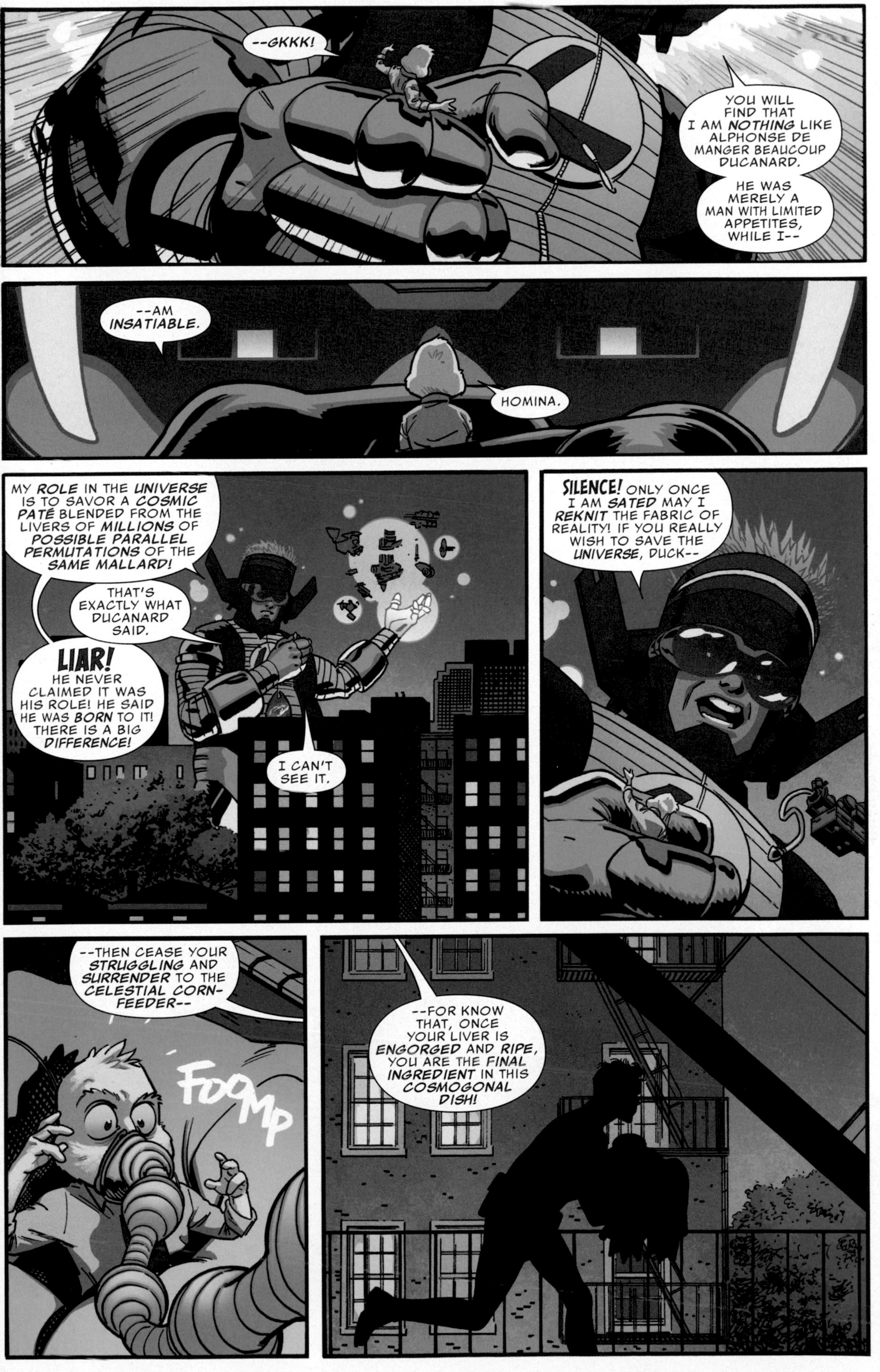
--GKKK!
YOU WILL FIND THAT I AM NOTHING LIKE ALPHONSE DE MANGER BEAUCOUP DUCANARD.
HE WAS MERELY A MAN WITH LIMITED APPETITES, WHILE I--
--AM INSATIABLE.
HOMINA.
MY ROLE IN THE UNIVERSE IS TO SAVOR A COSMIC PATÉ BLENDED FROM THE LIVERS OF MILLIONS OF POSSIBLE PARALLEL PERMUTATIONS OF THE SAME MALLARD!
THAT'S EXACTLY WHAT DUCANARD SAID.
LIAR! HE NEVER CLAIMED IT WAS HIS ROLE! HE SAID HE WAS BORN TO IT! THERE IS A BIG DIFFERENCE!
I CAN'T SEE IT.
SILENCE! ONLY ONCE I AM SATED MAY I REKNIT THE FABRIC OF REALITY! IF YOU REALLY WISH TO SAVE THE UNIVERSE, DUCK--
--THEN CEASE YOUR STRUGGLING AND SURRENDER TO THE CELESTIAL CORN-FEEDER--
FOOMP
--FOR KNOW THAT, ONCE YOUR LIVER IS ENGORGED AND RIPE, YOU ARE THE FINAL INGREDIENT IN THIS COSMOGONAL DISH!

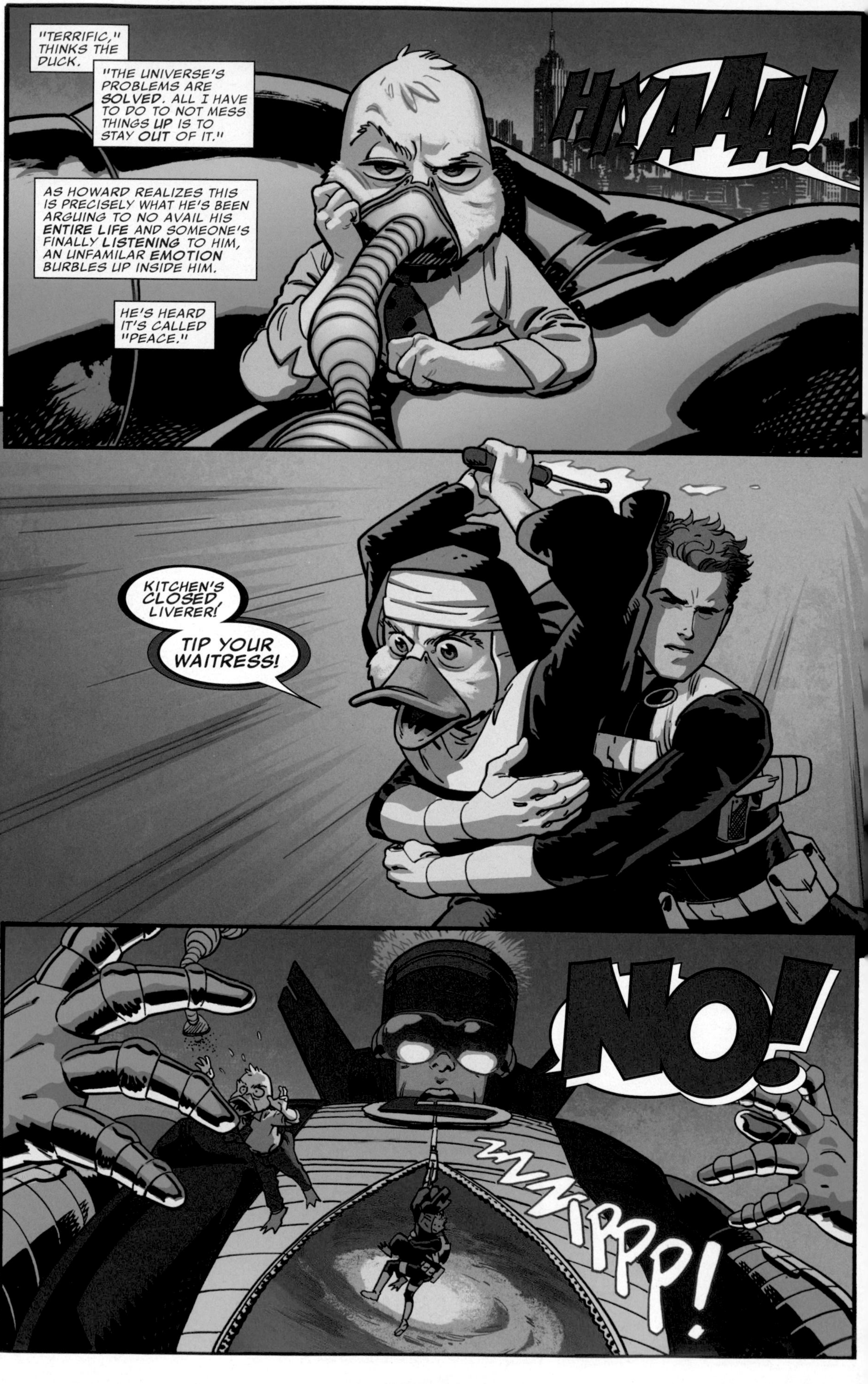
"TERRIFIC," THINKS THE DUCK.
"THE UNIVERSE'S PROBLEMS ARE SOLVED. ALL I HAVE TO DO TO NOT MESS THINGS UP IS TO STAY OUT OF IT."
HIYAAAA!
AS HOWARD REALIZES THIS IS PRECISELY WHAT HE'S BEEN ARGUING TO NO AVAIL HIS ENTIRE LIFE AND SOMEONE'S FINALLY LISTENING TO HIM, AN UNFAMILAR EMOTION BURBLES UP INSIDE HIM.
HE'S HEARD IT'S CALLED "PEACE."
KITCHEN'S CLOSED, LIVERER!
TIP YOUR WAITRESS!
NO!
ZZZZIPPP!

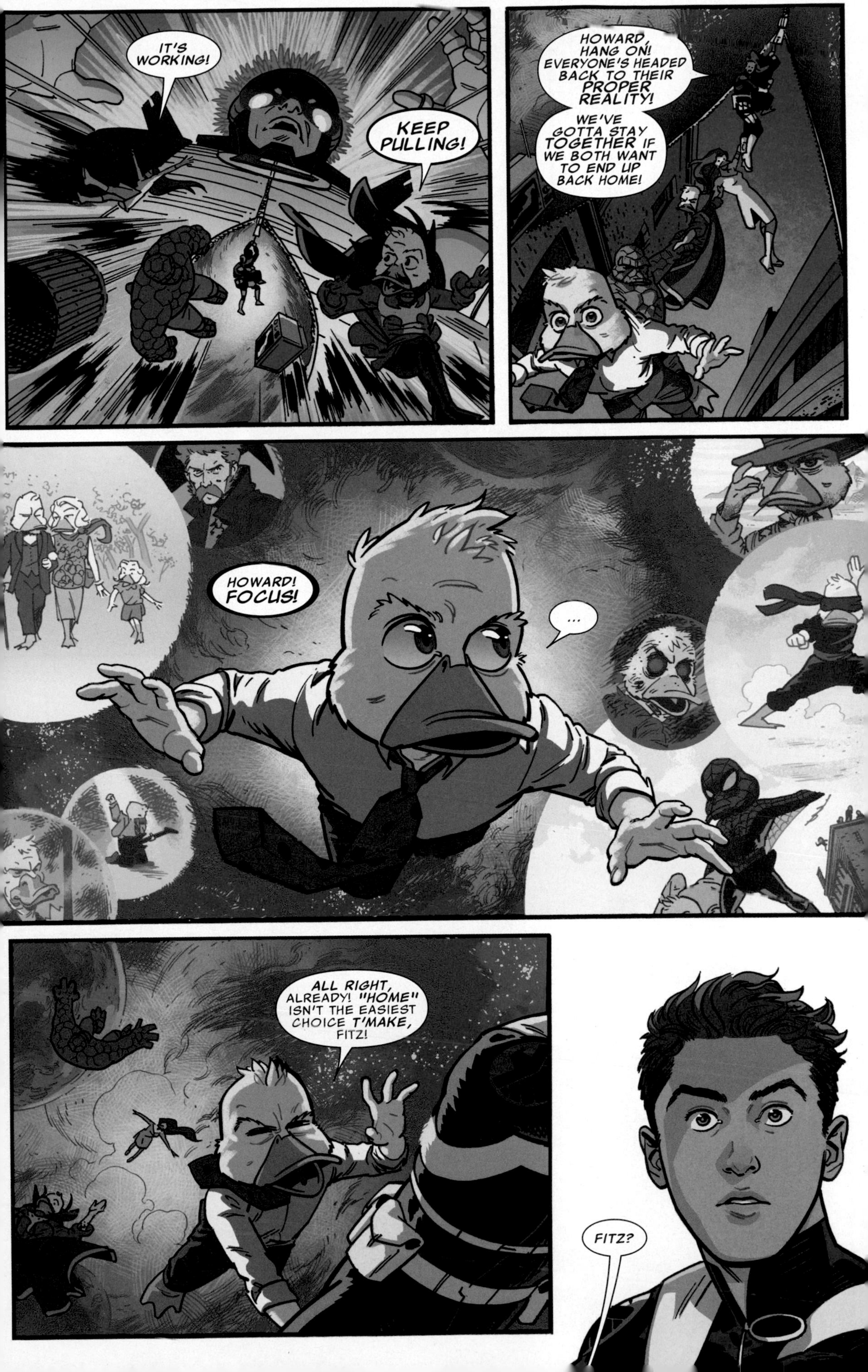
IT'S WORKING!
KEEP PULLING!
HOWARD, HANG ON! EVERYONE'S HEADED BACK TO THEIR PROPER REALITY!
WE'VE GOTTA STAY TOGETHER IF WE BOTH WANT TO END UP BACK HOME!
HOWARD! FOCUS!
...
ALL RIGHT, ALREADY! "HOME" ISN'T THE EASIEST CHOICE T'MAKE, FITZ!
FITZ?

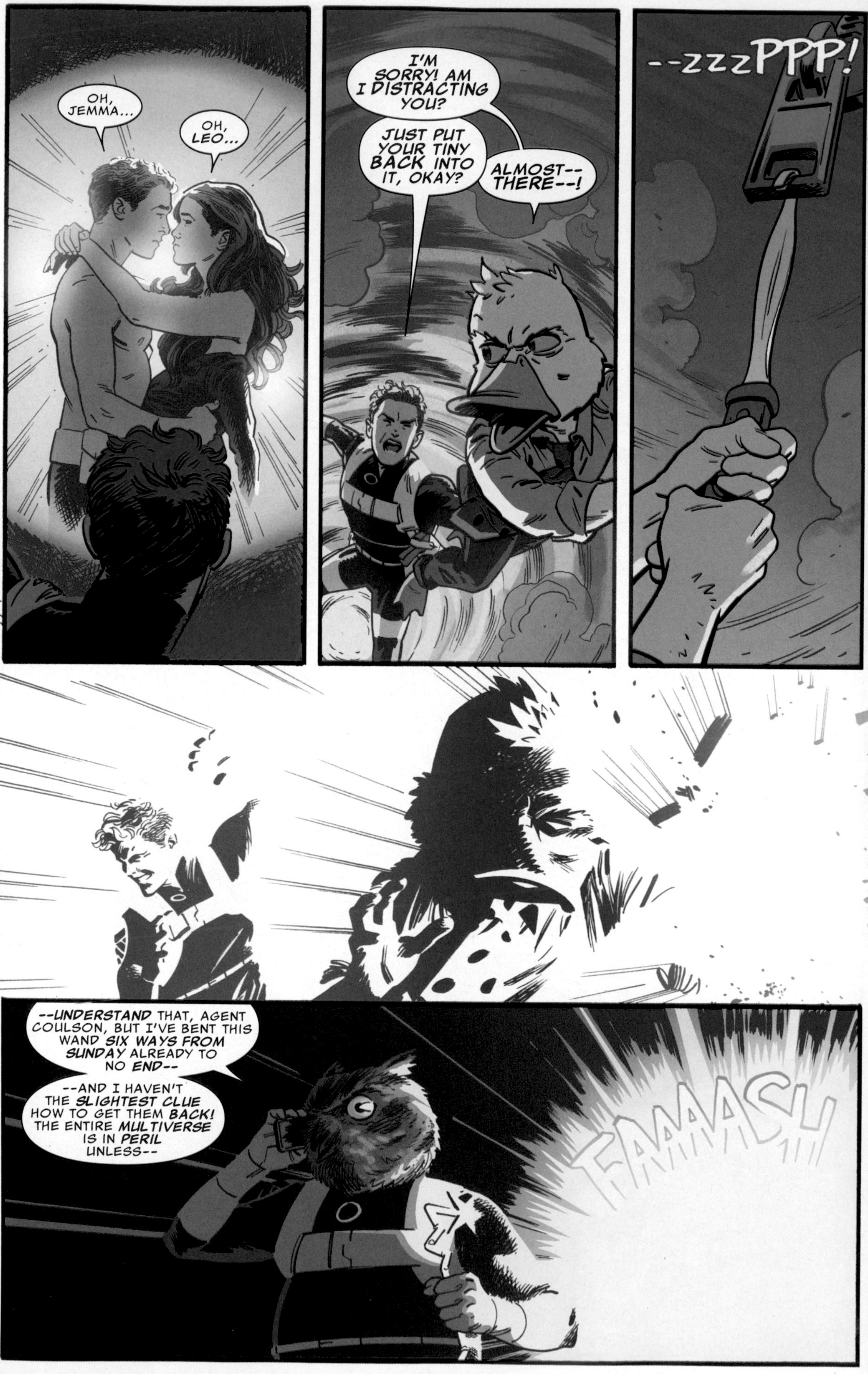
OH, JEMMA...
OH, LEO...
I'M SORRY! AM I DISTRACTING YOU?
JUST PUT YOUR TINY BACK INTO IT, OKAY?
ALMOST-- THERE--!
--zzzPPP!
--UNDERSTAND THAT, AGENT COULSON, BUT I'VE BENT THIS WAND SIX WAYS FROM SUNDAY ALREADY TO NO END--
--AND I HAVEN'T THE SLIGHTEST CLUE HOW TO GET THEM BACK! THE ENTIRE MULTIVERSE IS IN PERIL UNLESS--
FAAAASH

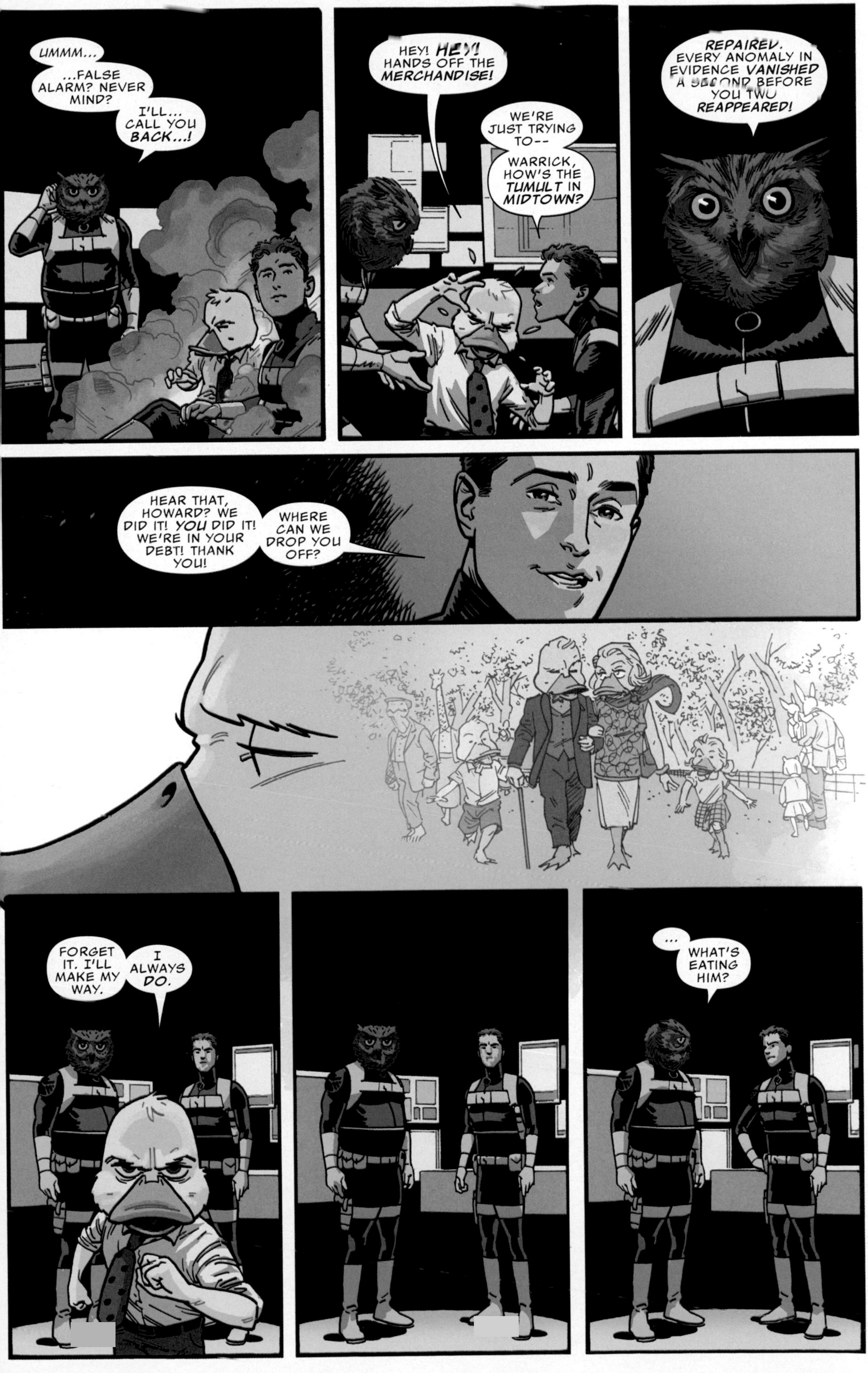
UMMM...
...FALSE ALARM? NEVER MIND?
I'LL... CALL YOU BACK...!
HEY! HEY! HANDS OFF THE MERCHANDISE!
WE'RE JUST TRYING TO--
WARRICK, HOW'S THE TUMULT IN MIDTOWN?
REPAIRED. EVERY ANOMALY IN EVIDENCE VANISHED A SECOND BEFORE YOU TWO REAPPEARED!
HEAR THAT, HOWARD? WE DID IT! YOU DID IT! WE'RE IN YOUR DEBT! THANK YOU!
WHERE CAN WE DROP YOU OFF?
FORGET IT. I'LL MAKE MY WAY.
I ALWAYS DO.
...
WHAT'S EATING HIM?

11. ACTIVE MISSION: FORTUNE'S FAVOR

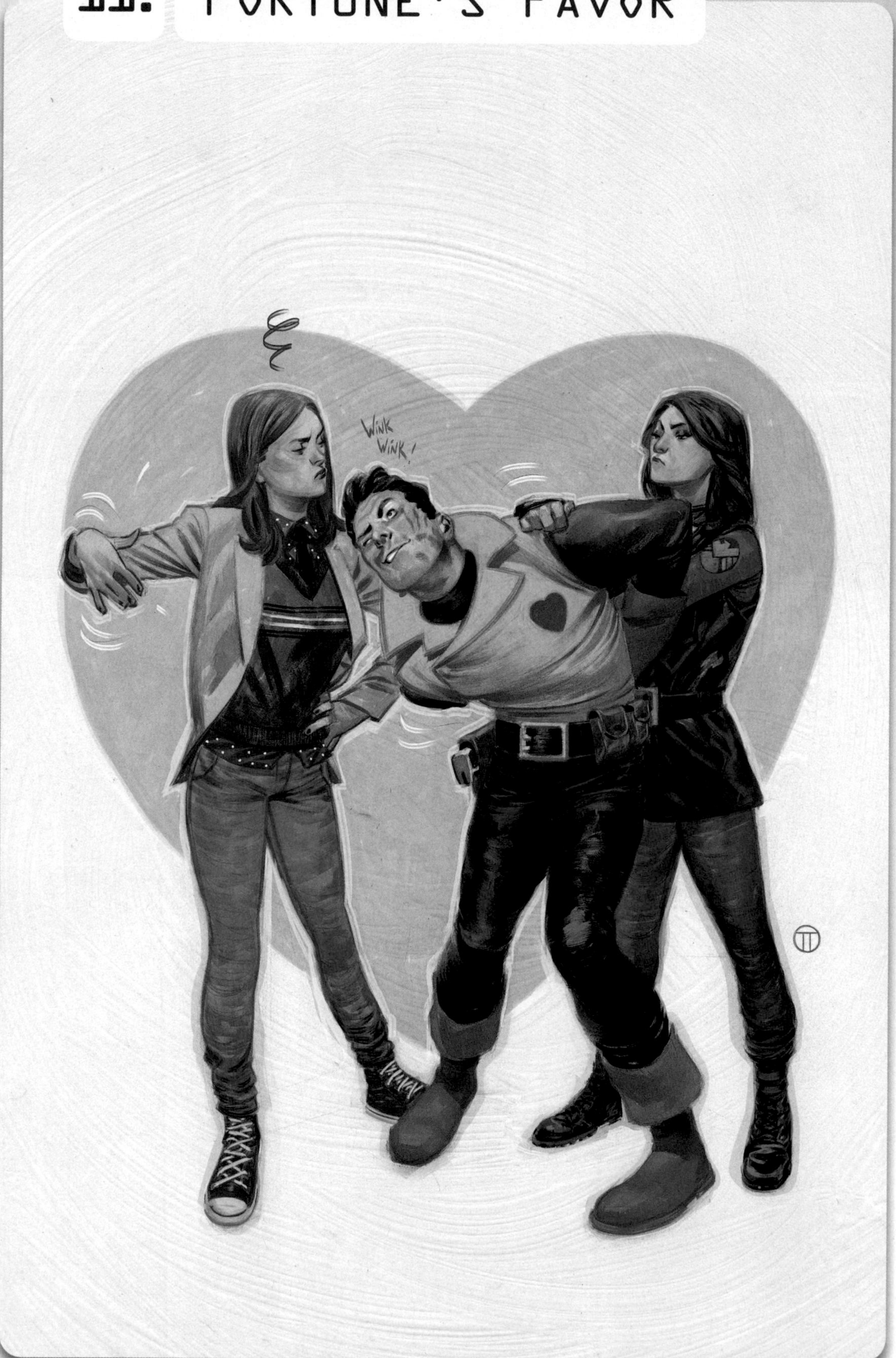
WINK WINK!

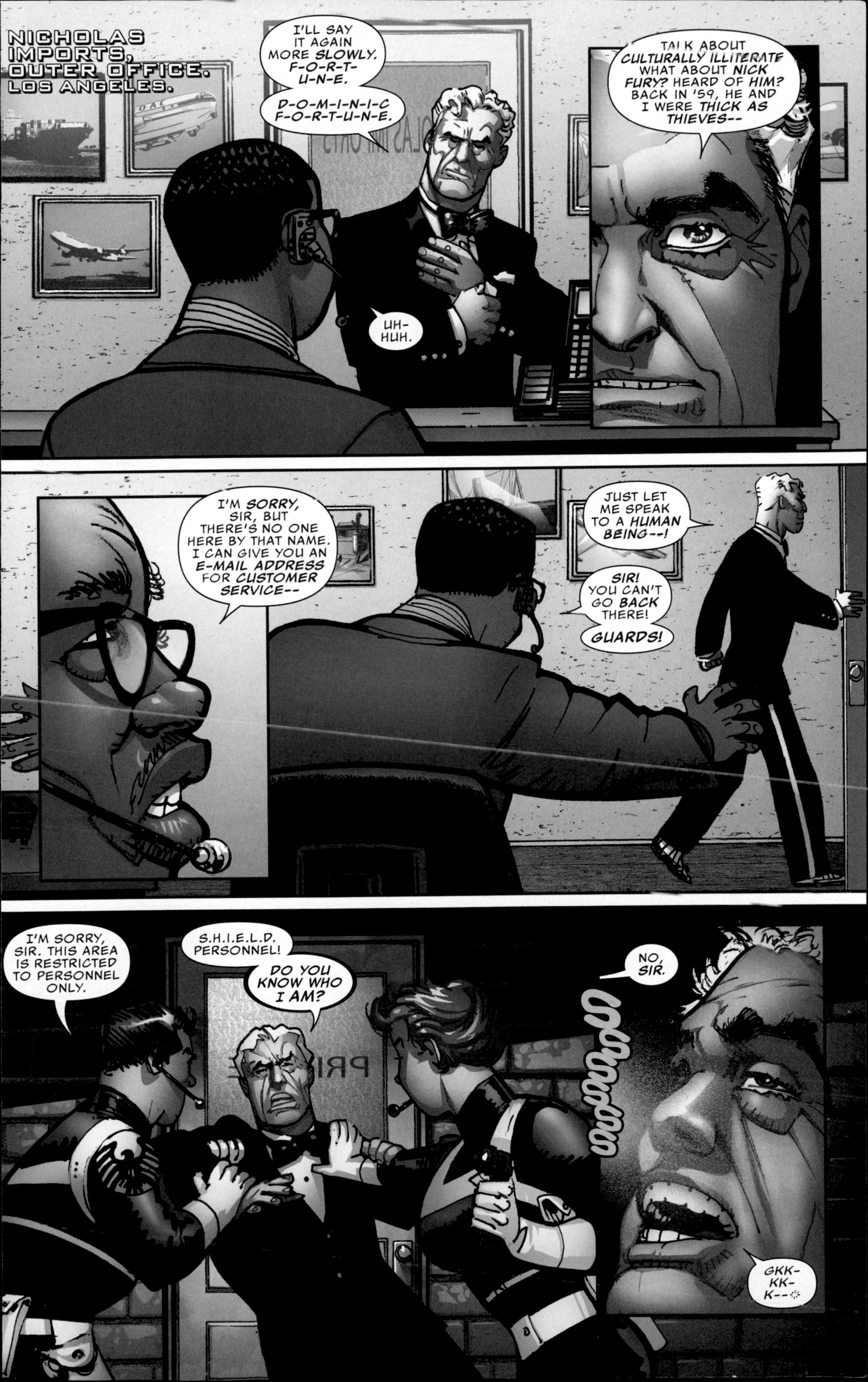

NICHOLAS IMPORTS, OUTER OFFICE. LOS ANGELES.
I'LL SAY IT AGAIN MORE SLOWLY. F-O-R-T-U-N-E.
D-O-M-I-N-I-C F-O-R-T-U-N-E.
UH-HUH.
TALK ABOUT CULTURALLY ILLITERATE WHAT ABOUT NICK FURY? HEARD OF HIM? BACK IN '59, HE AND I WERE THICK AS THIEVES--
I'M SORRY, SIR, BUT THERE'S NO ONE HERE BY THAT NAME. I CAN GIVE YOU AN E-MAIL ADDRESS FOR CUSTOMER SERVICE--
JUST LET ME SPEAK TO A HUMAN BEING--!
SIR! YOU CAN'T GO BACK THERE!
GUARDS!
I'M SORRY, SIR. THIS AREA IS RESTRICTED TO PERSONNEL ONLY.
S.H.I.E.L.D. PERSONNEL!
DO YOU KNOW WHO I AM?
NO, SIR.
GKK-KK-K--

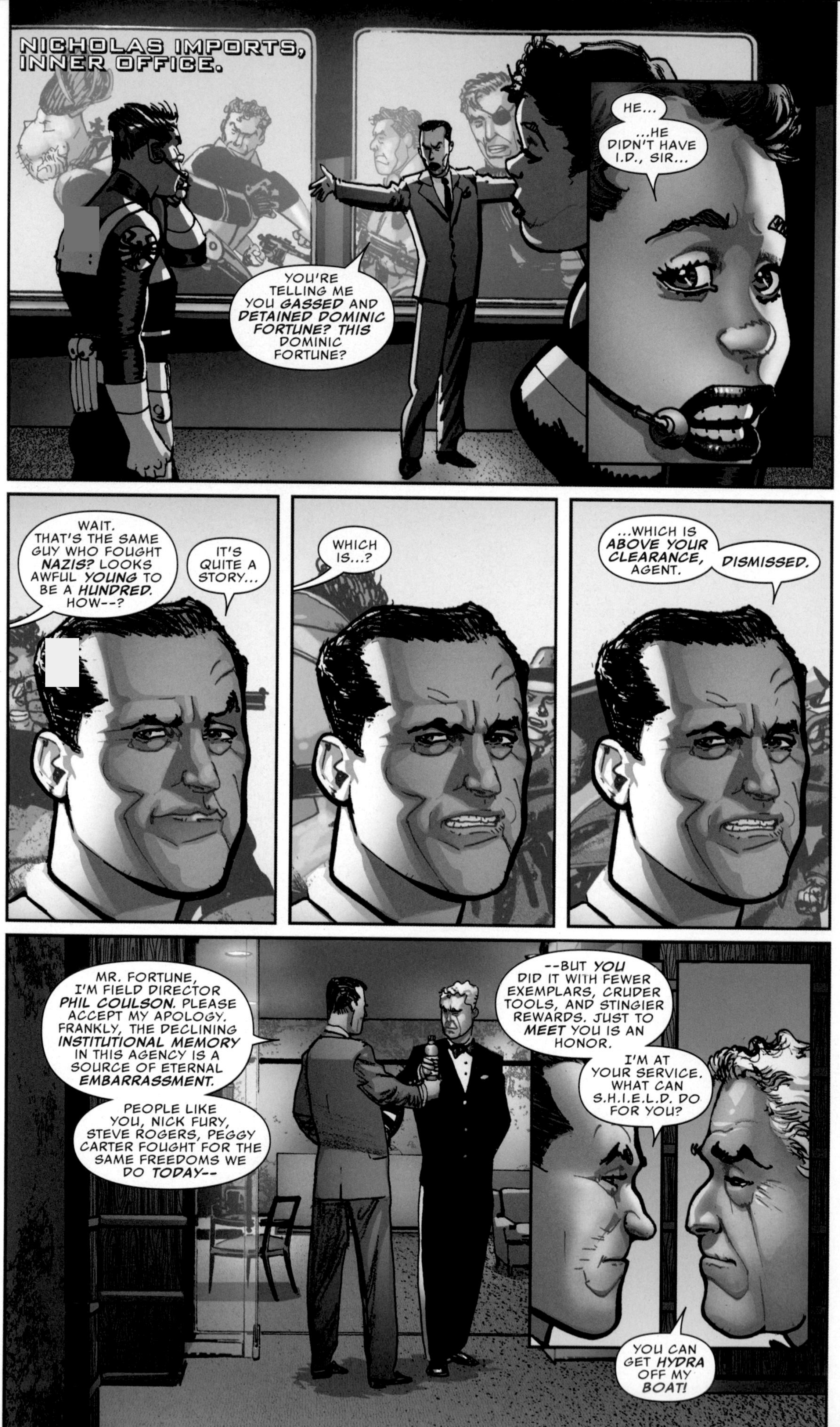
NICHOLAS IMPORTS, INNER OFFICE.
YOU'RE TELLING ME YOU GASSED AND DETAINED DOMINIC FORTUNE? THIS DOMINIC FORTUNE?
HE...
...HE DIDN'T HAVE I.D., SIR...
WAIT. THAT'S THE SAME GUY WHO FOUGHT NAZIS? LOOKS AWFUL YOUNG TO BE A HUNDRED. HOW--?
IT'S QUITE A STORY...
WHICH IS...?
...WHICH IS ABOVE YOUR CLEARANCE, AGENT.
DISMISSED.
MR. FORTUNE, I'M FIELD DIRECTOR PHIL COULSON. PLEASE ACCEPT MY APOLOGY. FRANKLY, THE DECLINING INSTITUTIONAL MEMORY IN THIS AGENCY IS A SOURCE OF ETERNAL EMBARRASSMENT.
PEOPLE LIKE YOU, NICK FURY, STEVE ROGERS, PEGGY CARTER FOUGHT FOR THE SAME FREEDOMS WE DO TODAY--
--BUT YOU DID IT WITH FEWER EXEMPLARS, CRUDER TOOLS, AND STINGIER REWARDS. JUST TO MEET YOU IS AN HONOR.
I'M AT YOUR SERVICE. WHAT CAN S.H.I.E.L.D. DO FOR YOU?
YOU CAN GET HYDRA OFF MY BOAT!

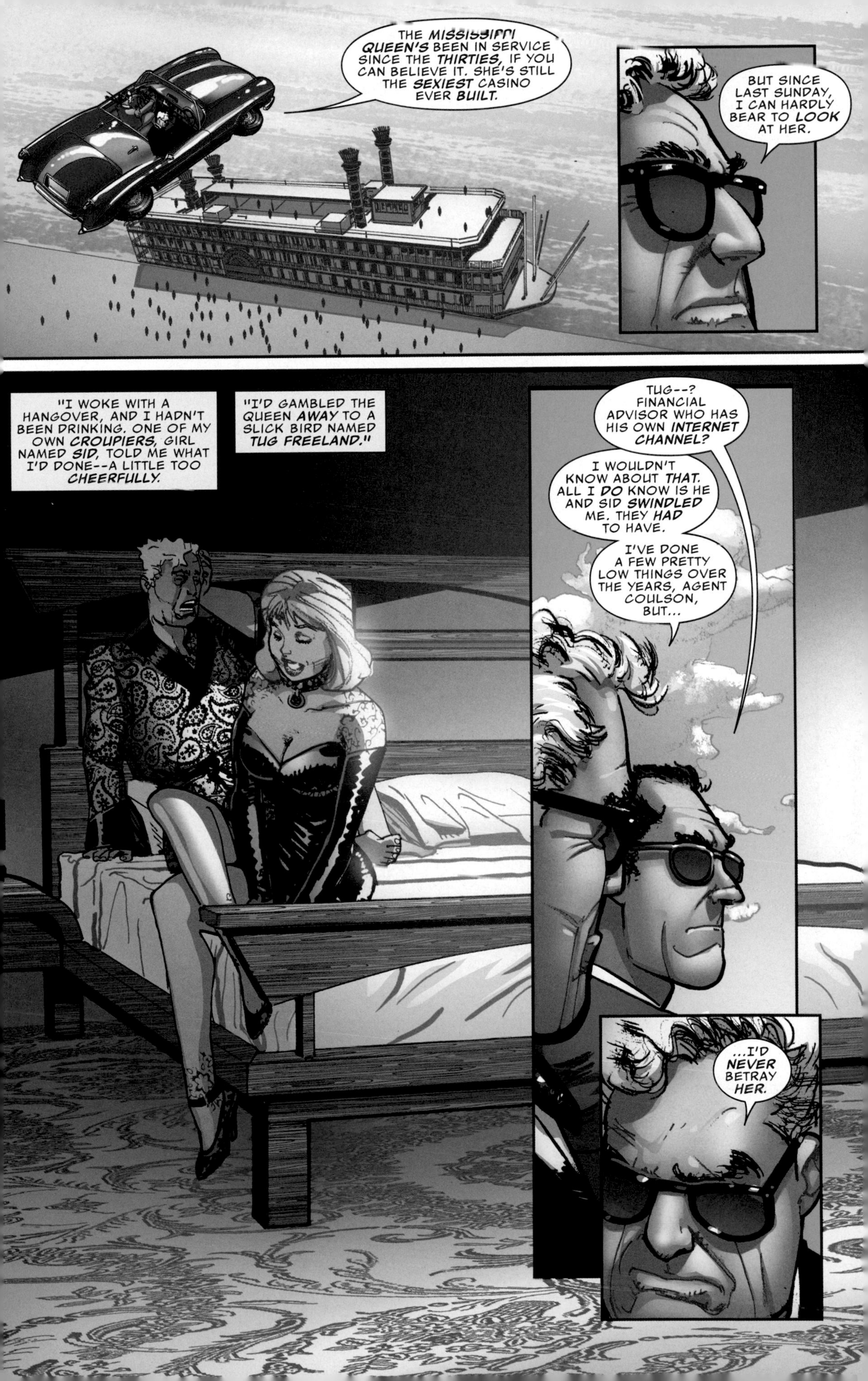
THE MISSISSIPPI QUEEN'S BEEN IN SERVICE SINCE THE THIRTIES, IF YOU CAN BELIEVE IT. SHE'S STILL THE SEXIEST CASINO EVER BUILT.
BUT SINCE LAST SUNDAY, I CAN HARDLY BEAR TO LOOK AT HER.
"I WOKE WITH A HANGOVER, AND I HADN'T BEEN DRINKING. ONE OF MY OWN CROUPIERS, GIRL NAMED SID, TOLD ME WHAT I'D DONE--A LITTLE TOO CHEERFULLY.
"I'D GAMBLED THE QUEEN AWAY TO A SLICK BIRD NAMED TUG FREELAND."
TUG--? FINANCIAL ADVISOR WHO HAS HIS OWN INTERNET CHANNEL?
I WOULDN'T KNOW ABOUT THAT. ALL I DO KNOW IS HE AND SID SWINDLED ME. THEY HAD TO HAVE.
I'VE DONE A FEW PRETTY LOW THINGS OVER THE YEARS, AGENT COULSON, BUT...
...I'D NEVER BETRAY HER.

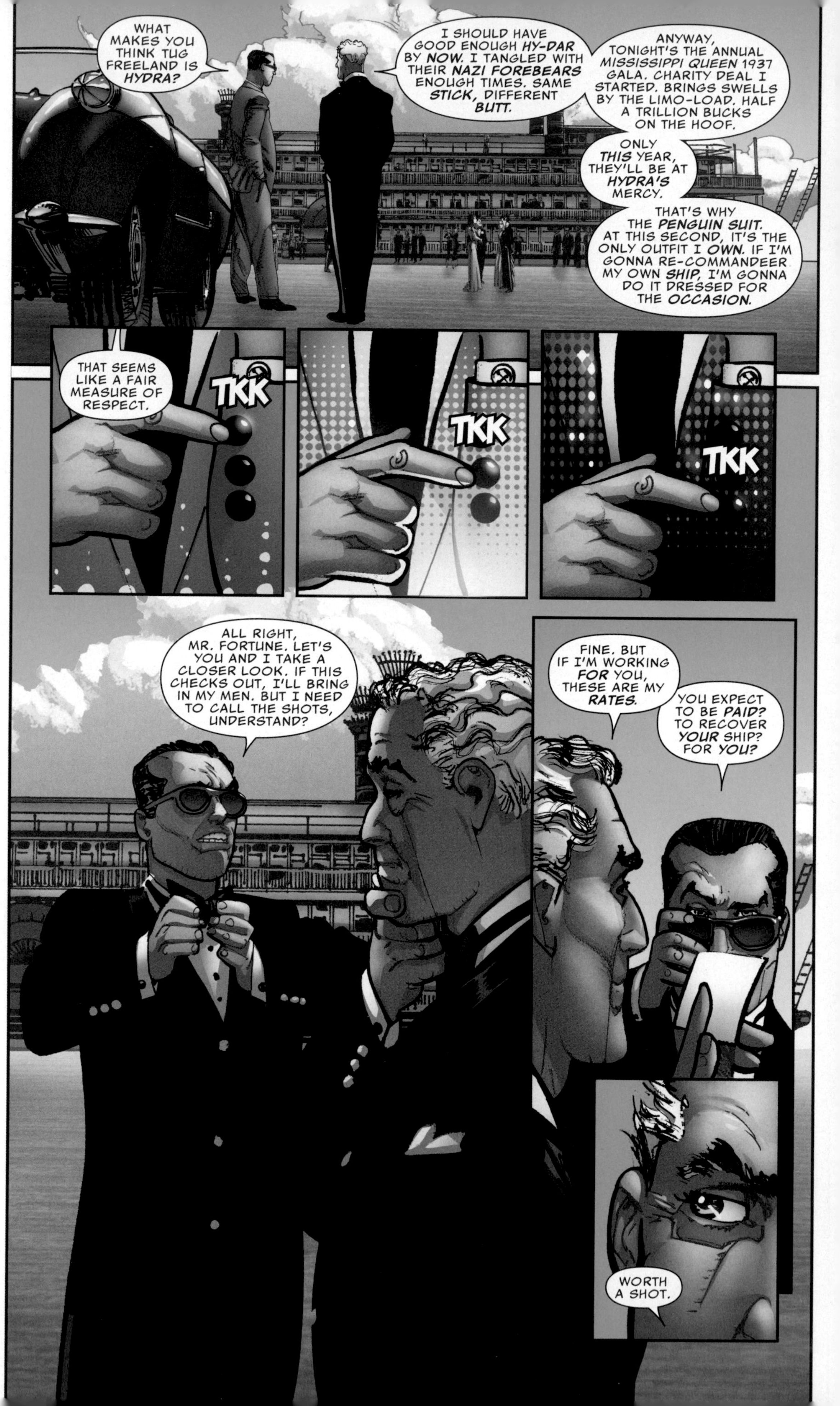
WHAT MAKES YOU THINK TUG FREELAND IS HYDRA?
I SHOULD HAVE GOOD ENOUGH HY-DAR BY NOW. I TANGLED WITH THEIR NAZI FOREBEARS ENOUGH TIMES. SAME STICK, DIFFERENT BUTT.
ANYWAY, TONIGHT'S THE ANNUAL MISSISSIPPI QUEEN 1937 GALA. CHARITY DEAL I STARTED. BRINGS SWELLS BY THE LIMO-LOAD. HALF A TRILLION BUCKS ON THE HOOF.
ONLY THIS YEAR, THEY'LL BE AT HYDRA'S MERCY.
THAT'S WHY THE PENGUIN SUIT. AT THIS SECOND, IT'S THE ONLY OUTFIT I OWN. IF I'M GONNA RE-COMMANDEER MY OWN SHIP, I'M GONNA DO IT DRESSED FOR THE OCCASION.
THAT SEEMS LIKE A FAIR MEASURE OF RESPECT.
TKK
TKK
TKK
ALL RIGHT, MR. FORTUNE. LET'S YOU AND I TAKE A CLOSER LOOK. IF THIS CHECKS OUT, I'LL BRING IN MY MEN. BUT I NEED TO CALL THE SHOTS, UNDERSTAND?
FINE. BUT IF I'M WORKING FOR YOU, THESE ARE MY RATES.
YOU EXPECT TO BE PAID? TO RECOVER YOUR SHIP? FOR YOU?
WORTH A SHOT.

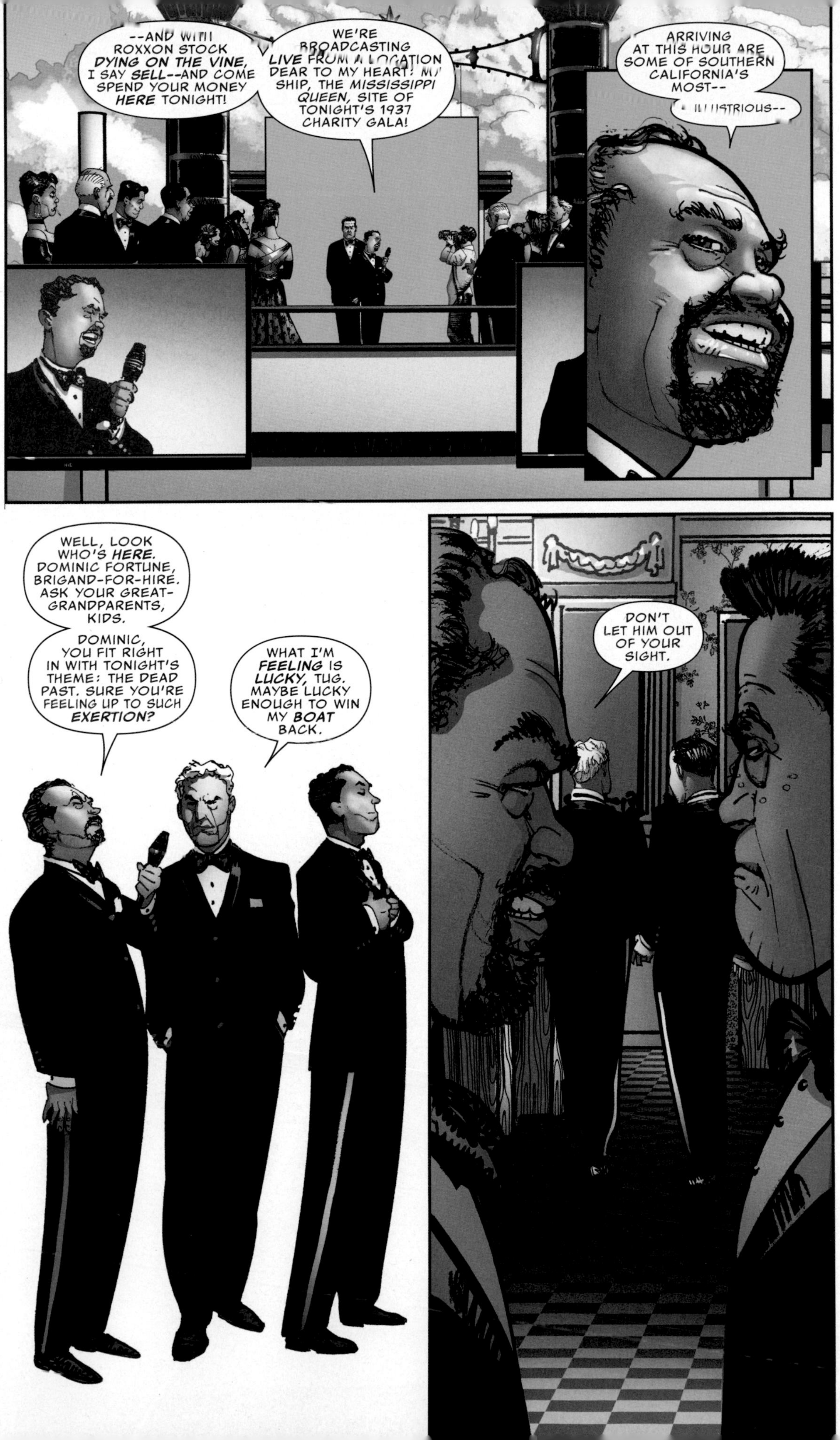
--AND WITH ROXXON STOCK DYING ON THE VINE, I SAY SELL--AND COME SPEND YOUR MONEY HERE TONIGHT!
WE'RE BROADCASTING LIVE FROM A LOCATION DEAR TO MY HEART: MY SHIP, THE MISSISSIPPI QUEEN, SITE OF TONIGHT'S 1937 CHARITY GALA!
ARRIVING AT THIS HOUR ARE SOME OF SOUTHERN CALIFORNIA'S MOST--
ILLUSTRIOUS--
WELL, LOOK WHO'S HERE. DOMINIC FORTUNE, BRIGAND-FOR-HIRE. ASK YOUR GREAT-GRANDPARENTS, KIDS.
DOMINIC, YOU FIT RIGHT IN WITH TONIGHT'S THEME: THE DEAD PAST. SURE YOU'RE FEELING UP TO SUCH EXERTION?
WHAT I'M FEELING IS LUCKY, TUG. MAYBE LUCKY ENOUGH TO WIN MY BOAT BACK.
DON'T LET HIM OUT OF YOUR SIGHT.

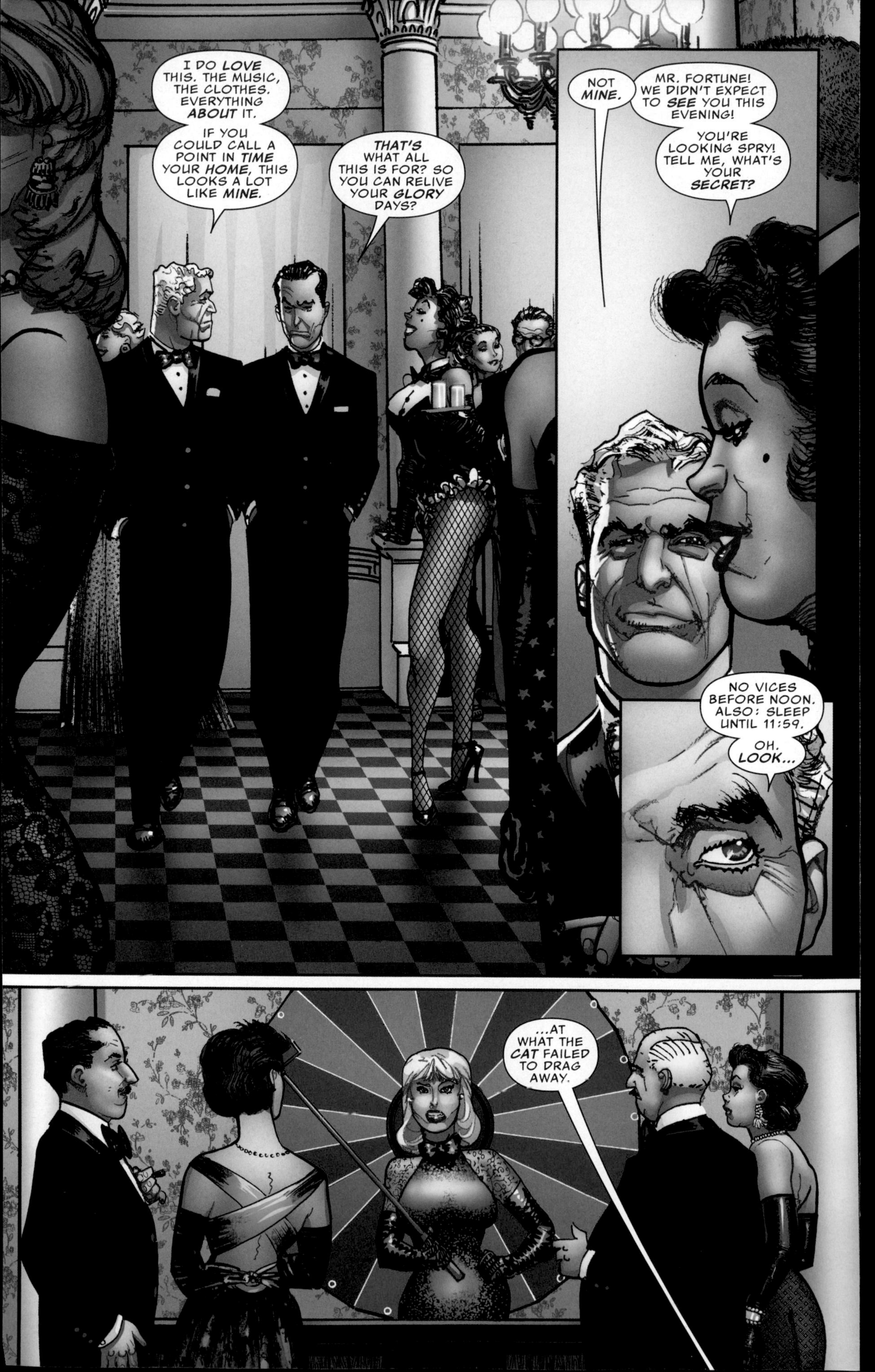
I DO LOVE THIS. THE MUSIC, THE CLOTHES. EVERYTHING ABOUT IT.
IF YOU COULD CALL A POINT IN TIME YOUR HOME, THIS LOOKS A LOT LIKE MINE.
THAT'S WHAT ALL THIS IS FOR? SO YOU CAN RELIVE YOUR GLORY DAYS?
NOT MINE.
MR. FORTUNE! WE DIDN'T EXPECT TO SEE YOU THIS EVENING!
YOU'RE LOOKING SPRY! TELL ME, WHAT'S YOUR SECRET?
NO VICES BEFORE NOON. ALSO: SLEEP UNTIL 11:59.
OH. LOOK...
...AT WHAT THE CAT FAILED TO DRAG AWAY.

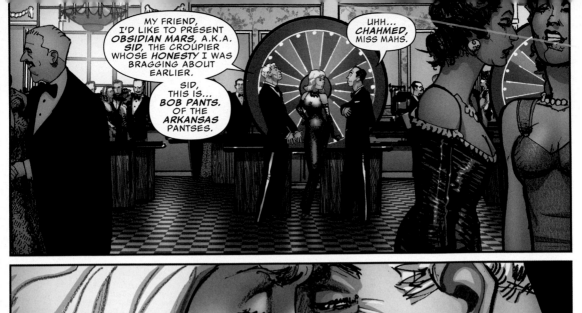

MY FRIEND, I'D LIKE TO PRESENT *OBSIDIAN MARS*, A.K.A. *SID*, THE CROUPIER WHOSE *HONESTY* I WAS BRAGGING ABOUT EARLIER.

SID, THIS IS... *BOB PANTS.* OF THE *ARKANSAS* PANTSES.

UHH... CHAHMED, MISS MAHS.

WHAT ARE *YOU* DOING HERE, DOMINIC?

MAKING SURE YOU KEEP YOUR *THUMB* OFF THE WHEEL.

NOW, BOB AND I ARE OFF TO *MINGLE*-- BUT DON'T WORRY, WE WON'T BE *FAR.*

THAT IS THE *WORST* SOUTHERN DRAWL I EVER HEARD.

YOU PUT ME ON THE SPOT. AND *PANTS? REALLY?*

I EXPECT A SPYMASTER TO BE LESS *FLAPPABLE.* VERY DISAPPOINTING.

JAKE. OVER *HERE.*

GO GET *TUG.*

BUT HE TOLD ME TO KEEP AN EYE ON--

-:HUCCH:-

GET. TUG.

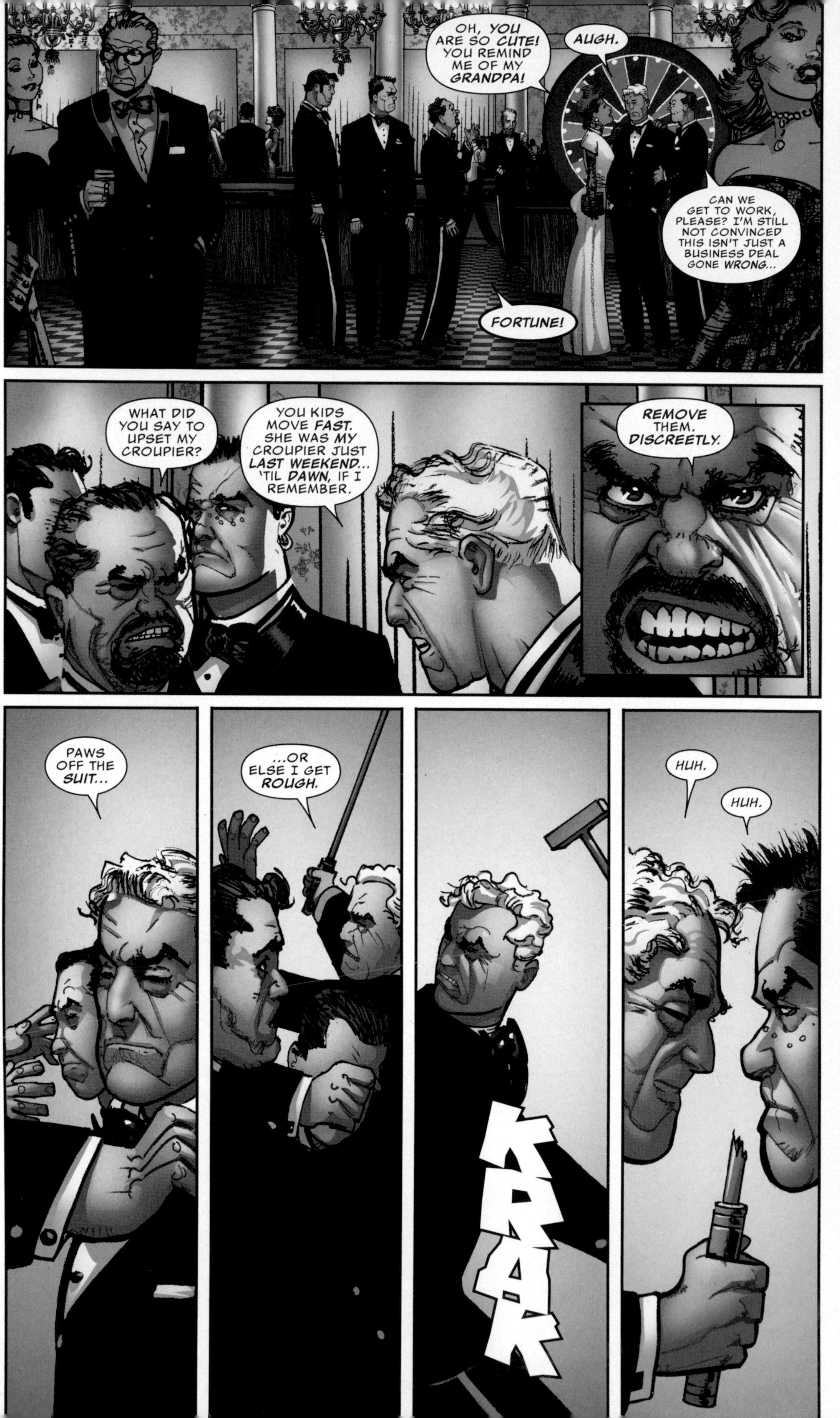
OH, YOU ARE SO CUTE! YOU REMIND ME OF MY GRANDPA!
AUGH.
CAN WE GET TO WORK, PLEASE? I'M STILL NOT CONVINCED THIS ISN'T JUST A BUSINESS DEAL GONE WRONG...
FORTUNE!
WHAT DID YOU SAY TO UPSET MY CROUPIER?
YOU KIDS MOVE FAST. SHE WAS MY CROUPIER JUST LAST WEEKEND... 'TIL DAWN, IF I REMEMBER.
REMOVE THEM. DISCREETLY.
PAWS OFF THE SUIT...
...OR ELSE I GET ROUGH.
KRAK
HUH.
HUH.

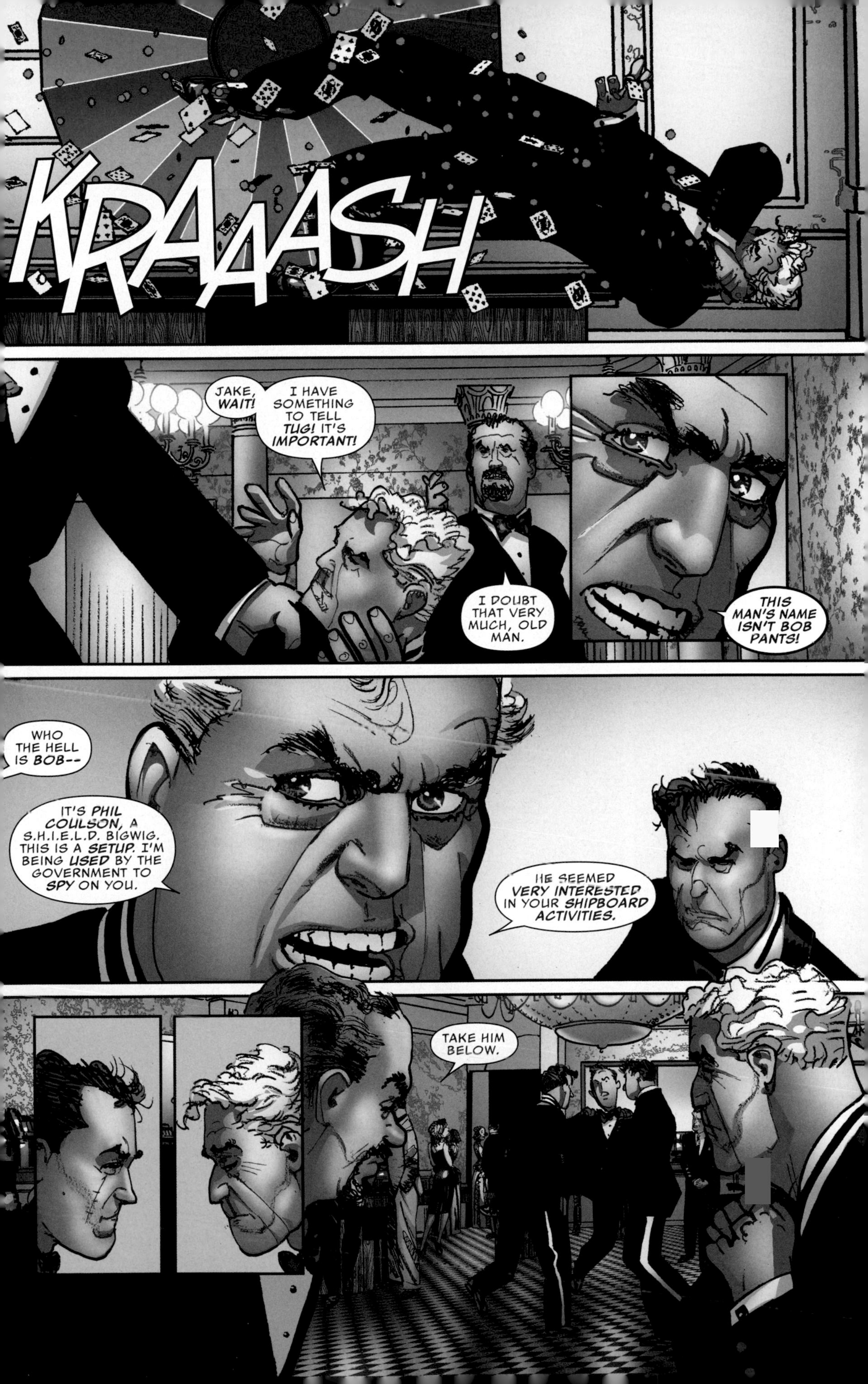
KRAAASH
JAKE, WAIT!
I HAVE SOMETHING TO TELL TUG! IT'S IMPORTANT!
I DOUBT THAT VERY MUCH, OLD MAN.
THIS MAN'S NAME ISN'T BOB PANTS!
WHO THE HELL IS BOB--
IT'S PHIL COULSON, A S.H.I.E.L.D. BIGWIG. THIS IS A SETUP. I'M BEING USED BY THE GOVERNMENT TO SPY ON YOU.
HE SEEMED VERY INTERESTED IN YOUR SHIPBOARD ACTIVITIES.
TAKE HIM BELOW.

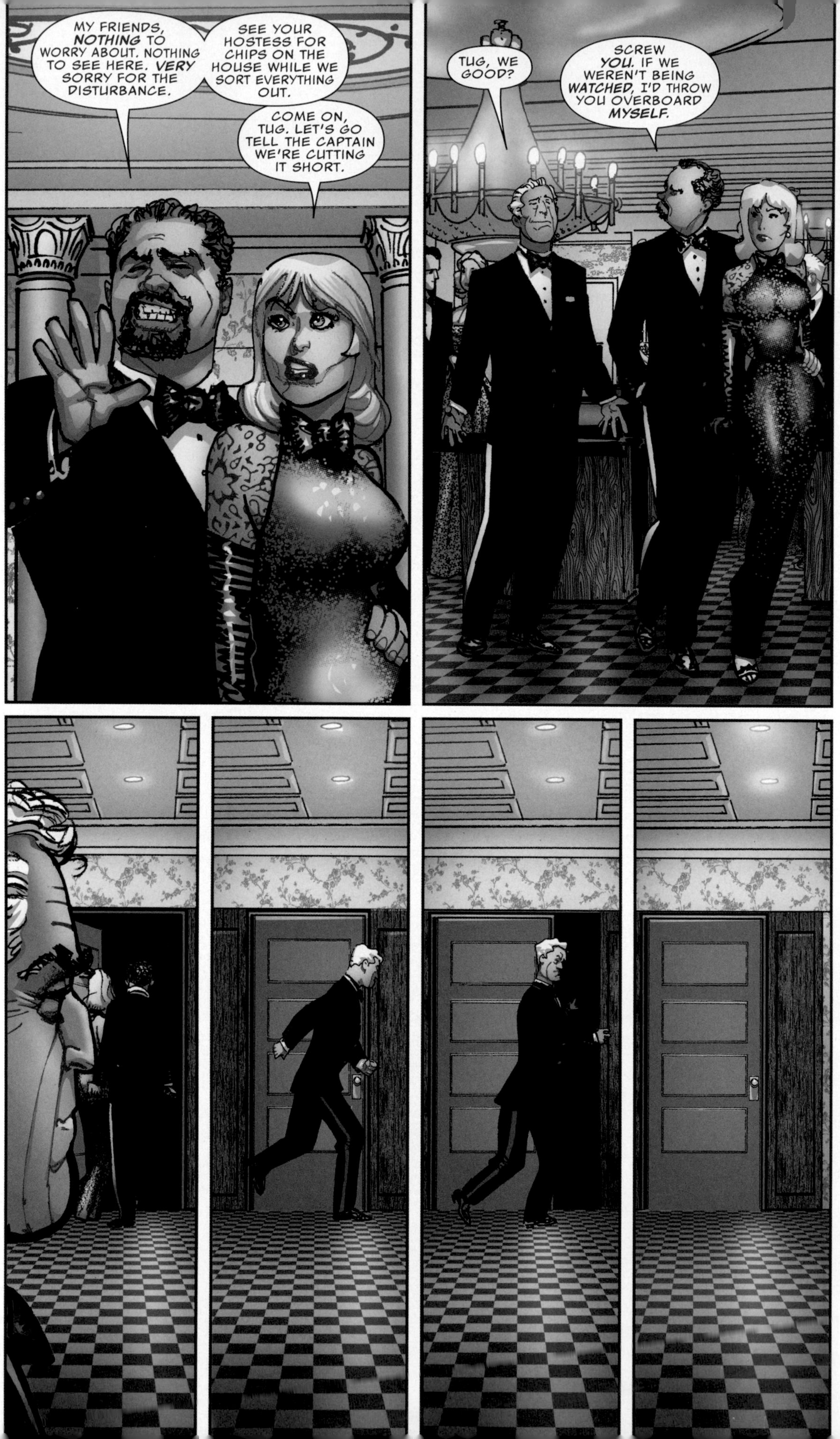
MY FRIENDS, NOTHING TO WORRY ABOUT. NOTHING TO SEE HERE. VERY SORRY FOR THE DISTURBANCE.
SEE YOUR HOSTESS FOR CHIPS ON THE HOUSE WHILE WE SORT EVERYTHING OUT.
COME ON, TUG. LET'S GO TELL THE CAPTAIN WE'RE CUTTING IT SHORT.
TUG, WE GOOD?
SCREW YOU. IF WE WEREN'T BEING WATCHED, I'D THROW YOU OVERBOARD MYSELF.

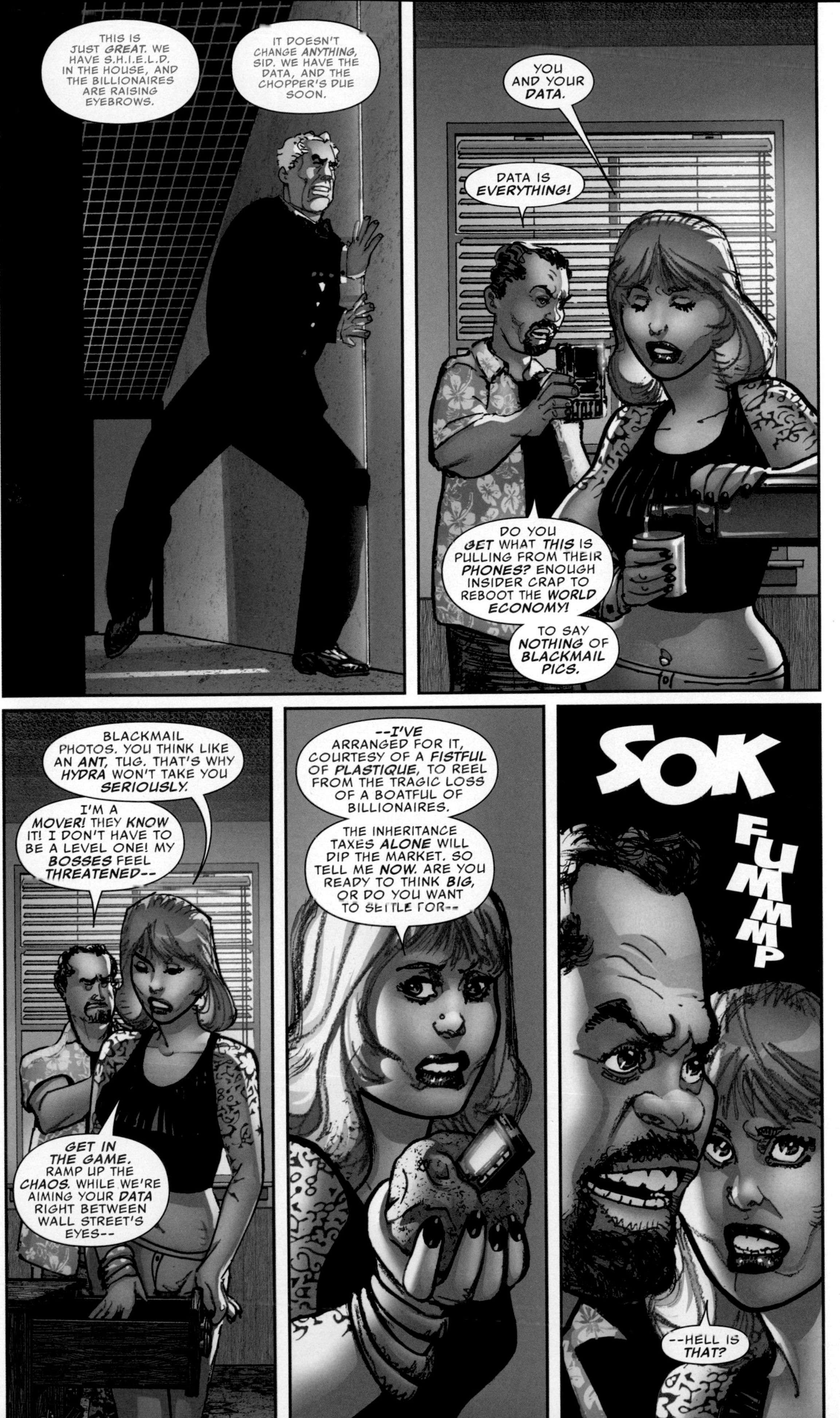
THIS IS JUST GREAT. WE HAVE S.H.I.E.L.D. IN THE HOUSE, AND THE BILLIONAIRES ARE RAISING EYEBROWS.
IT DOESN'T CHANGE ANYTHING, SID. WE HAVE THE DATA, AND THE CHOPPER'S DUE SOON.
YOU AND YOUR DATA.
DATA IS EVERYTHING!
DO YOU GET WHAT THIS IS PULLING FROM THEIR PHONES? ENOUGH INSIDER CRAP TO REBOOT THE WORLD ECONOMY!
TO SAY NOTHING OF BLACKMAIL PICS.
BLACKMAIL PHOTOS. YOU THINK LIKE AN ANT, TUG. THAT'S WHY HYDRA WON'T TAKE YOU SERIOUSLY.
I'M A MOVER! THEY KNOW IT! I DON'T HAVE TO BE A LEVEL ONE! MY BOSSES FEEL THREATENED--
GET IN THE GAME. RAMP UP THE CHAOS. WHILE WE'RE AIMING YOUR DATA RIGHT BETWEEN WALL STREET'S EYES--
--I'VE ARRANGED FOR IT, COURTESY OF A FISTFUL OF PLASTIQUE, TO REEL FROM THE TRAGIC LOSS OF A BOATFUL OF BILLIONAIRES.
THE INHERITANCE TAXES ALONE WILL DIP THE MARKET. SO TELL ME NOW. ARE YOU READY TO THINK BIG, OR DO YOU WANT TO SETTLE FOR--
SOK
FUMMMP
--HELL IS THAT?

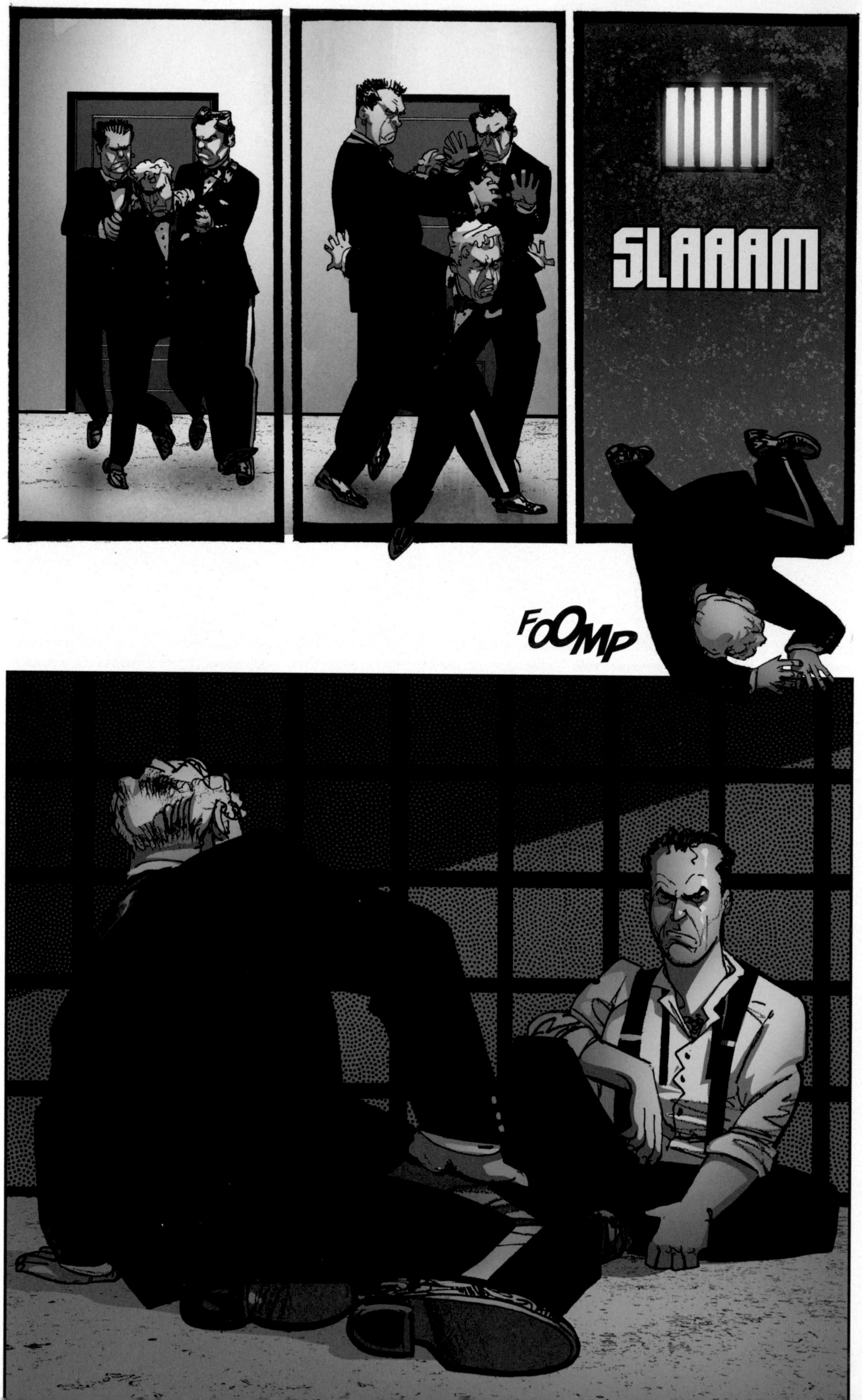
SLAAAM
FOOMP

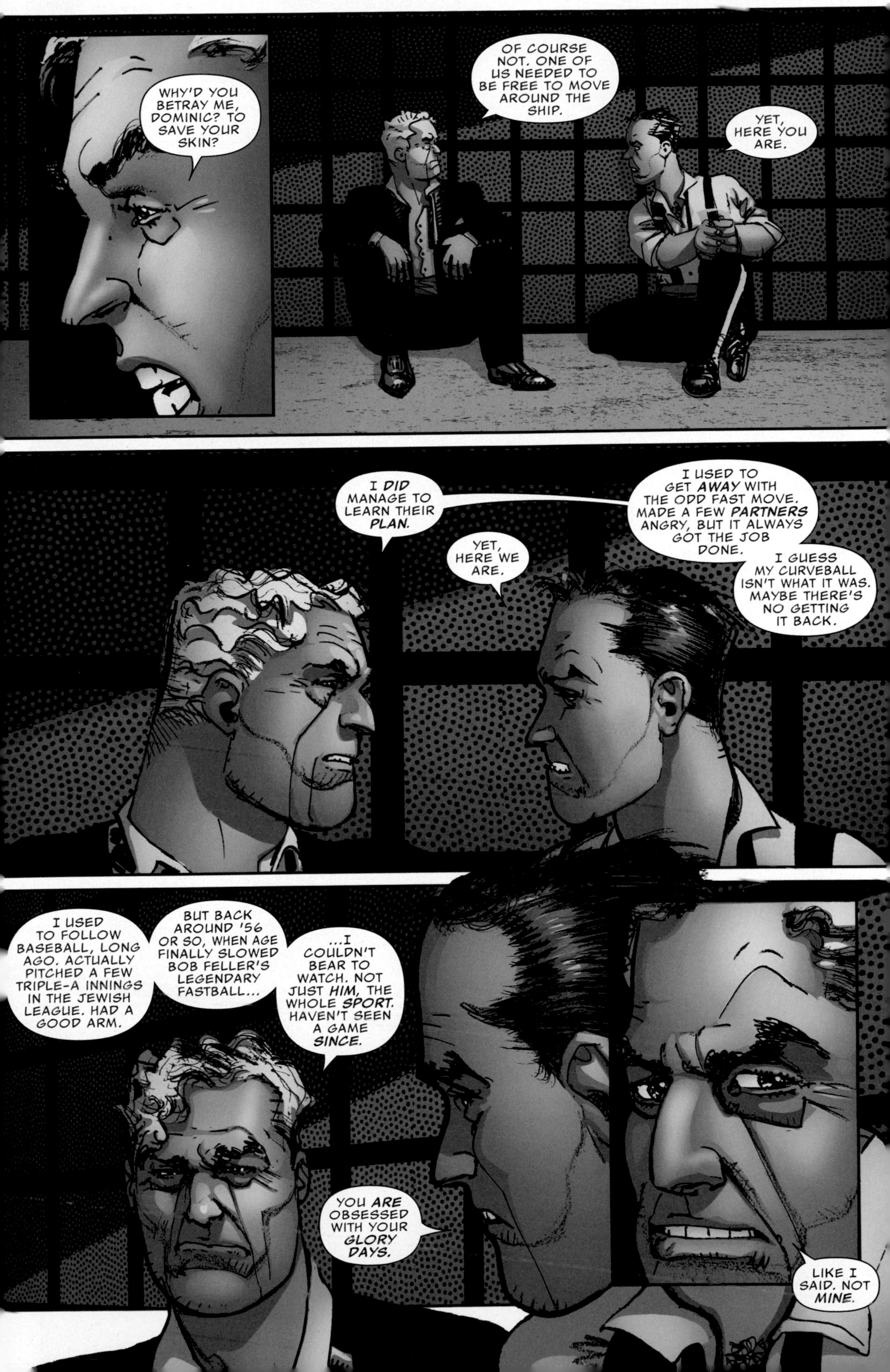
WHY'D YOU BETRAY ME, DOMINIC? TO SAVE YOUR SKIN?
OF COURSE NOT. ONE OF US NEEDED TO BE FREE TO MOVE AROUND THE SHIP.
YET, HERE YOU ARE.
I DID MANAGE TO LEARN THEIR PLAN.
I USED TO GET AWAY WITH THE ODD FAST MOVE. MADE A FEW PARTNERS ANGRY, BUT IT ALWAYS GOT THE JOB DONE.
YET, HERE WE ARE.
I GUESS MY CURVEBALL ISN'T WHAT IT WAS. MAYBE THERE'S NO GETTING IT BACK.
I USED TO FOLLOW BASEBALL, LONG AGO. ACTUALLY PITCHED A FEW TRIPLE-A INNINGS IN THE JEWISH LEAGUE. HAD A GOOD ARM.
BUT BACK AROUND '56 OR SO, WHEN AGE FINALLY SLOWED BOB FELLER'S LEGENDARY FASTBALL...
...I COULDN'T BEAR TO WATCH. NOT JUST HIM, THE WHOLE SPORT. HAVEN'T SEEN A GAME SINCE.
YOU ARE OBSESSED WITH YOUR GLORY DAYS.
LIKE I SAID. NOT MINE.

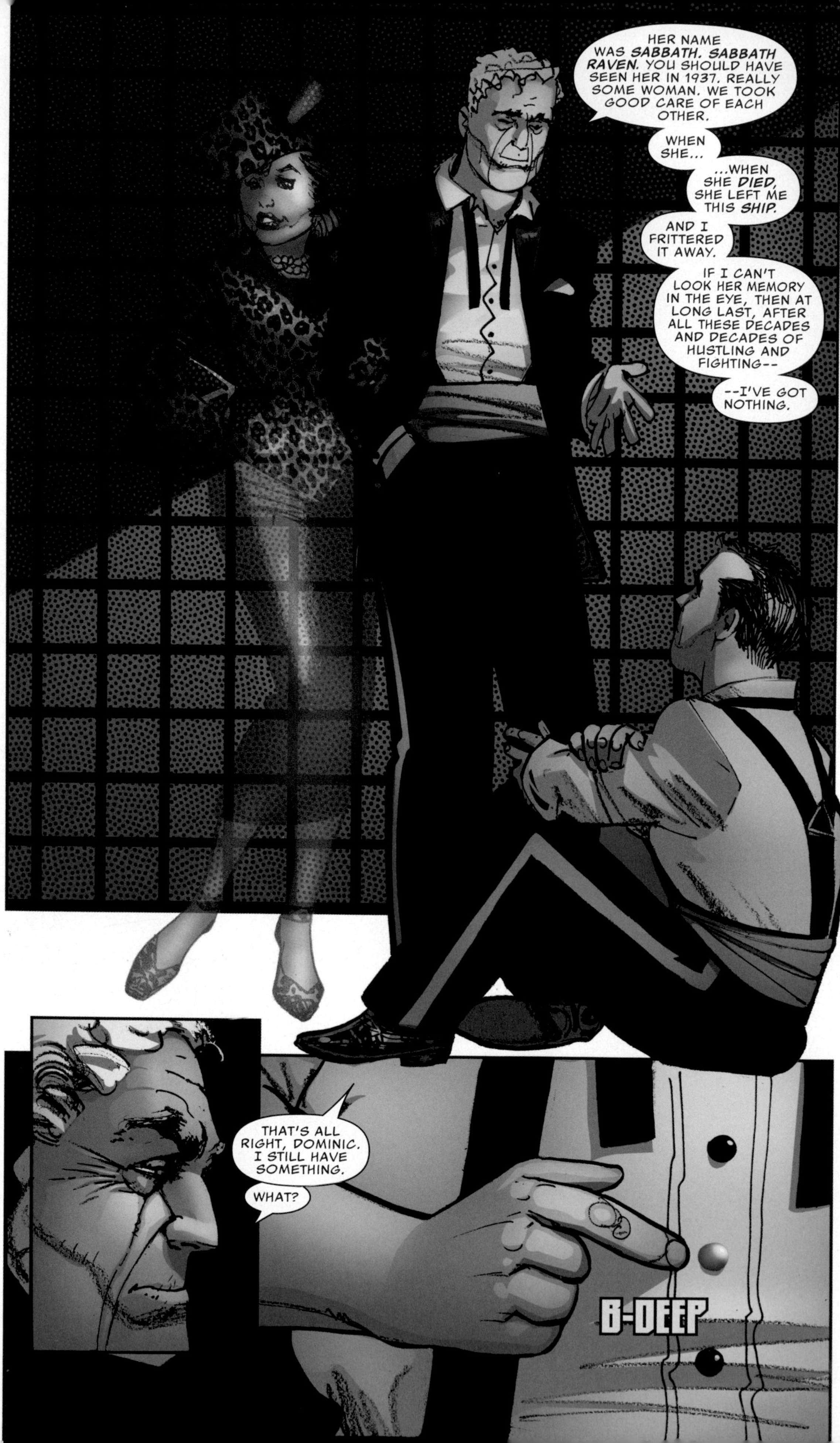
HER NAME WAS SABBATH. SABBATH RAVEN. YOU SHOULD HAVE SEEN HER IN 1937. REALLY SOME WOMAN. WE TOOK GOOD CARE OF EACH OTHER.
WHEN SHE...
...WHEN SHE DIED, SHE LEFT ME THIS SHIP.
AND I FRITTERED IT AWAY.
IF I CAN'T LOOK HER MEMORY IN THE EYE, THEN AT LONG LAST, AFTER ALL THESE DECADES AND DECADES OF HUSTLING AND FIGHTING--
--I'VE GOT NOTHING.
THAT'S ALL RIGHT, DOMINIC. I STILL HAVE SOMETHING.
WHAT?
B-DEEP

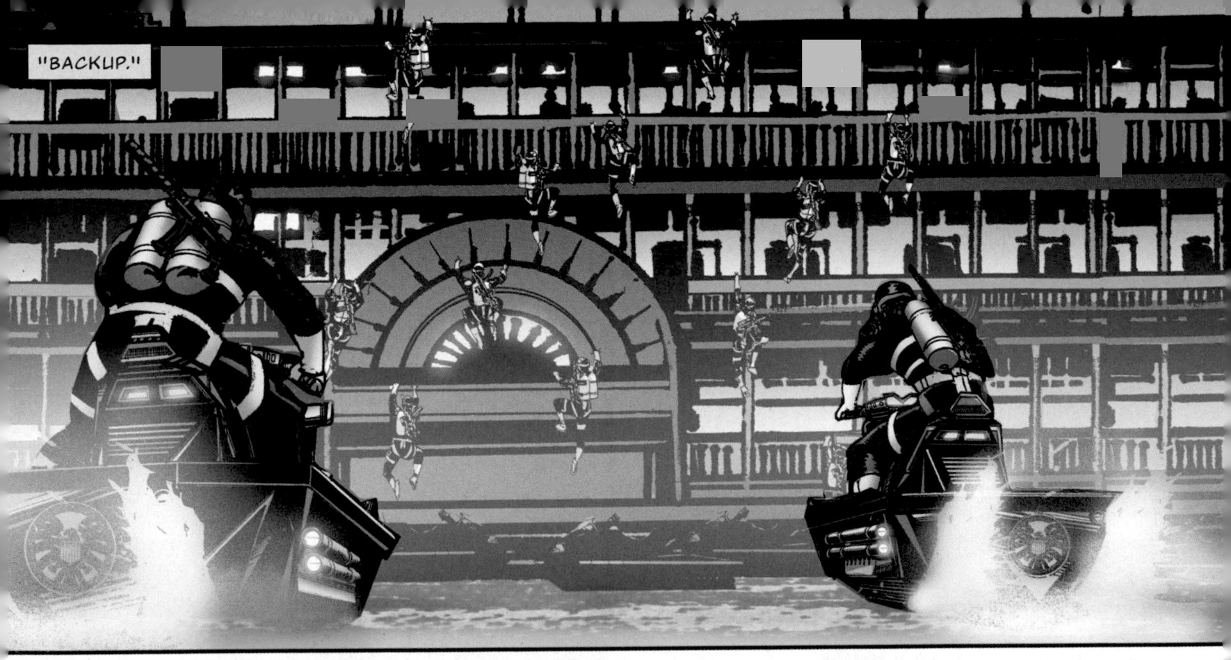
"BACKUP."

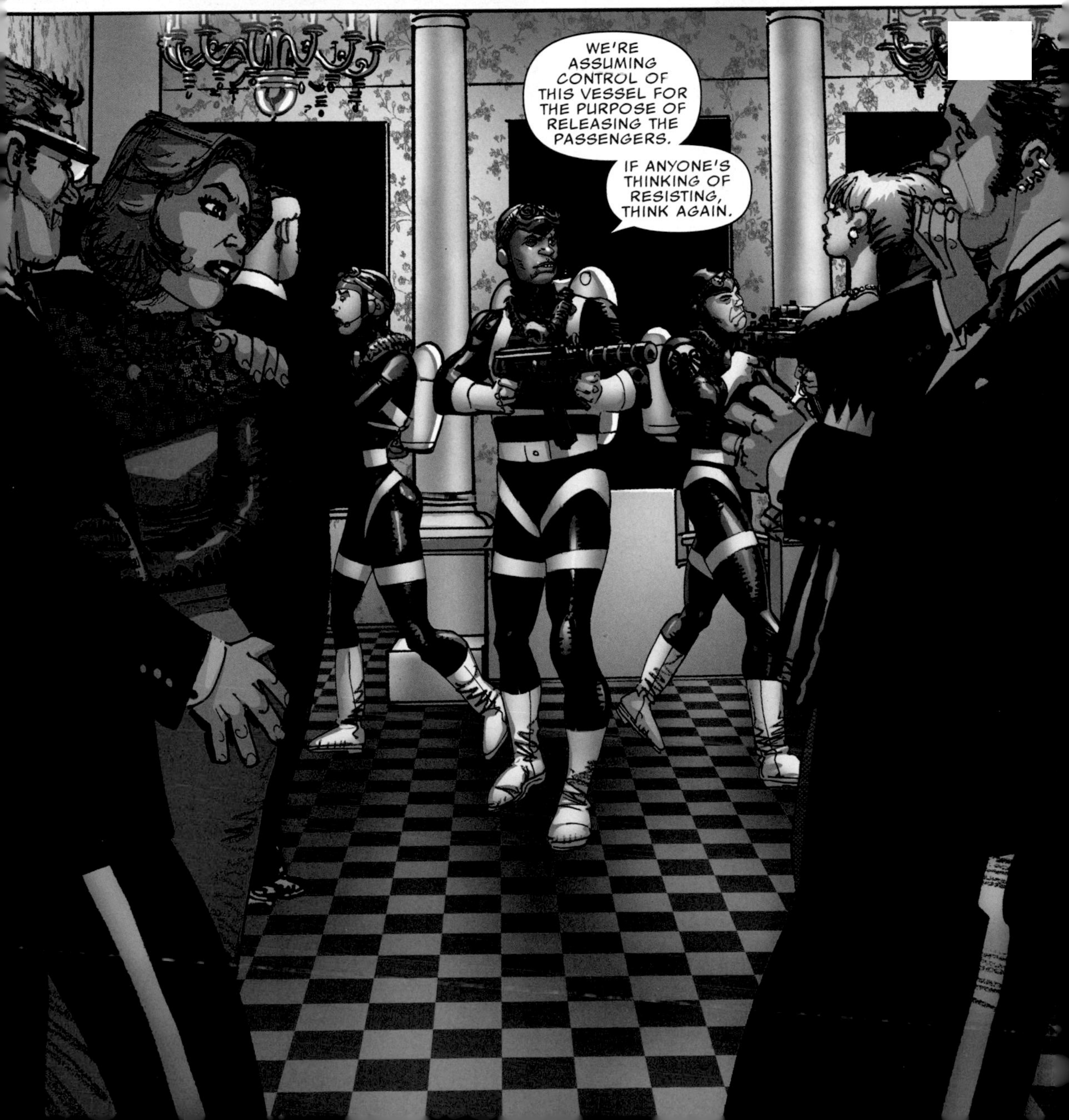
WE'RE ASSUMING CONTROL OF THIS VESSEL FOR THE PURPOSE OF RELEASING THE PASSENGERS.
IF ANYONE'S THINKING OF RESISTING, THINK AGAIN.

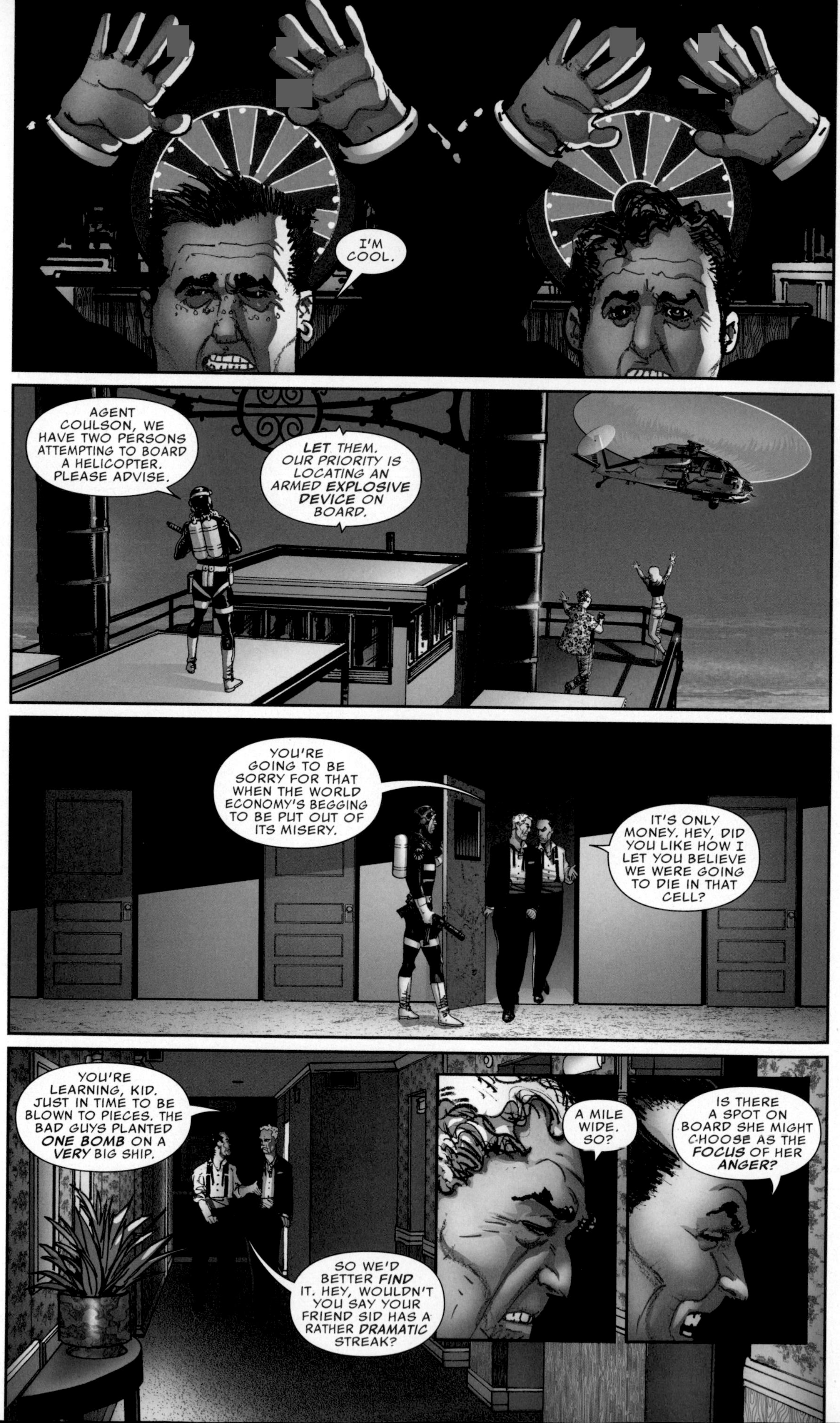
I'M COOL.
AGENT COULSON, WE HAVE TWO PERSONS ATTEMPTING TO BOARD A HELICOPTER. PLEASE ADVISE.
LET THEM. OUR PRIORITY IS LOCATING AN ARMED EXPLOSIVE DEVICE ON BOARD.
YOU'RE GOING TO BE SORRY FOR THAT WHEN THE WORLD ECONOMY'S BEGGING TO BE PUT OUT OF ITS MISERY.
IT'S ONLY MONEY. HEY, DID YOU LIKE HOW I LET YOU BELIEVE WE WERE GOING TO DIE IN THAT CELL?
YOU'RE LEARNING, KID. JUST IN TIME TO BE BLOWN TO PIECES. THE BAD GUYS PLANTED ONE BOMB ON A VERY BIG SHIP.
SO WE'D BETTER FIND IT. HEY, WOULDN'T YOU SAY YOUR FRIEND SID HAS A RATHER DRAMATIC STREAK?
A MILE WIDE. SO?
IS THERE A SPOT ON BOARD SHE MIGHT CHOOSE AS THE FOCUS OF HER ANGER?

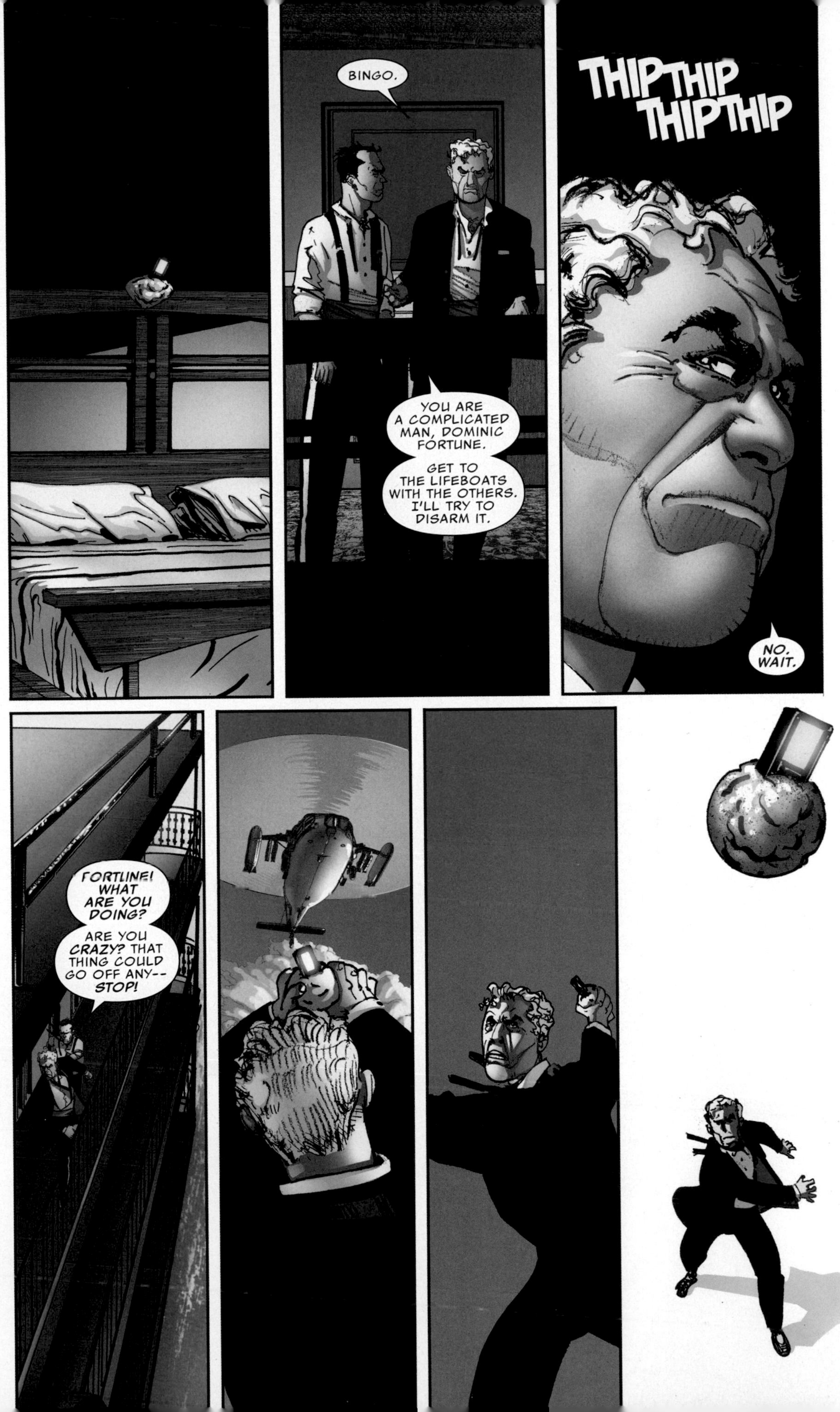
BINGO.
YOU ARE A COMPLICATED MAN, DOMINIC FORTUNE.
GET TO THE LIFEBOATS WITH THE OTHERS. I'LL TRY TO DISARM IT.
THIPTHIP THIPTHIP
NO. WAIT.
FORTUNE! WHAT ARE YOU DOING?
ARE YOU CRAZY? THAT THING COULD GO OFF ANY-- STOP!

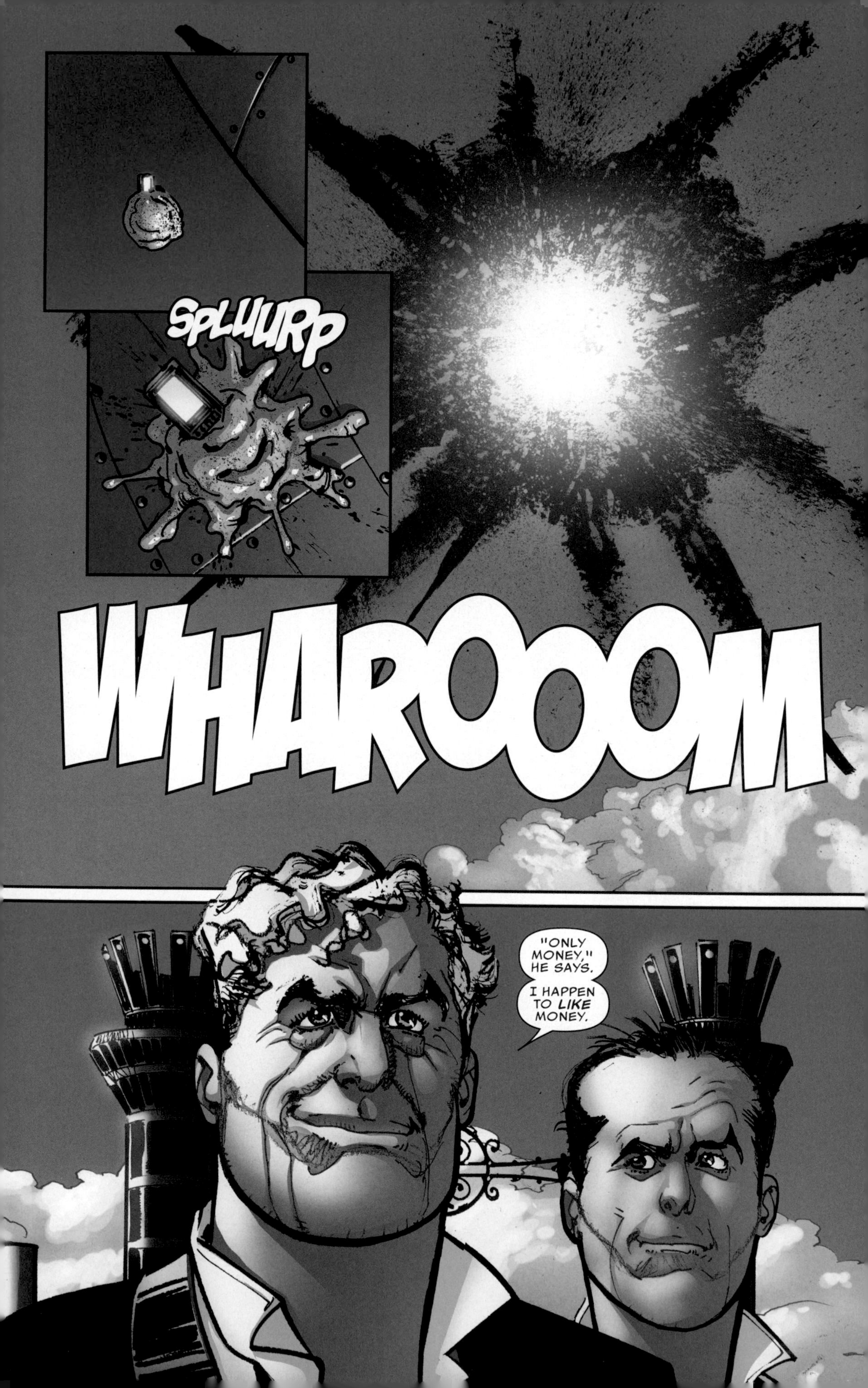
SPLUURP
WHAROOOM
"ONLY MONEY," HE SAYS.
I HAPPEN TO *LIKE* MONEY.

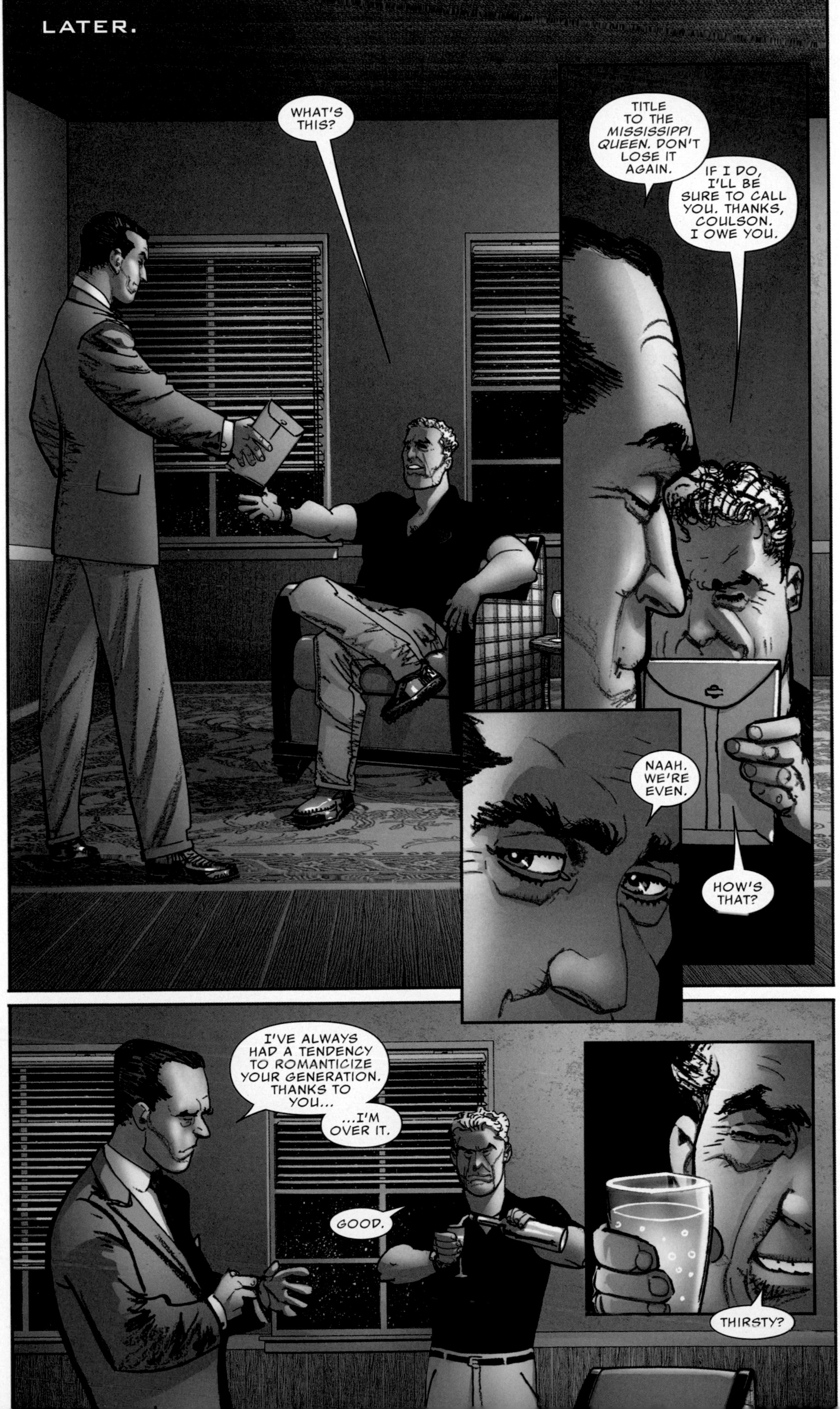
LATER.
WHAT'S THIS?
TITLE TO THE MISSISSIPPI QUEEN. DON'T LOSE IT AGAIN.
IF I DO, I'LL BE SURE TO CALL YOU. THANKS, COULSON. I OWE YOU.
NAAH. WE'RE EVEN.
HOW'S THAT?
I'VE ALWAYS HAD A TENDENCY TO ROMANTICIZE YOUR GENERATION. THANKS TO YOU...
...I'M OVER IT.
GOOD.
THIRSTY?

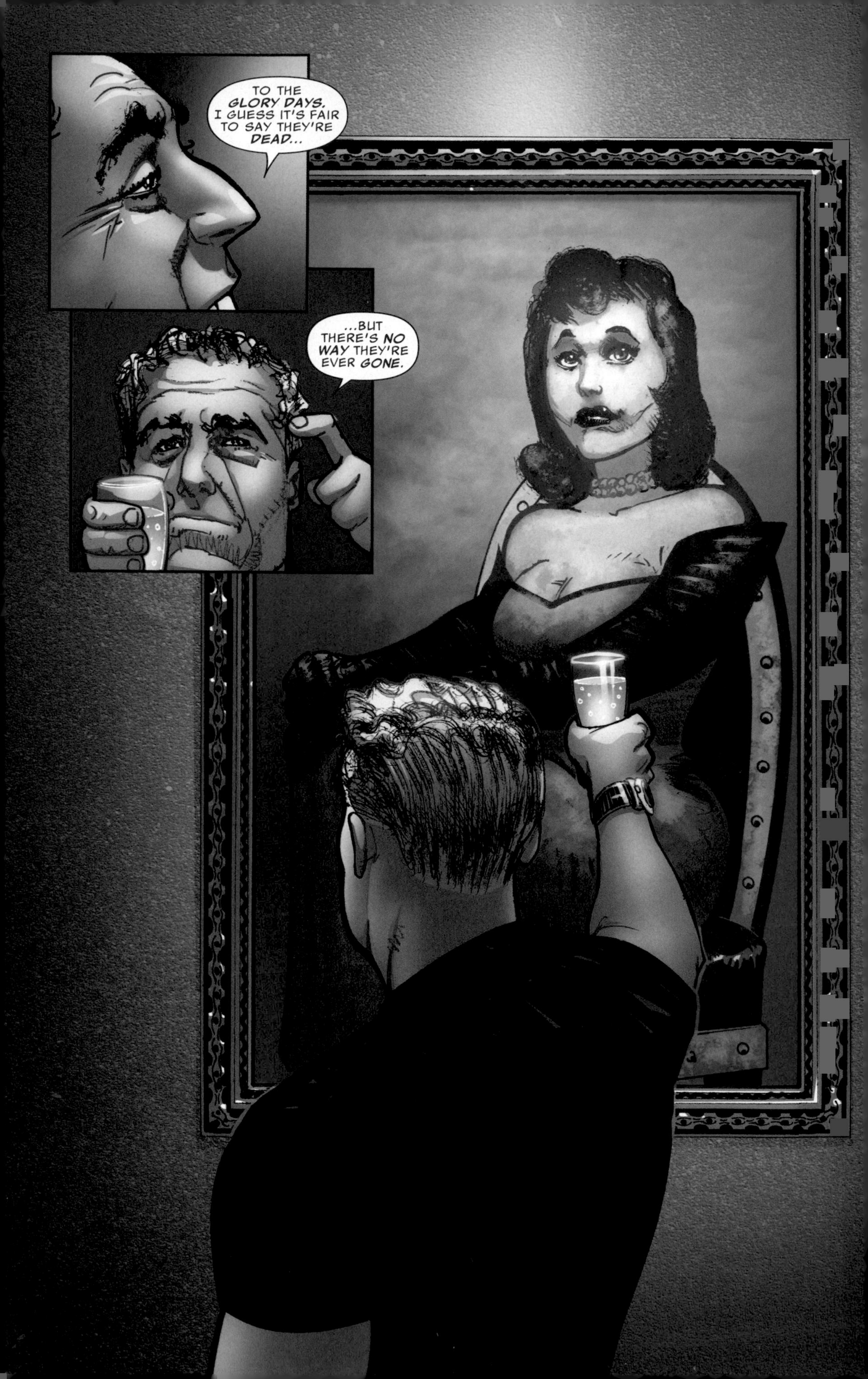
TO THE GLORY DAYS. I GUESS IT'S FAIR TO SAY THEY'RE DEAD...
...BUT THERE'S NO WAY THEY'RE EVER GONE.

12. ACTIVE MISSION: KINGSLAYER

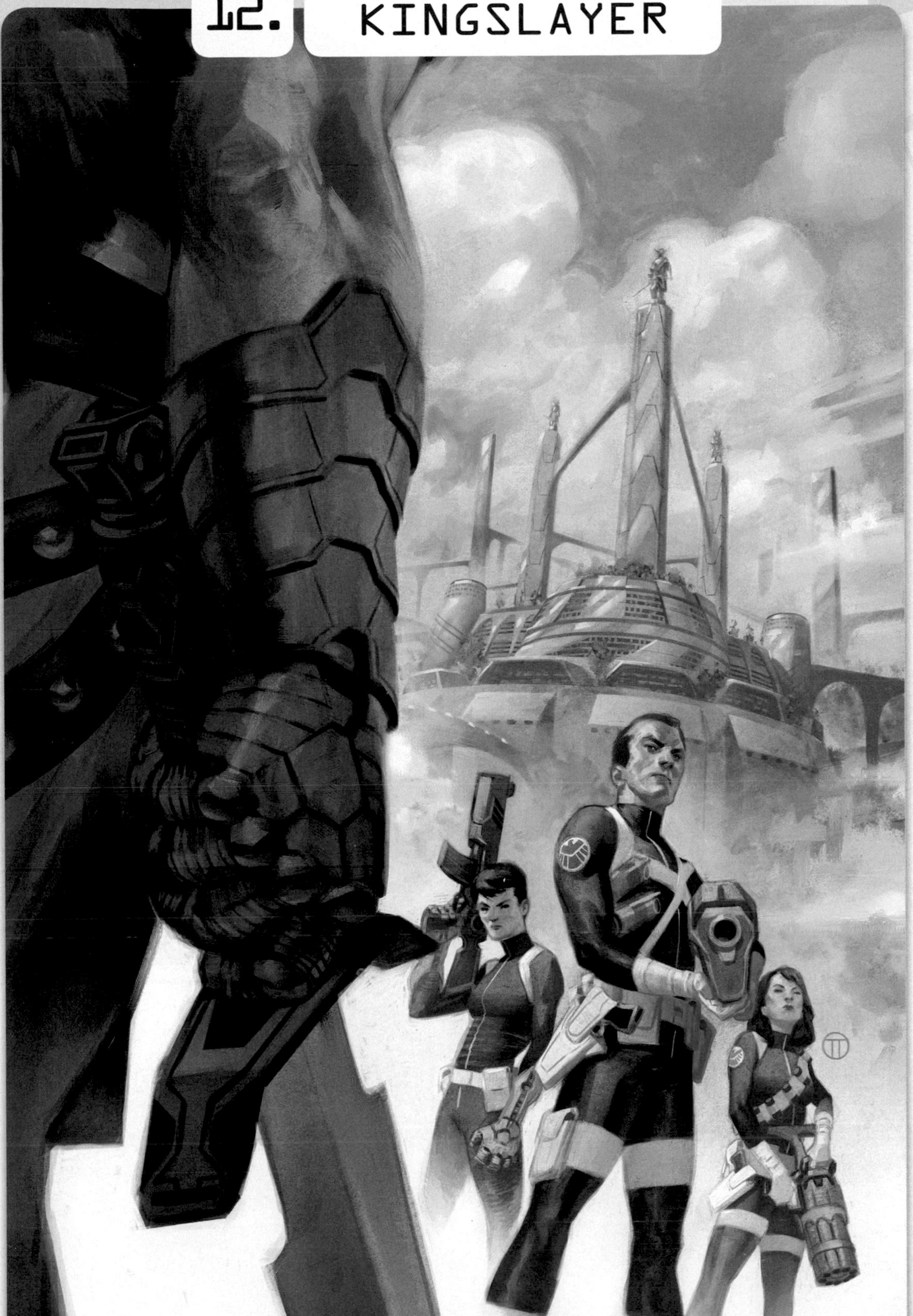

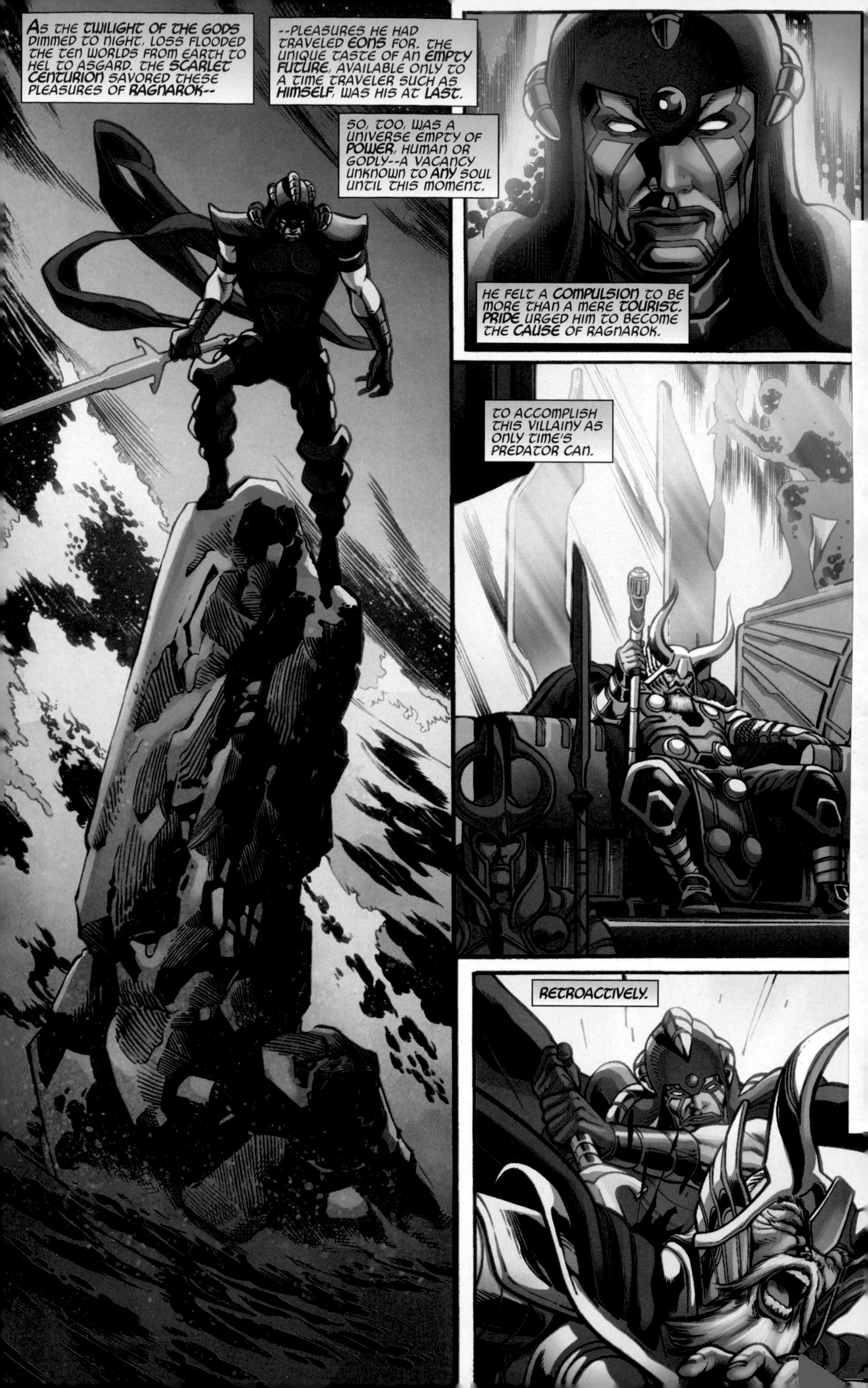
AS THE TWILIGHT OF THE GODS DIMMED TO NIGHT, LOSS FLOODED THE TEN WORLDS FROM EARTH TO HEL TO ASGARD. THE SCARLET CENTURION SAVORED THESE PLEASURES OF RAGNAROK--
--PLEASURES HE HAD TRAVELED EONS FOR. THE UNIQUE TASTE OF AN EMPTY FUTURE, AVAILABLE ONLY TO A TIME TRAVELER SUCH AS HIMSELF, WAS HIS AT LAST.
SO, TOO, WAS A UNIVERSE EMPTY OF POWER, HUMAN OR GODLY--A VACANCY UNKNOWN TO ANY SOUL UNTIL THIS MOMENT.
HE FELT A COMPULSION TO BE MORE THAN A MERE TOURIST. PRIDE URGED HIM TO BECOME THE CAUSE OF RAGNAROK.
TO ACCOMPLISH THIS VILLAINY AS ONLY TIME'S PREDATOR CAN.
RETROACTIVELY.

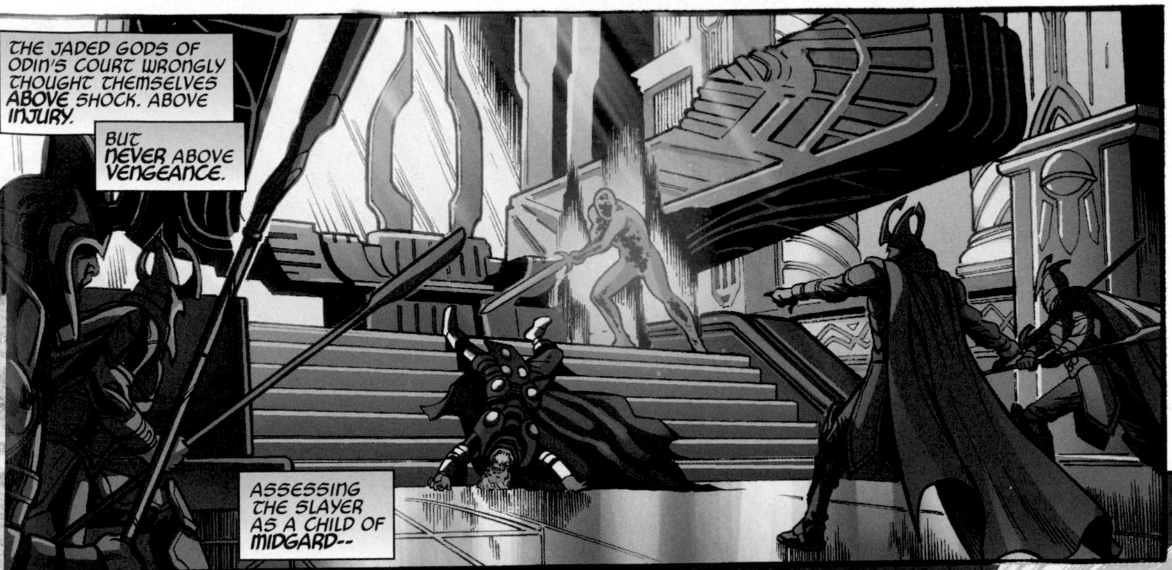
THE JADED GODS OF ODIN'S COURT WRONGLY THOUGHT THEMSELVES ABOVE SHOCK. ABOVE INJURY.
BUT NEVER ABOVE VENGEANCE.
ASSESSING THE SLAYER AS A CHILD OF MIDGARD--
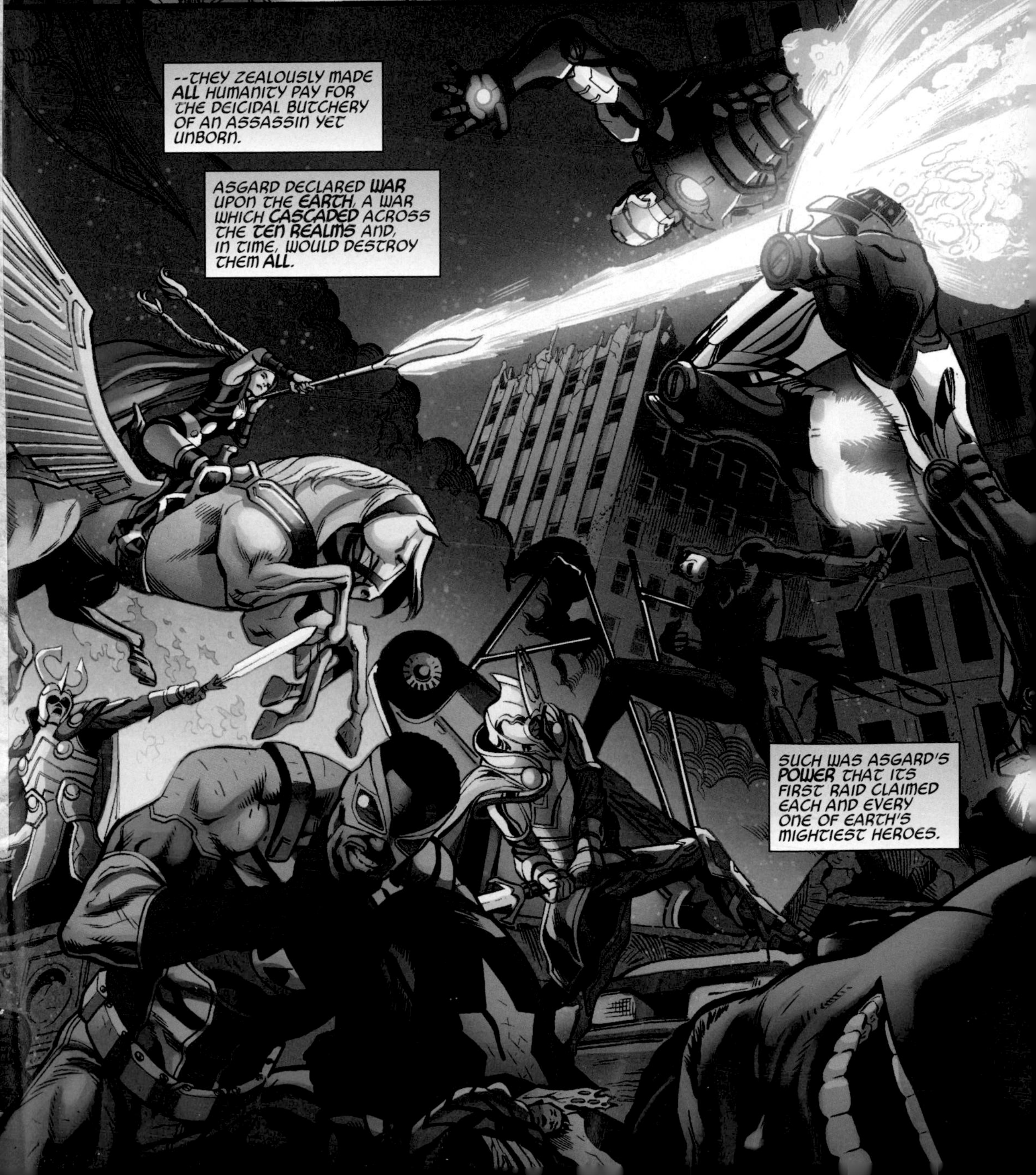
--THEY ZEALOUSLY MADE ALL HUMANITY PAY FOR THE DEICIDAL BUTCHERY OF AN ASSASSIN YET UNBORN.
ASGARD DECLARED WAR UPON THE EARTH, A WAR WHICH CASCADED ACROSS THE TEN REALMS AND, IN TIME, WOULD DESTROY THEM ALL.
SUCH WAS ASGARD'S POWER THAT ITS FIRST RAID CLAIMED EACH AND EVERY ONE OF EARTH'S MIGHTIEST HEROES.

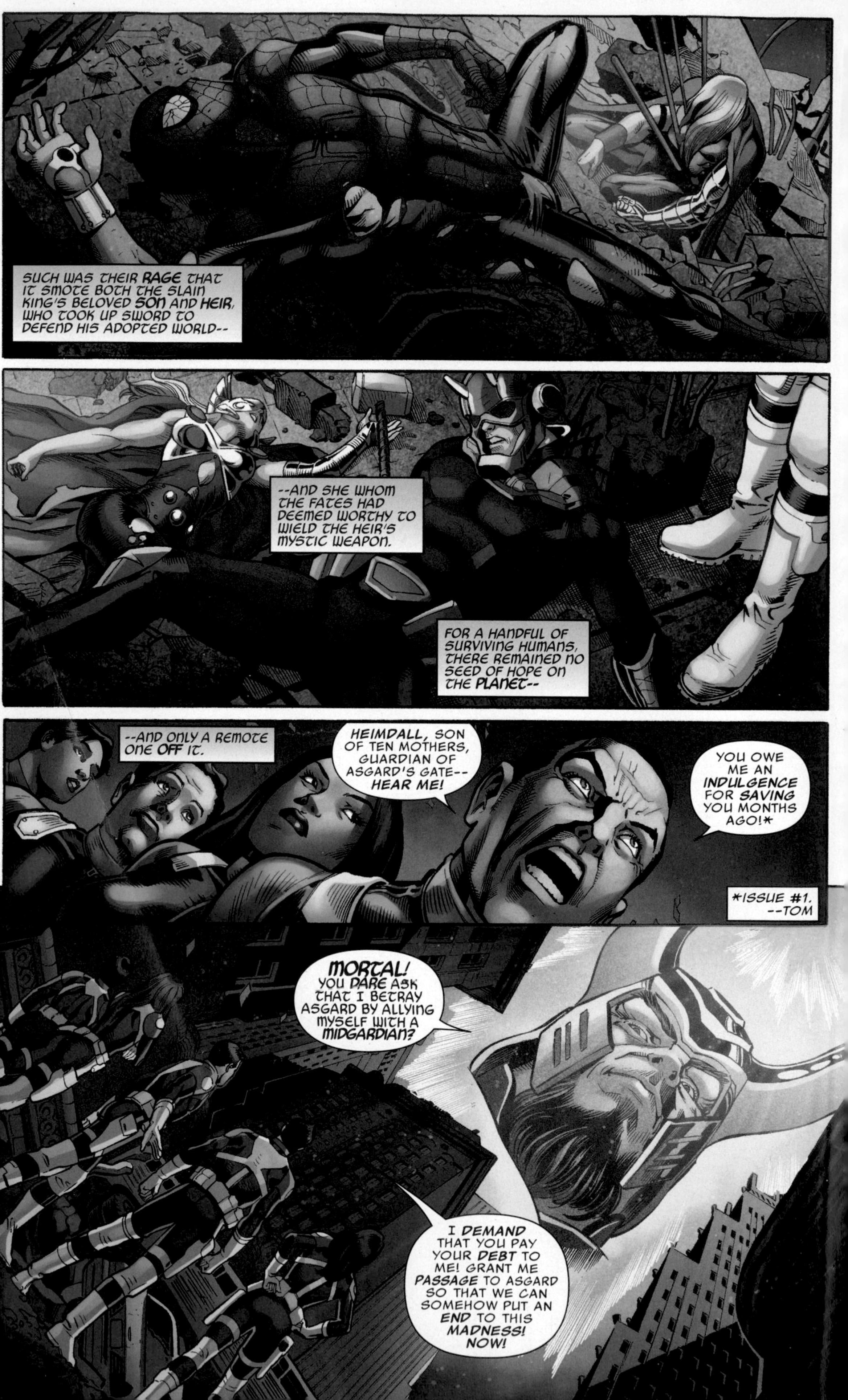
SUCH WAS THEIR RAGE THAT IT SMOTE BOTH THE SLAIN KING'S BELOVED SON AND HEIR, WHO TOOK UP SWORD TO DEFEND HIS ADOPTED WORLD--
--AND SHE WHOM THE FATES HAD DEEMED WORTHY TO WIELD THE HEIR'S MYSTIC WEAPON.
FOR A HANDFUL OF SURVIVING HUMANS, THERE REMAINED NO SEED OF HOPE ON THE PLANET--
--AND ONLY A REMOTE ONE OFF IT.
HEIMDALL, SON OF TEN MOTHERS, GUARDIAN OF ASGARD'S GATE-- HEAR ME!
YOU OWE ME AN INDULGENCE FOR SAVING YOU MONTHS AGO!*
*ISSUE #1. --TOM
MORTAL! YOU DARE ASK THAT I BETRAY ASGARD BY ALLYING MYSELF WITH A MIDGARDIAN?
I DEMAND THAT YOU PAY YOUR DEBT TO ME! GRANT ME PASSAGE TO ASGARD SO THAT WE CAN SOMEHOW PUT AN END TO THIS MADNESS! NOW!

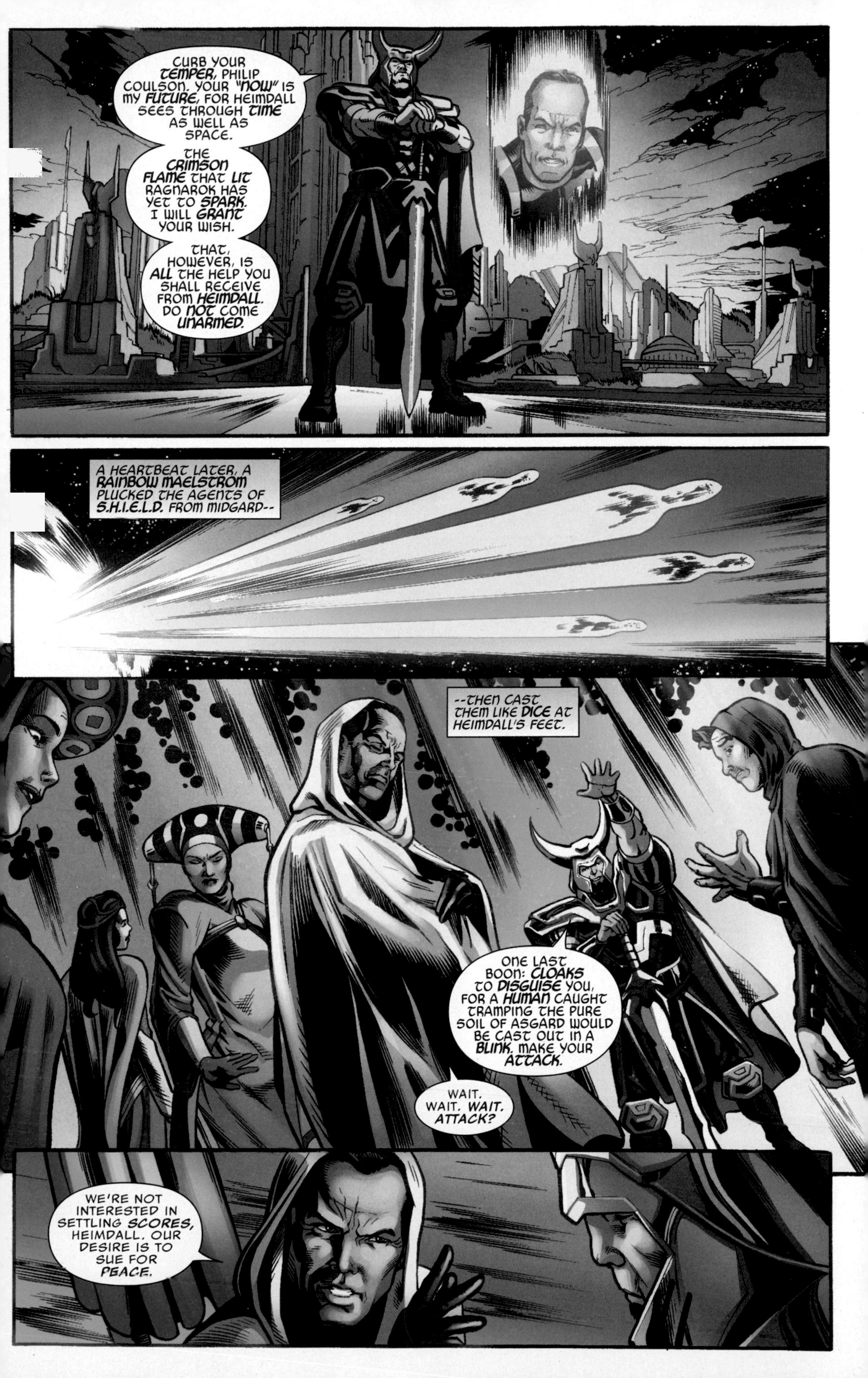
CURB YOUR TEMPER, PHILIP COULSON. YOUR "NOW" IS MY FUTURE, FOR HEIMDALL SEES THROUGH TIME AS WELL AS SPACE.
THE CRIMSON FLAME THAT LIT RAGNAROK HAS YET TO SPARK. I WILL GRANT YOUR WISH.
THAT, HOWEVER, IS ALL THE HELP YOU SHALL RECEIVE FROM HEIMDALL. DO NOT COME UNARMED.
A HEARTBEAT LATER, A RAINBOW MAELSTROM PLUCKED THE AGENTS OF S.H.I.E.L.D. FROM MIDGARD--
--THEN CAST THEM LIKE DICE AT HEIMDALL'S FEET.
ONE LAST BOON: CLOAKS TO DISGUISE YOU, FOR A HUMAN CAUGHT TRAMPING THE PURE SOIL OF ASGARD WOULD BE CAST OUT IN A BLINK. MAKE YOUR ATTACK.
WAIT. WAIT. WAIT. ATTACK?
WE'RE NOT INTERESTED IN SETTLING SCORES, HEIMDALL. OUR DESIRE IS TO SUE FOR PEACE.

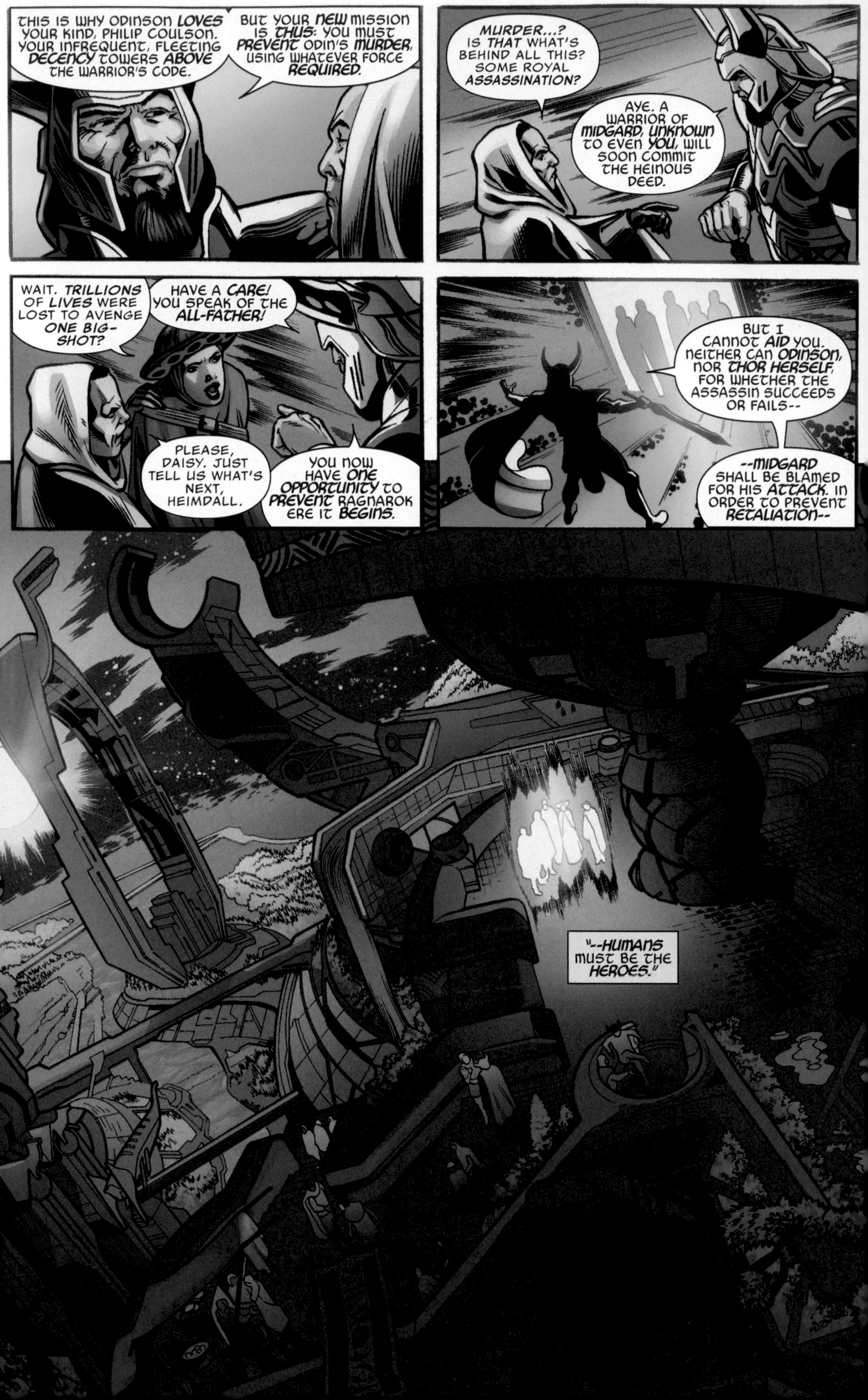
THIS IS WHY ODINSON LOVES YOUR KIND, PHILIP COULSON. YOUR INFREQUENT, FLEETING DECENCY TOWERS ABOVE THE WARRIOR'S CODE.
BUT YOUR NEW MISSION IS THUS: YOU MUST PREVENT ODIN'S MURDER, USING WHATEVER FORCE REQUIRED.
MURDER...? IS THAT WHAT'S BEHIND ALL THIS? SOME ROYAL ASSASSINATION?
AYE. A WARRIOR OF MIDGARD, UNKNOWN TO EVEN YOU, WILL SOON COMMIT THE HEINOUS DEED.
WAIT. TRILLIONS OF LIVES WERE LOST TO AVENGE ONE BIG-SHOT?
HAVE A CARE! YOU SPEAK OF THE ALL-FATHER!
PLEASE, DAISY. JUST TELL US WHAT'S NEXT, HEIMDALL.
YOU NOW HAVE ONE OPPORTUNITY TO PREVENT RAGNAROK ERE IT BEGINS.
BUT I CANNOT AID YOU. NEITHER CAN ODINSON, NOR THOR HERSELF, FOR WHETHER THE ASSASSIN SUCCEEDS OR FAILS--
--MIDGARD SHALL BE BLAMED FOR HIS ATTACK. IN ORDER TO PREVENT RETALIATION--
"--HUMANS MUST BE THE HEROES."

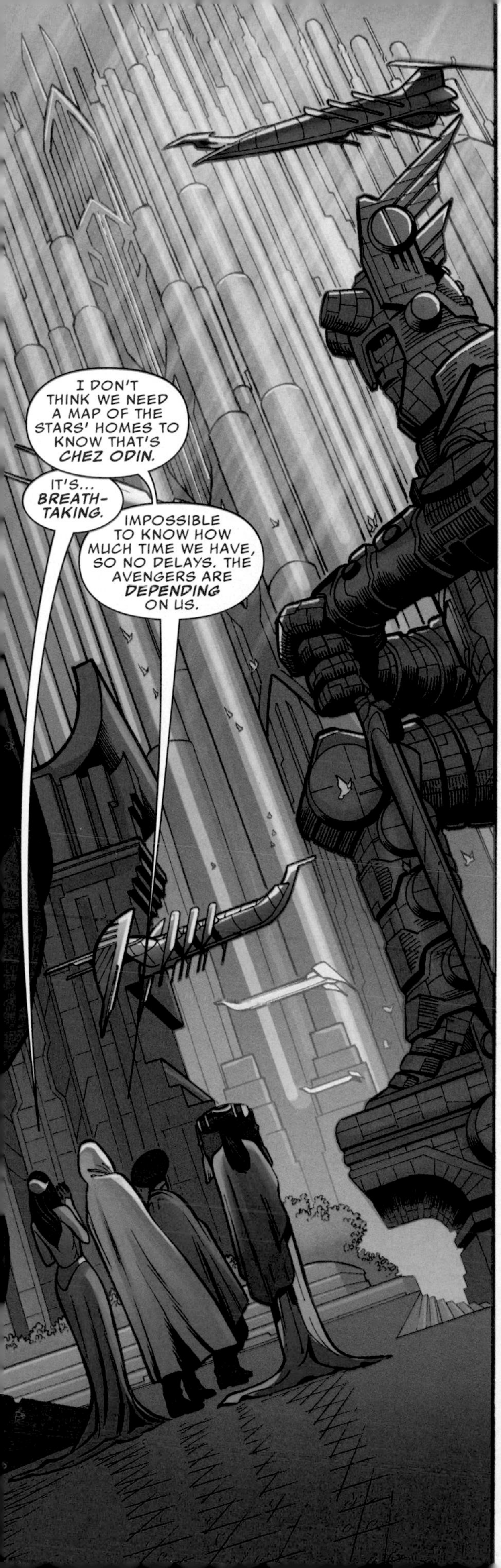
I DON'T THINK WE NEED A MAP OF THE STARS' HOMES TO KNOW THAT'S CHEZ ODIN.
IT'S... BREATH-TAKING.
IMPOSSIBLE TO KNOW HOW MUCH TIME WE HAVE, SO NO DELAYS. THE AVENGERS ARE DEPENDING ON US.
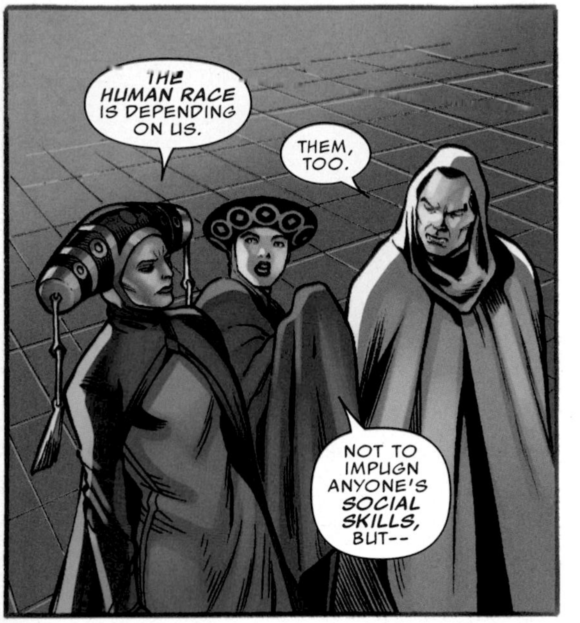
THE HUMAN RACE IS DEPENDING ON US.
THEM, TOO.
NOT TO IMPUGN ANYONE'S SOCIAL SKILLS, BUT--
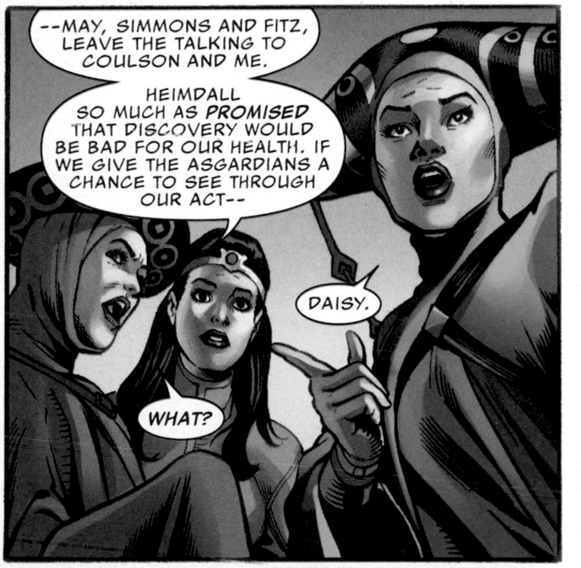
--MAY, SIMMONS AND FITZ, LEAVE THE TALKING TO COULSON AND ME.
HEIMDALL SO MUCH AS PROMISED THAT DISCOVERY WOULD BE BAD FOR OUR HEALTH. IF WE GIVE THE ASGARDIANS A CHANCE TO SEE THROUGH OUR ACT--
DAISY.
WHAT?
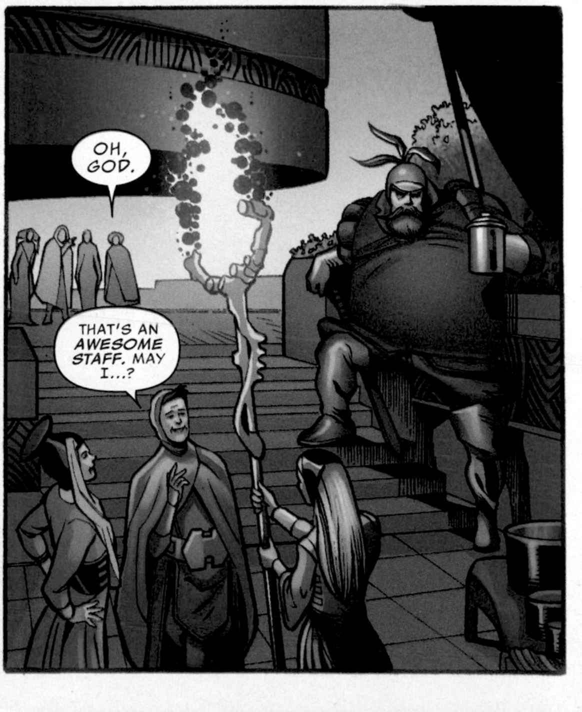
OH, GOD.
THAT'S AN AWESOME STAFF. MAY I...?

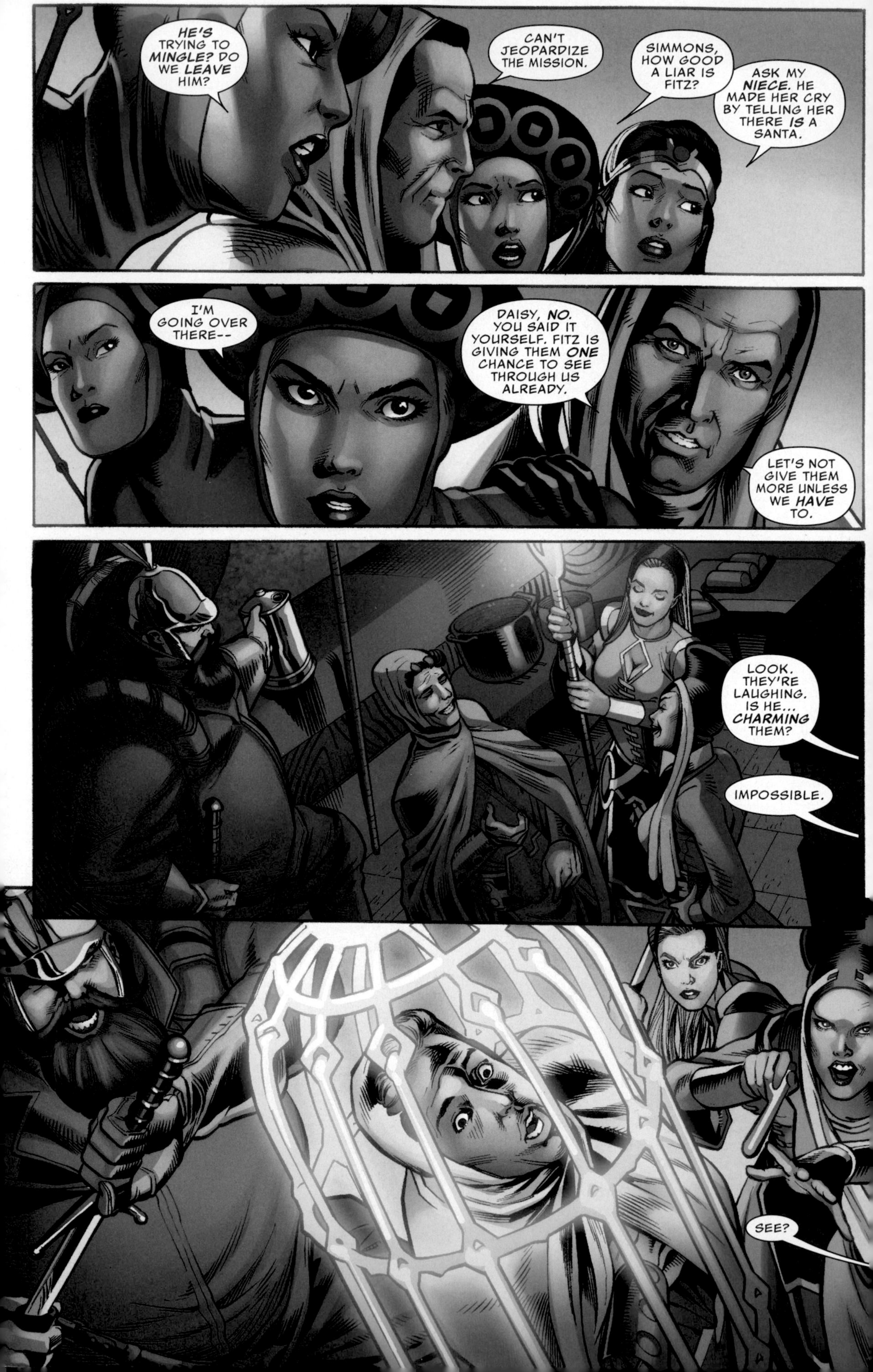
HE'S TRYING TO MINGLE? DO WE LEAVE HIM?
CAN'T JEOPARDIZE THE MISSION.
SIMMONS, HOW GOOD A LIAR IS FITZ?
ASK MY NIECE. HE MADE HER CRY BY TELLING HER THERE IS A SANTA.
I'M GOING OVER THERE--
DAISY, NO. YOU SAID IT YOURSELF. FITZ IS GIVING THEM ONE CHANCE TO SEE THROUGH US ALREADY.
LET'S NOT GIVE THEM MORE UNLESS WE HAVE TO.
LOOK. THEY'RE LAUGHING. IS HE... CHARMING THEM?
IMPOSSIBLE.
SEE?

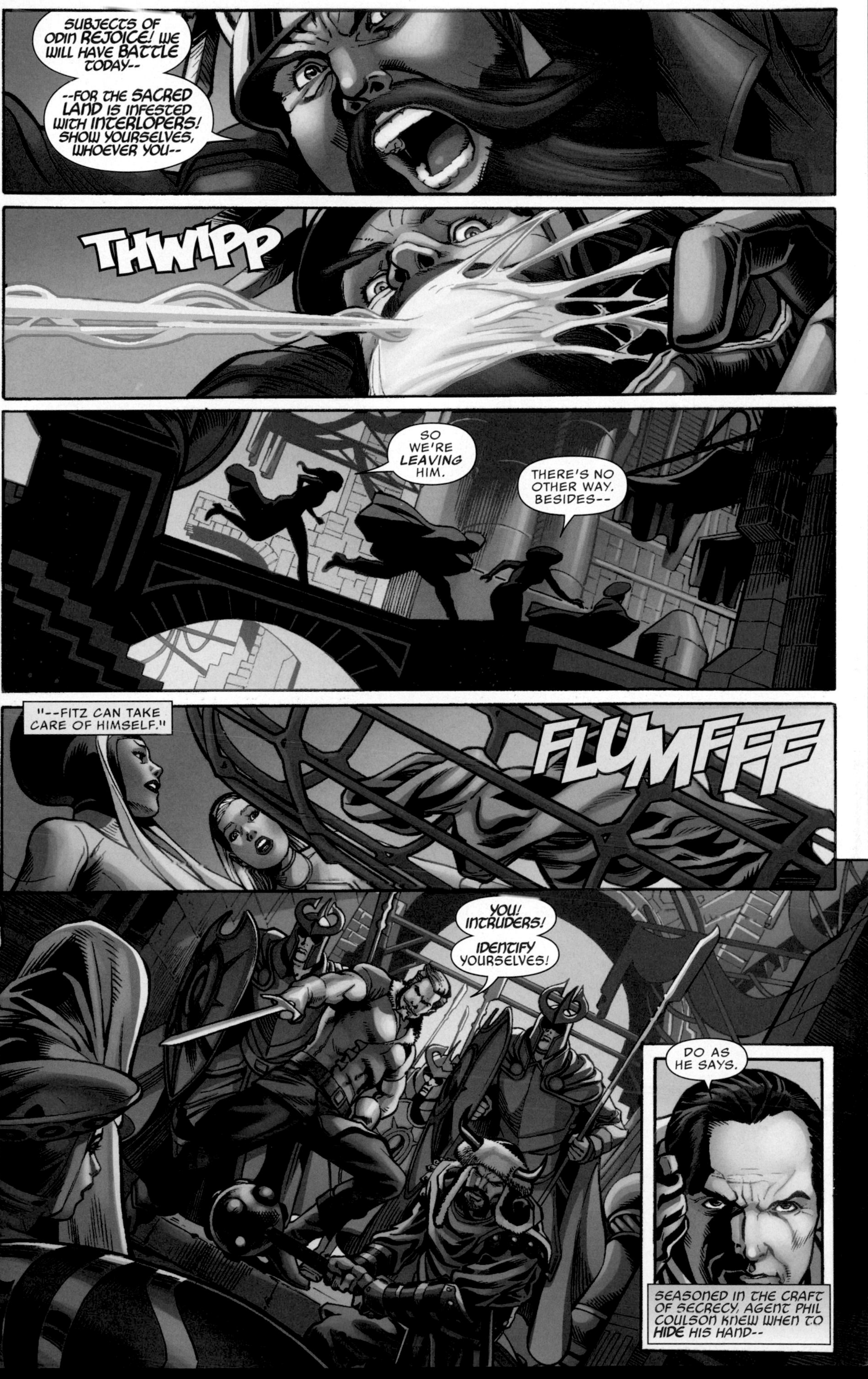
SUBJECTS OF ODIN REJOICE! WE WILL HAVE BATTLE TODAY--
--FOR THE SACRED LAND IS INFESTED WITH INTERLOPERS! SHOW YOURSELVES, WHOEVER YOU--
THWIPP
SO WE'RE LEAVING HIM.
THERE'S NO OTHER WAY. BESIDES--
"--FITZ CAN TAKE CARE OF HIMSELF."
FLUMFFF
YOU! INTRUDERS!
IDENTIFY YOURSELVES!
DO AS HE SAYS.
SEASONED IN THE CRAFT OF SECRECY, AGENT PHIL COULSON KNEW WHEN TO HIDE HIS HAND--

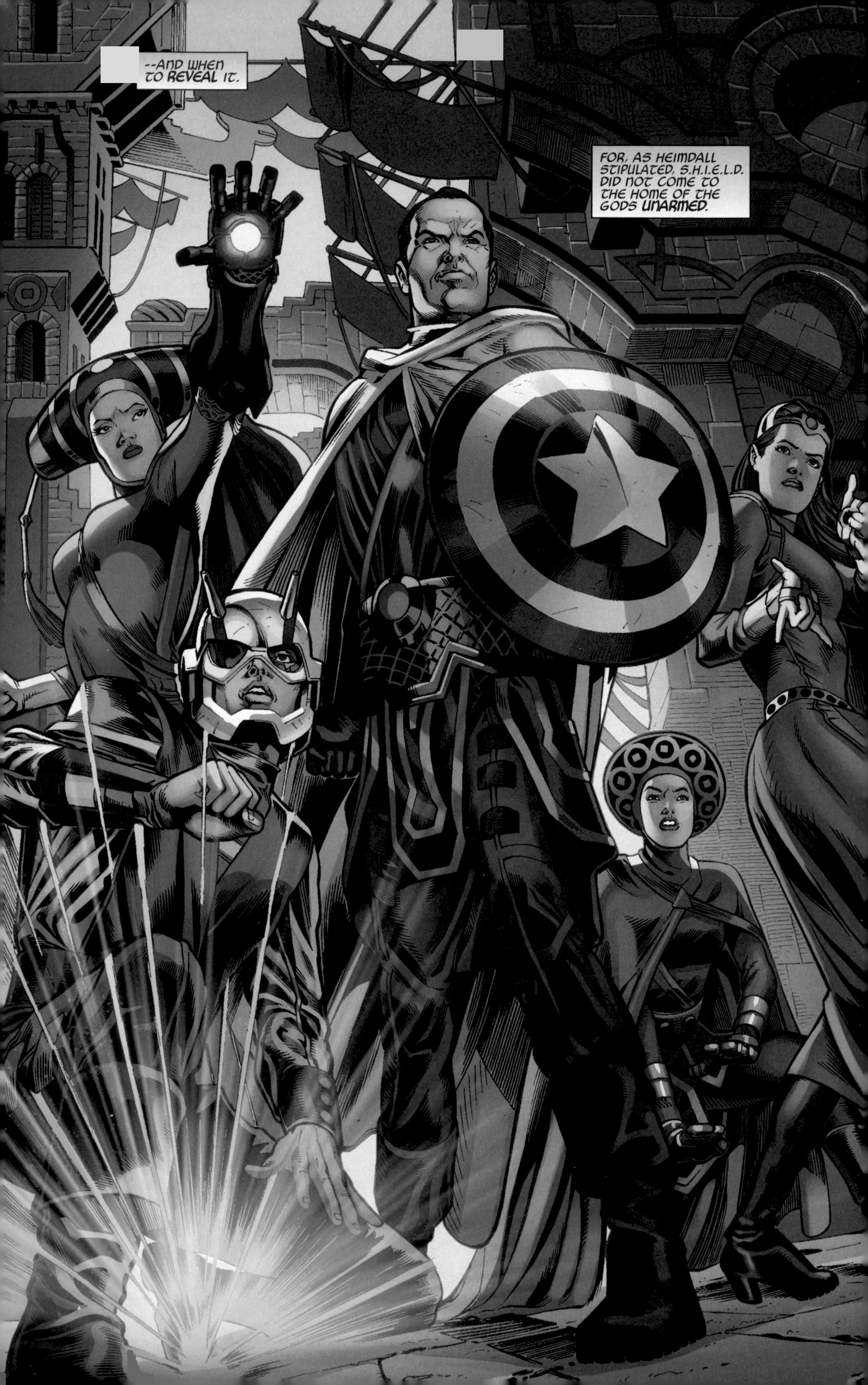
--AND WHEN TO REVEAL IT.
FOR, AS HEIMDALL STIPULATED, S.H.I.E.L.D. DID NOT COME TO THE HOME OF THE GODS UNARMED.

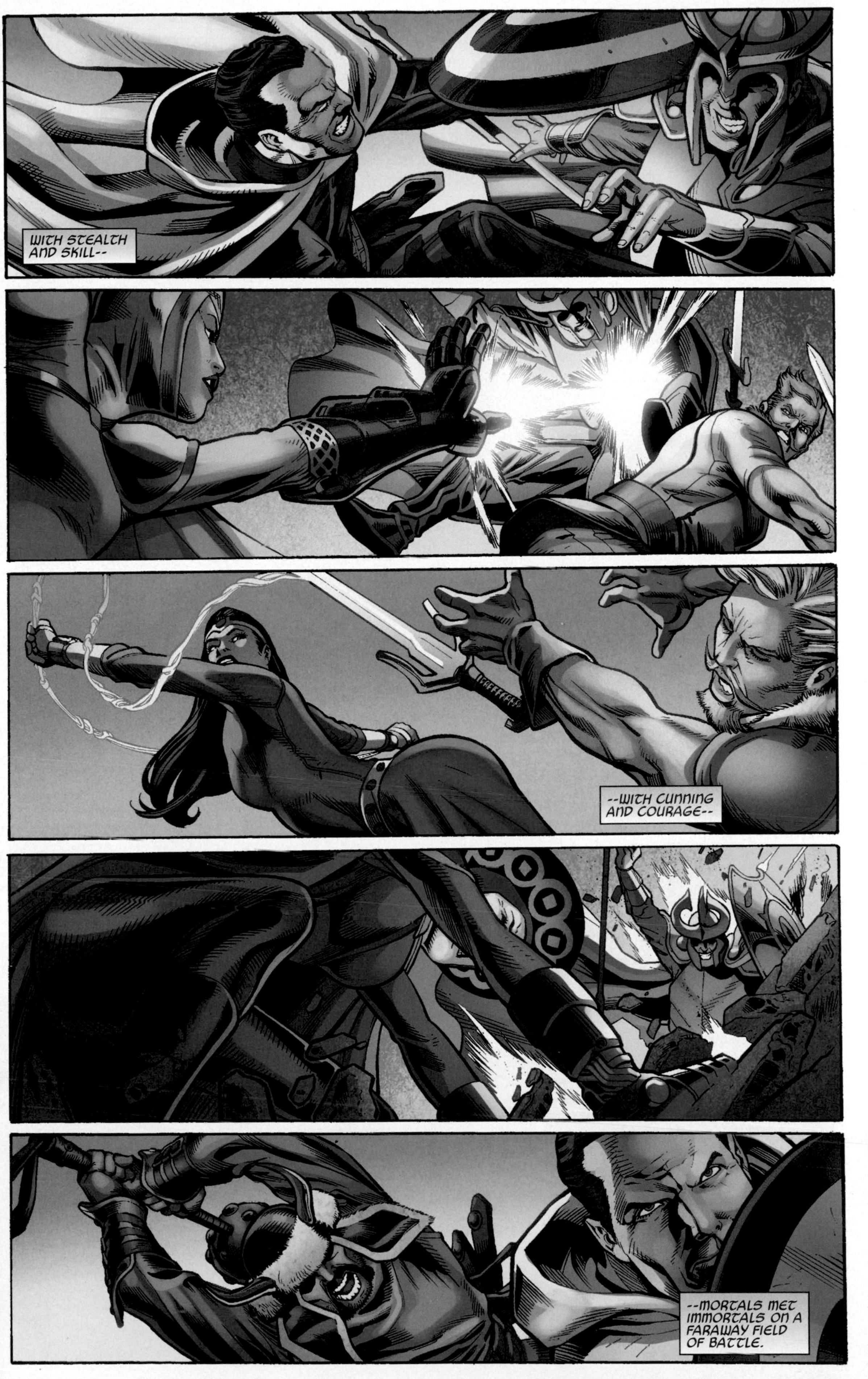
WITH STEALTH AND SKILL--
--WITH CUNNING AND COURAGE--
--MORTALS MET IMMORTALS ON A FARAWAY FIELD OF BATTLE.

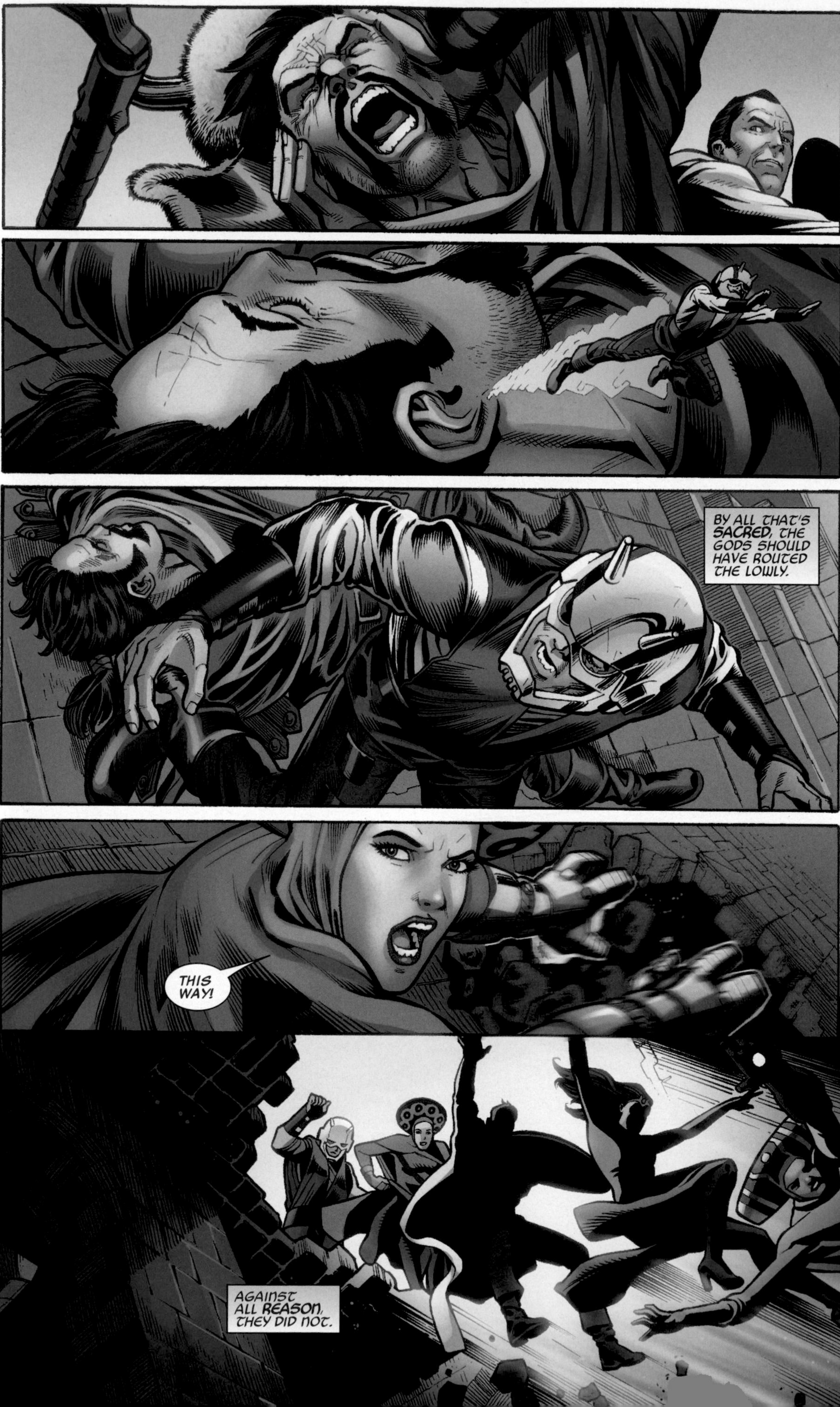
BY ALL THAT'S SACRED, THE GODS SHOULD HAVE ROUTED THE LOWLY.
THIS WAY!
AGAINST ALL REASON, THEY DID NOT.

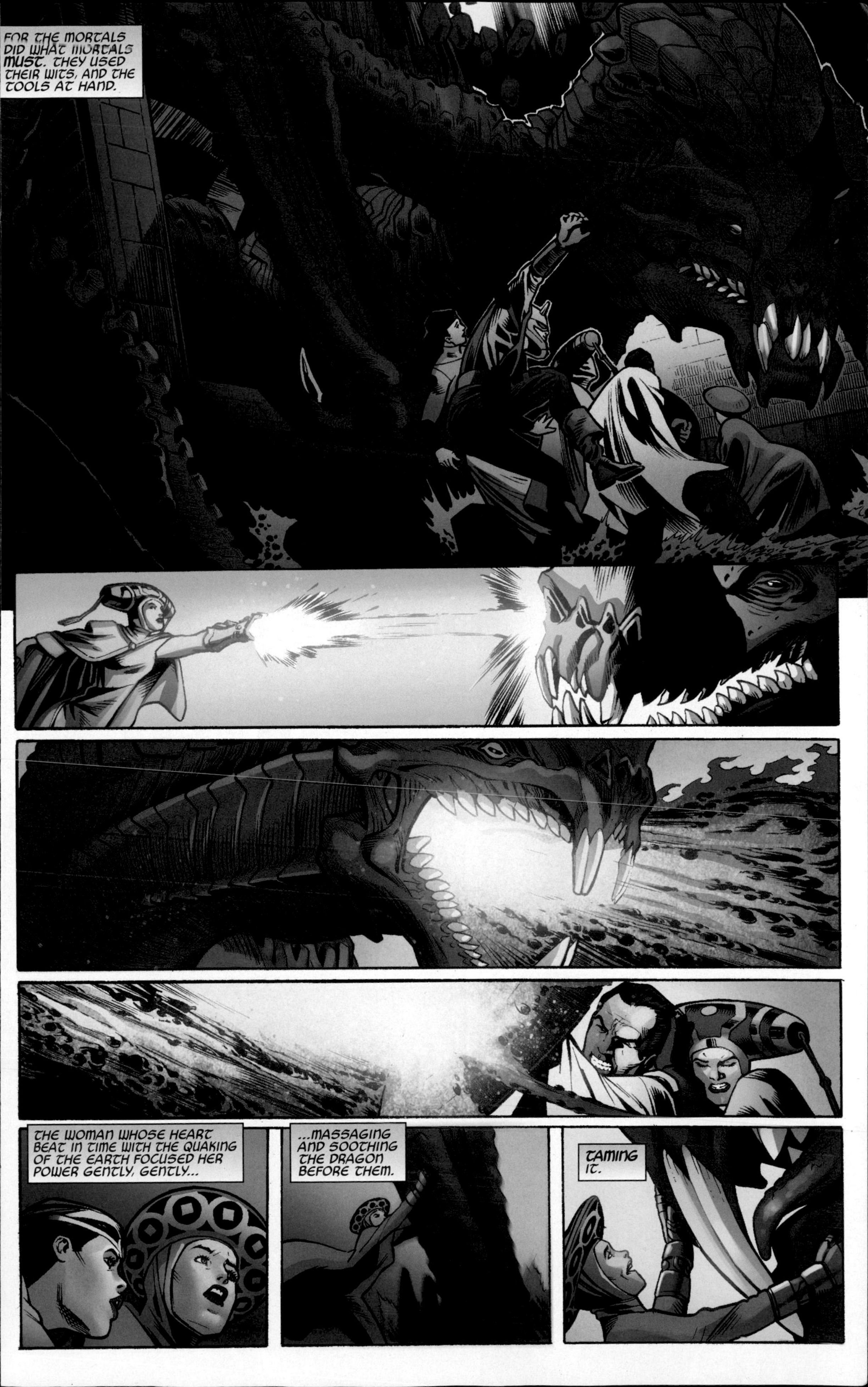
FOR THE MORTALS DID WHAT MORTALS MUST. THEY USED THEIR WITS, AND THE TOOLS AT HAND.
THE WOMAN WHOSE HEART BEAT IN TIME WITH THE QUAKING OF THE EARTH FOCUSED HER POWER GENTLY, GENTLY...
...MASSAGING AND SOOTHING THE DRAGON BEFORE THEM.
TAMING IT.

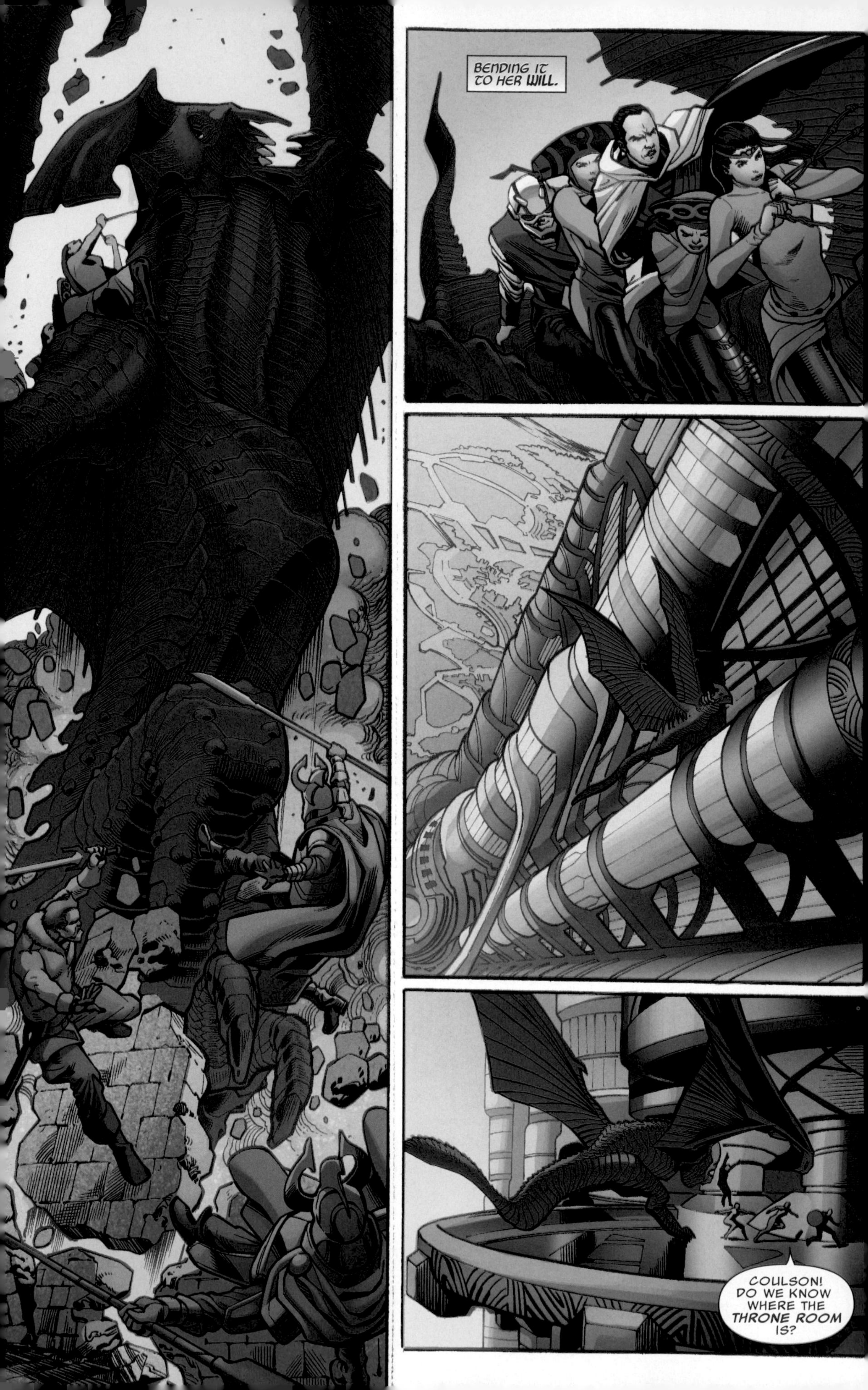
BENDING IT TO HER WILL.
COULSON! DO WE KNOW WHERE THE THRONE ROOM IS?

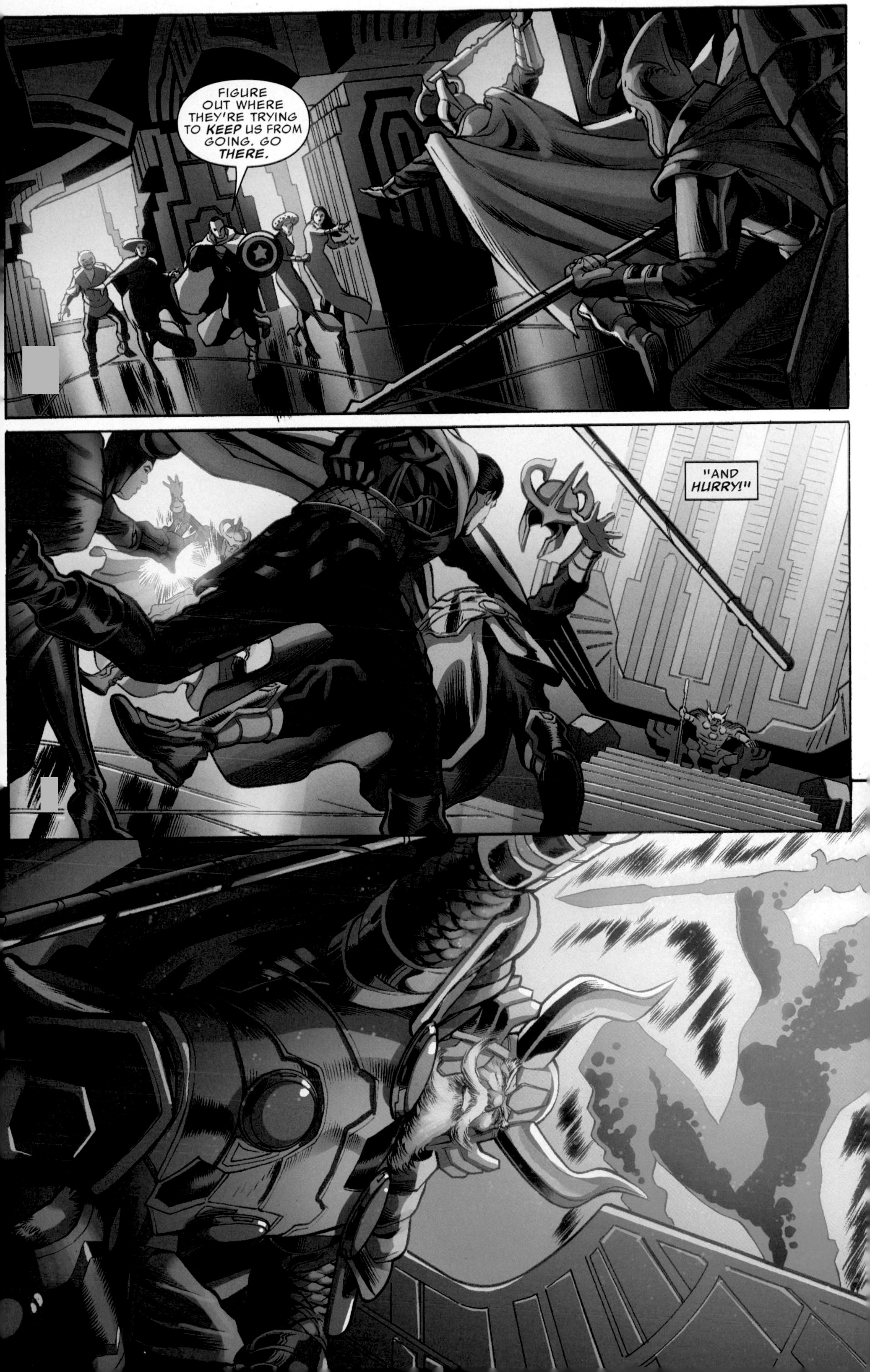
FIGURE OUT WHERE THEY'RE TRYING TO KEEP US FROM GOING. GO THERE.
"AND HURRY!"

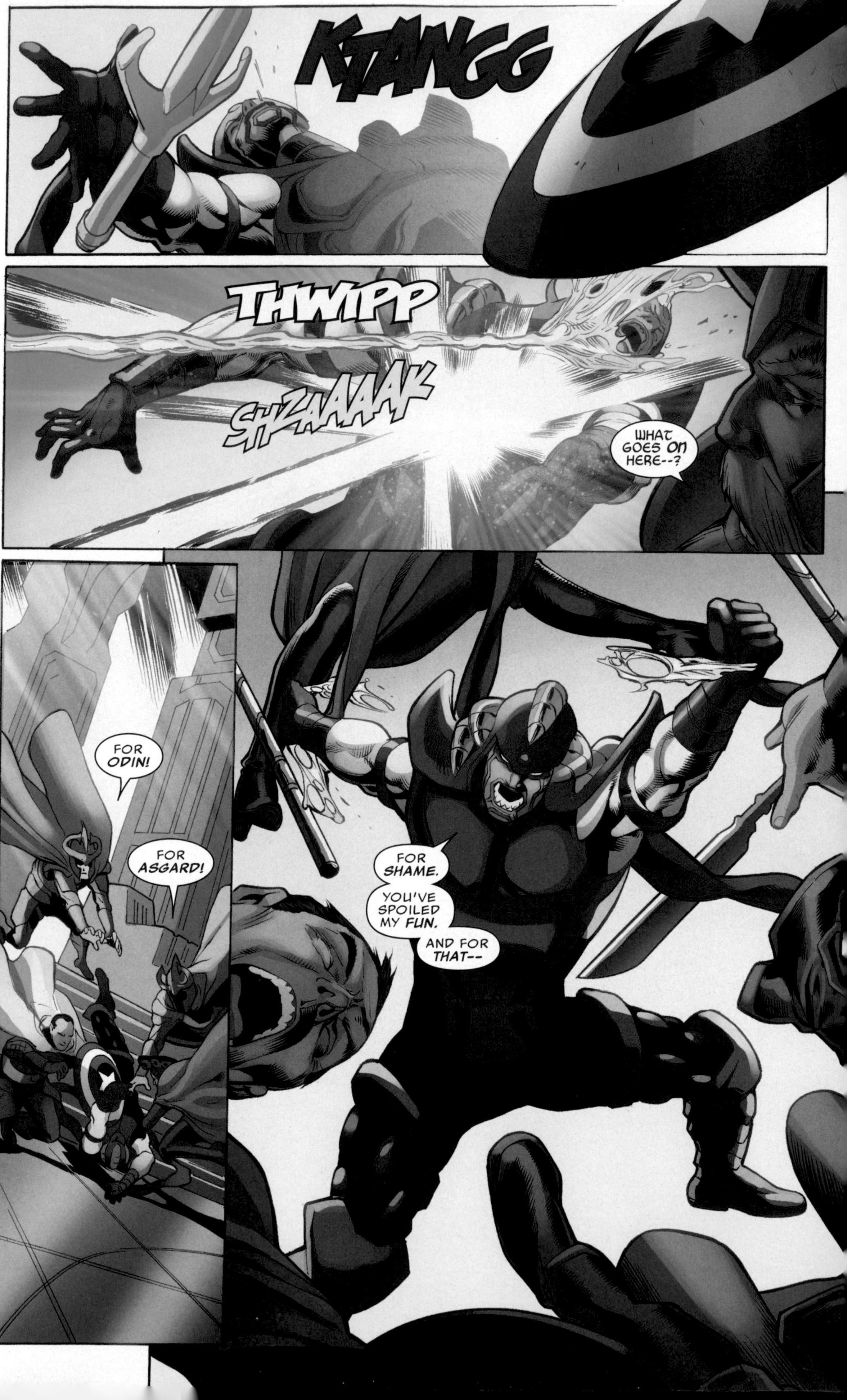
KTANGG
THWIPP
SHZAAAAK
WHAT GOES ON HERE--?
FOR ODIN!
FOR ASGARD!
FOR SHAME.
YOU'VE SPOILED MY FUN.
AND FOR THAT--

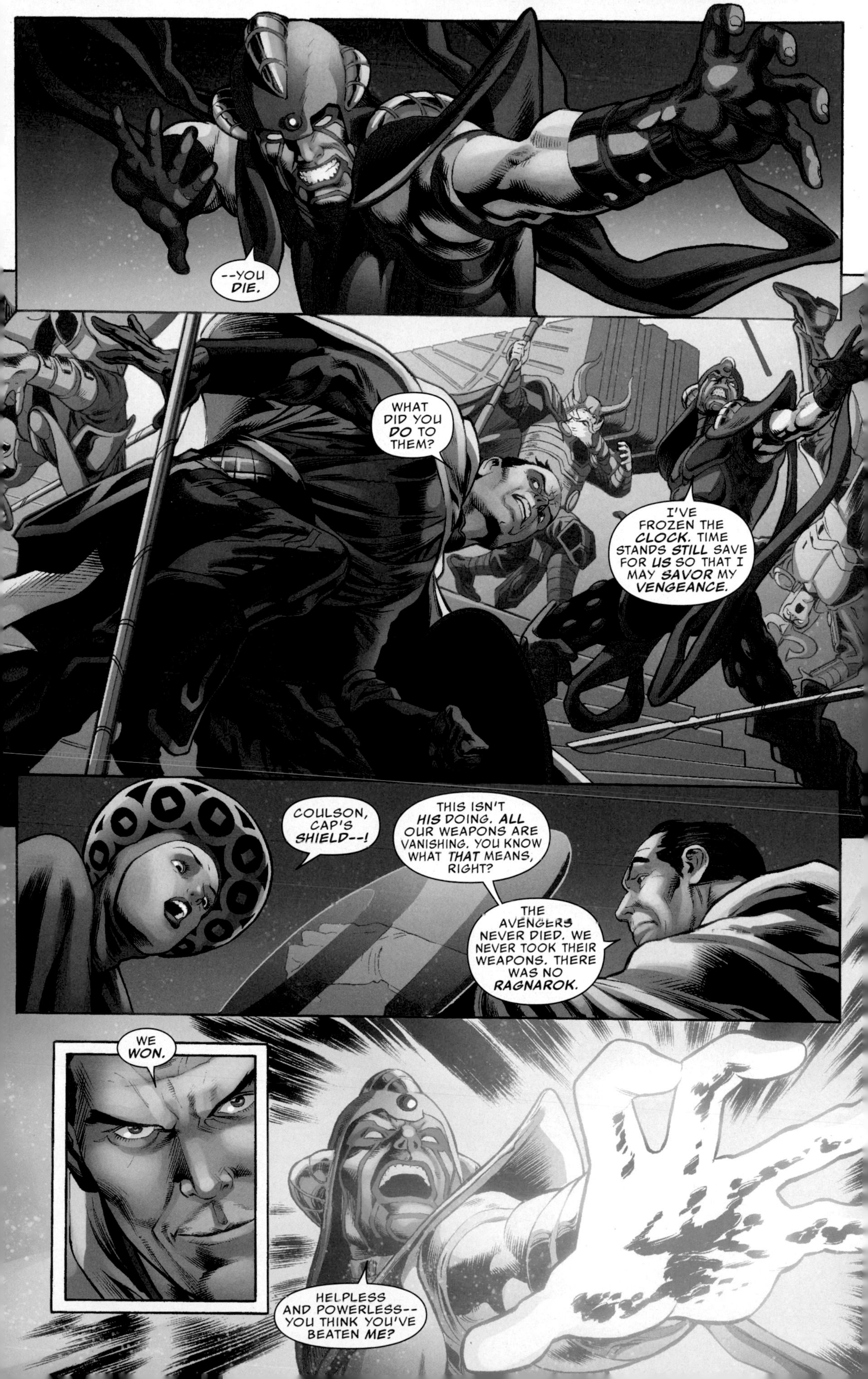
--YOU DIE.
WHAT DID YOU DO TO THEM?
I'VE FROZEN THE CLOCK. TIME STANDS STILL SAVE FOR US SO THAT I MAY SAVOR MY VENGEANCE.
COULSON, CAP'S SHIELD--!
THIS ISN'T HIS DOING. ALL OUR WEAPONS ARE VANISHING. YOU KNOW WHAT THAT MEANS, RIGHT?
THE AVENGERS NEVER DIED. WE NEVER TOOK THEIR WEAPONS. THERE WAS NO RAGNAROK.
WE WON.
HELPLESS AND POWERLESS--YOU THINK YOU'VE BEATEN ME?

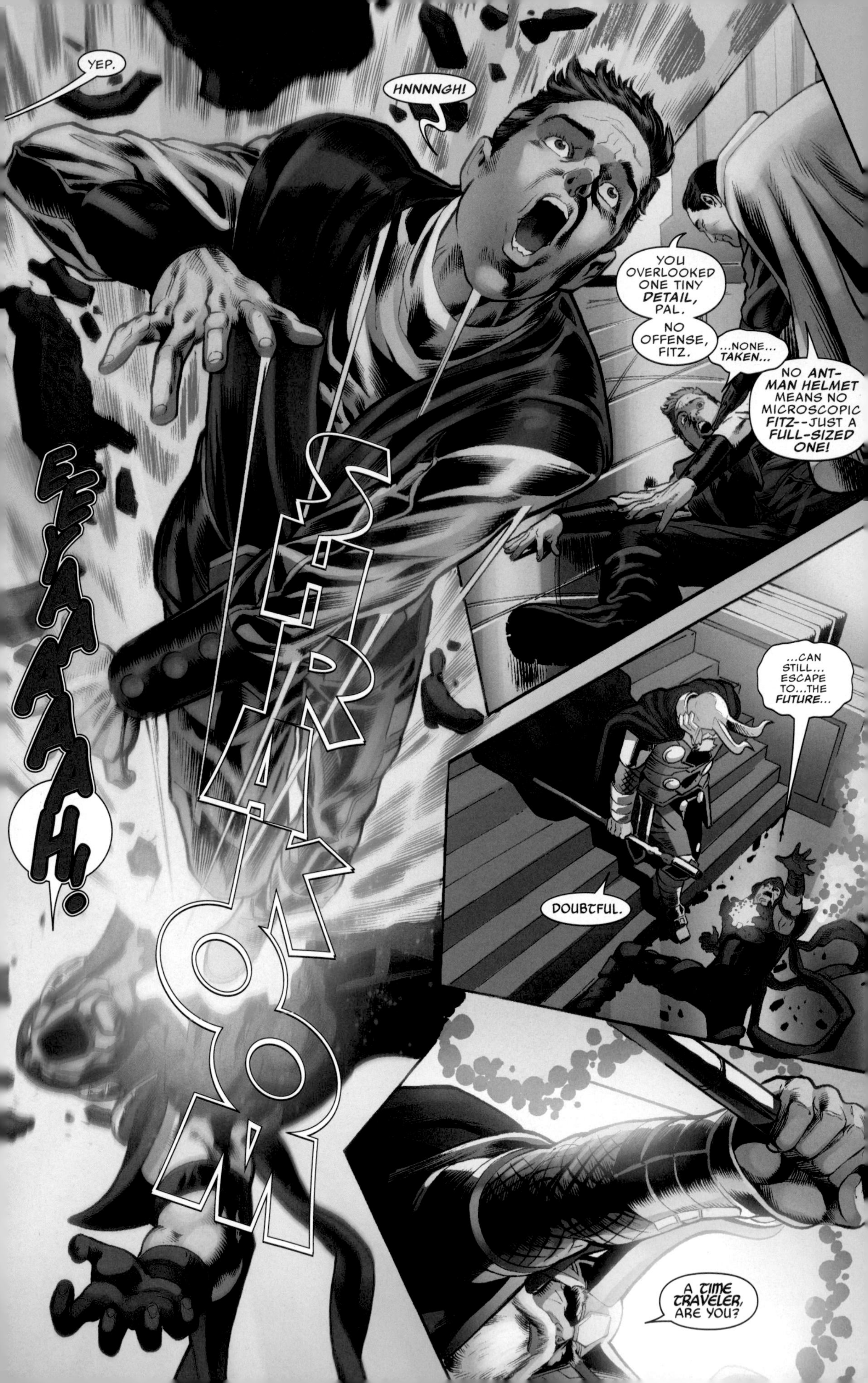

YEP.
HNNNNGH!
YOU OVERLOOKED ONE TINY DETAIL, PAL.
NO OFFENSE, FITZ.
...NONE... TAKEN...
NO ANT-MAN HELMET MEANS NO MICROSCOPIC FITZ--JUST A FULL-SIZED ONE!
...CAN STILL... ESCAPE TO...THE FUTURE...
DOUBTFUL.
A TIME TRAVELER, ARE YOU?

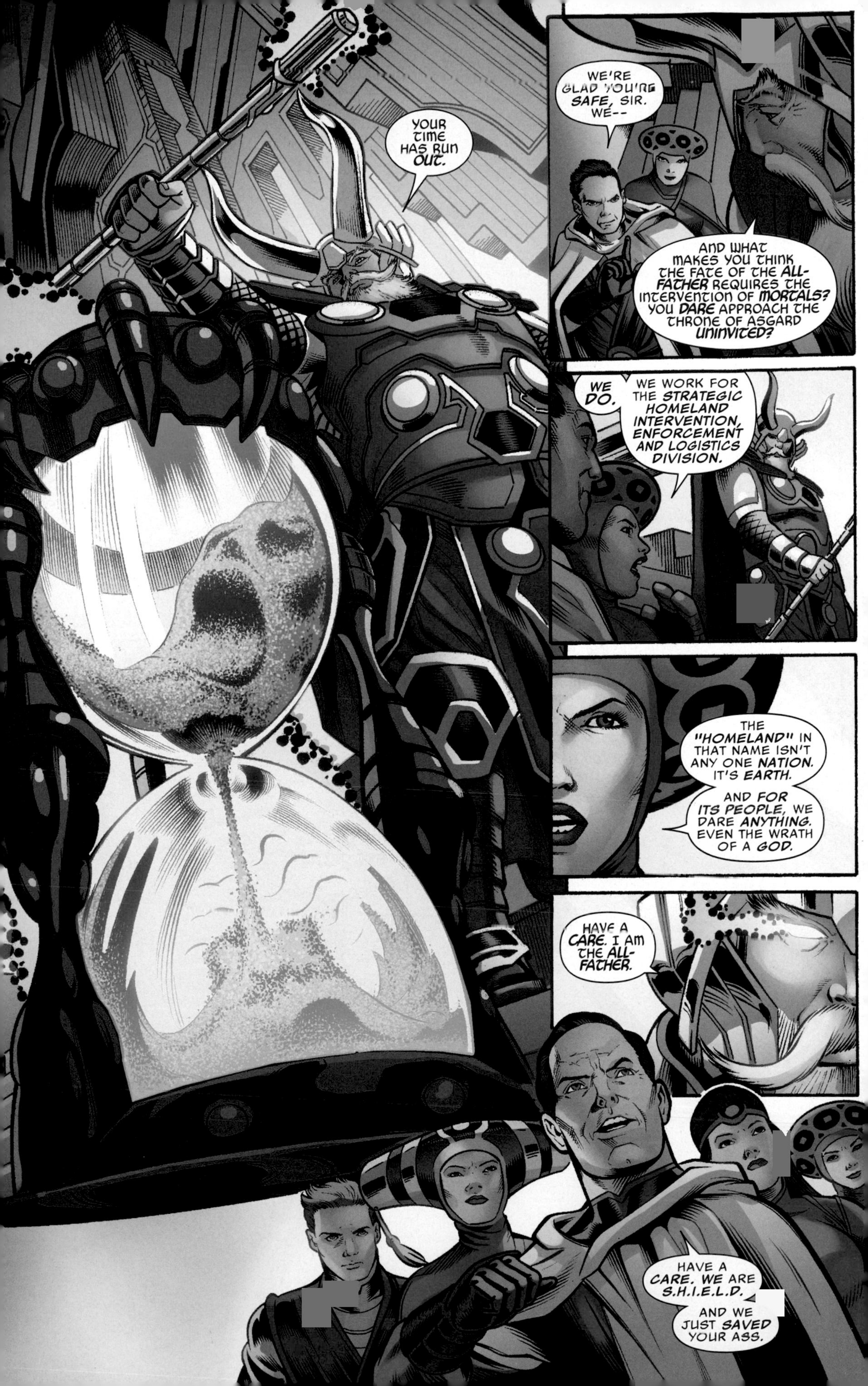
YOUR TIME HAS RUN OUT.
WE'RE GLAD YOU'RE SAFE, SIR. WE--
AND WHAT MAKES YOU THINK THE FATE OF THE ALL-FATHER REQUIRES THE INTERVENTION OF MORTALS? YOU DARE APPROACH THE THRONE OF ASGARD UNINVITED?
WE DO.
WE WORK FOR THE STRATEGIC HOMELAND INTERVENTION, ENFORCEMENT AND LOGISTICS DIVISION.
THE "HOMELAND" IN THAT NAME ISN'T ANY ONE NATION. IT'S EARTH.
AND FOR ITS PEOPLE, WE DARE ANYTHING. EVEN THE WRATH OF A GOD.
HAVE A CARE. I AM THE ALL-FATHER.
HAVE A CARE. WE ARE S.H.I.E.L.D.
AND WE JUST SAVED YOUR ASS.

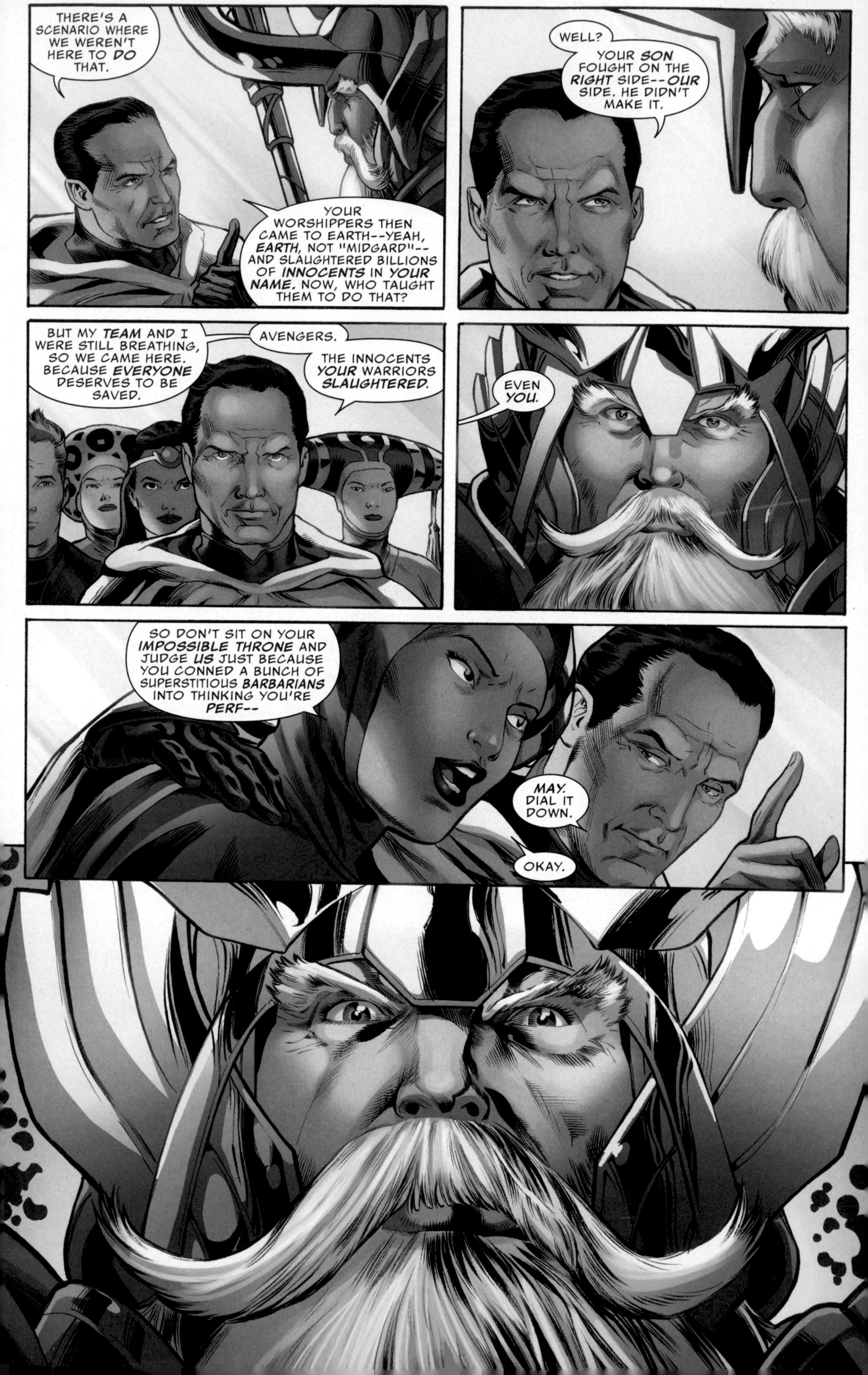
THERE'S A SCENARIO WHERE WE WEREN'T HERE TO DO THAT.
YOUR WORSHIPPERS THEN CAME TO EARTH--YEAH, EARTH, NOT "MIDGARD"--AND SLAUGHTERED BILLIONS OF INNOCENTS IN YOUR NAME. NOW, WHO TAUGHT THEM TO DO THAT?
WELL?
YOUR SON FOUGHT ON THE RIGHT SIDE--OUR SIDE. HE DIDN'T MAKE IT.
BUT MY TEAM AND I WERE STILL BREATHING, SO WE CAME HERE. BECAUSE EVERYONE DESERVES TO BE SAVED.
AVENGERS.
THE INNOCENTS YOUR WARRIORS SLAUGHTERED.
EVEN YOU.
SO DON'T SIT ON YOUR IMPOSSIBLE THRONE AND JUDGE US JUST BECAUSE YOU CONNED A BUNCH OF SUPERSTITIOUS BARBARIANS INTO THINKING YOU'RE PERF--
MAY. DIAL IT DOWN.
OKAY.

WE'RE HOME.

IN ONE PIECE.

EVERYTHING'S IN ONE PIECE. WE SAVED *TEN* WORLDS.

FITZ, GIVE ME YOUR PUNCH CARD.

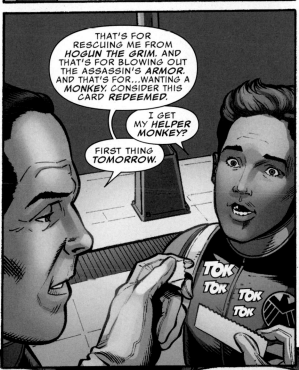

THAT'S FOR RESCUING ME FROM *HOGUN THE GRIM.* AND THAT'S FOR BLOWING OUT THE ASSASSIN'S *ARMOR.* AND THAT'S FOR...WANTING A *MONKEY.* CONSIDER THIS CARD *REDEEMED.*

I GET MY *HELPER MONKEY?*

FIRST THING *TOMORROW.*

TOK TOK TOK TOK

RIGHT NOW, THE *REST* OF YOU ARE BUYING MS. JOHNSON AND ME A *STIFF DRINK.*

BECAUSE...?

BECAUSE WE JUST TOLD OFF THE HEAD OF *ASGARD* WITHOUT BROWNING OUR *PANTS.*

KIRBY'S BAR

CLINK

JUST ANOTHER DAY AT THE OFFICE, THEN.

I'VE HAD WORSE.

TO THE HOMELAND.

 Th End.

9\.

VARIANT ART FILE BY:
JACK KIRBY, JIM STERANKO
& PAUL MOUNTS

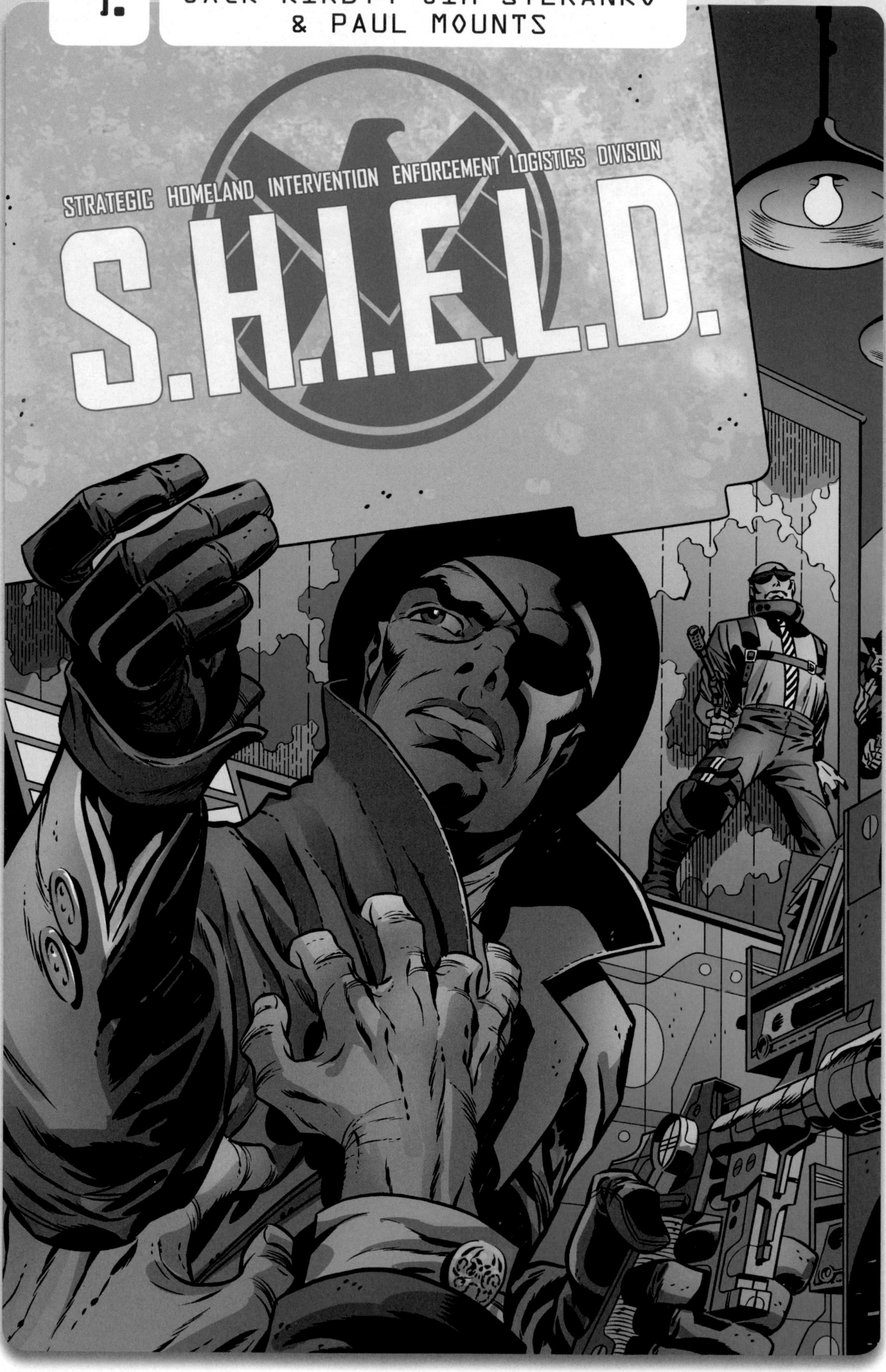
STRATEGIC HOMELAND INTERVENTION ENFORCEMENT LOGISTICS DIVISION
S.H.I.E.L.D.

ACCESSING HIDDEN FILES...

IN 1965, JACK KIRBY CAME UP WITH AN IDEA TO DO A CONTEMPORARY VERSION OF SGT. FURY AS A SUPER-SPY. HE CREATED THE FOLLOWING TWO PAGES AS A PILOT TO PRESENT TO EDITOR STAN LEE. STAN LIKED THE BASIC IDEA, BUT HAD SEVERAL OF HIS OWN – AND SO THE MAN CALLED D.E.A.T.H. DEVELOPED INTO NICK FURY, AGENT OF S.H.I.E.L.D., AND THE TWO PILOT PAGES WERE NEVER USED.

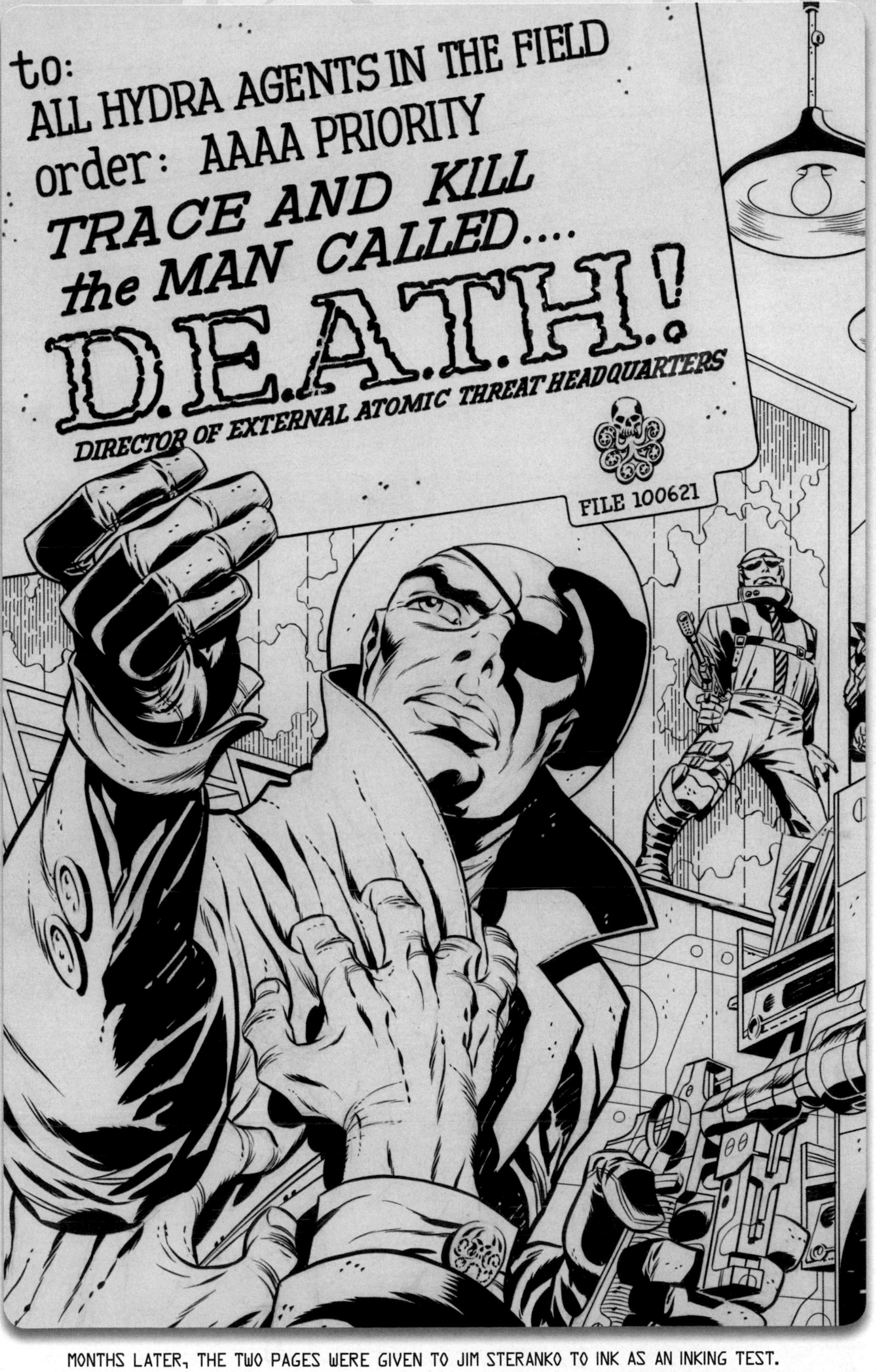
to:
ALL HYDRA AGENTS IN THE FIELD
order: AAAA PRIORITY
TRACE AND KILL
the MAN CALLED....
D.E.A.T.H!
DIRECTOR OF EXTERNAL ATOMIC THREAT HEADQUARTERS
FILE 100621

MONTHS LATER, THE TWO PAGES WERE GIVEN TO JIM STERANKO TO INK AS AN INKING TEST.

KIRBY INCLUDED COPIOUS NOTES IN HIS PRESENTATION, BOTH AS CAPTIONS AND BORDER NOTES THAT CLARIFY THE ACTION. WE HAVE TYPESET THESE ORIGINAL NOTES BELOW FOR EASIER READING.

THIS MAN'S NAME IS NICK FURY. HE HAS JUST INVADED A CELL OF "HYDRA," A SECRET ORGANIZATION--AND READ THE ORDER FOR HIS OWN DEATH!
CLICK
N. FURY 100621
BUT DEATH HOLDS NO FEAR FOR MEN LIKE FURY! IT'S MERELY A WORD--MOLDED INTO A TITLE WHICH HE BEARS WITH HONOR AND SERVICE...
ZIT
KRAK
HIS HONOR IS HIS RECORD! HIS SERVICE IS IN THE CAUSE OF ALL FREE MANKIND...
NICK, ONCE FOUGHT, WHAT HE THOUGHT WAS A BIG WAR. HE WAS SERGEANT OF THE FAMOUS COMMANDO UNIT KNOWN AS THE "HOWLERS"! AND SCORES OF NAZIS CALLED HIM OTHER NAMES--BEFORE THEY DIED...
THEN CAME PEACE--AND THE "BOMB" AND BIGGER BIGGER BOMBS--AND THE BIGGER, SECRET WAR TO KEEP THE BOMBS FROM GOING OFF. IN THIS WAR NICK IS STILL FIGHTING--AGAINST SILENT BUT DEADLY ENEMIES
IT IS INDEED A NEW WORLD--OF MEGATON AND OVERKILL--OF WEAPONS MADE TO FIT THE AGE
BA-LAM

NICK HEARS SOUND KNOWS HE'S BEEN DISCOVERED

FIRES AT ASSAILANTS AS HE DIVES

MAN IS HIT--OTHER MAN FIRES

FURY BURSTS THRU DOOR AND GRABS TAPE OFF WALL WHICH HE PULLS OFF AS HE RUNS

HE HAS TAPED WALL ON WAY INTO HIDEOUT--NOW BY PULLING IT OFF, HE CAN FIND HIS WAY OUT OF MAZE OF CORRIDORS QUICKLY...

HE FIXES GUN-PART WHICH CAN HELP HIM FIRE AROUND CORNER AT PURSUER